AVENGERS MECH STRIKE

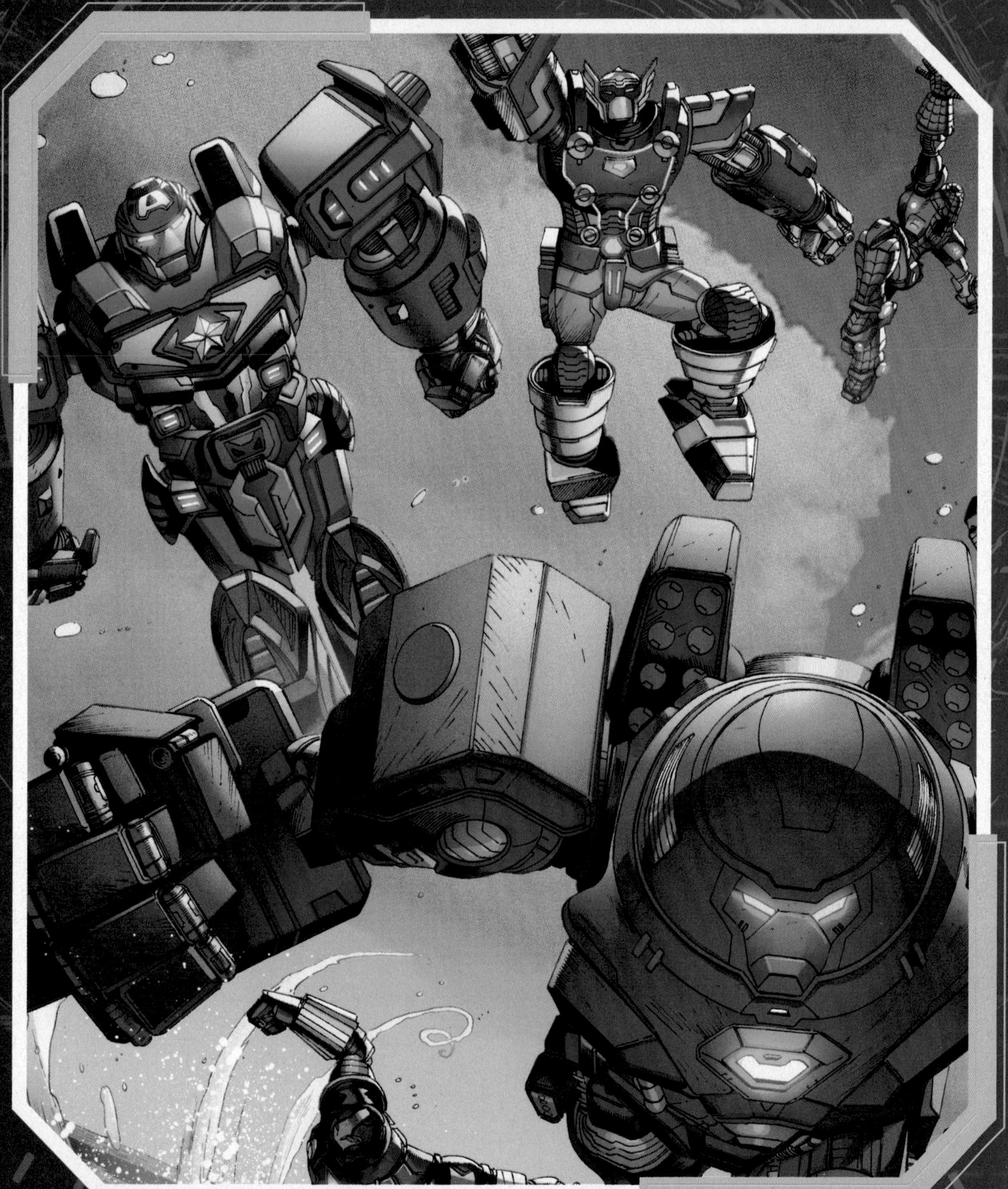

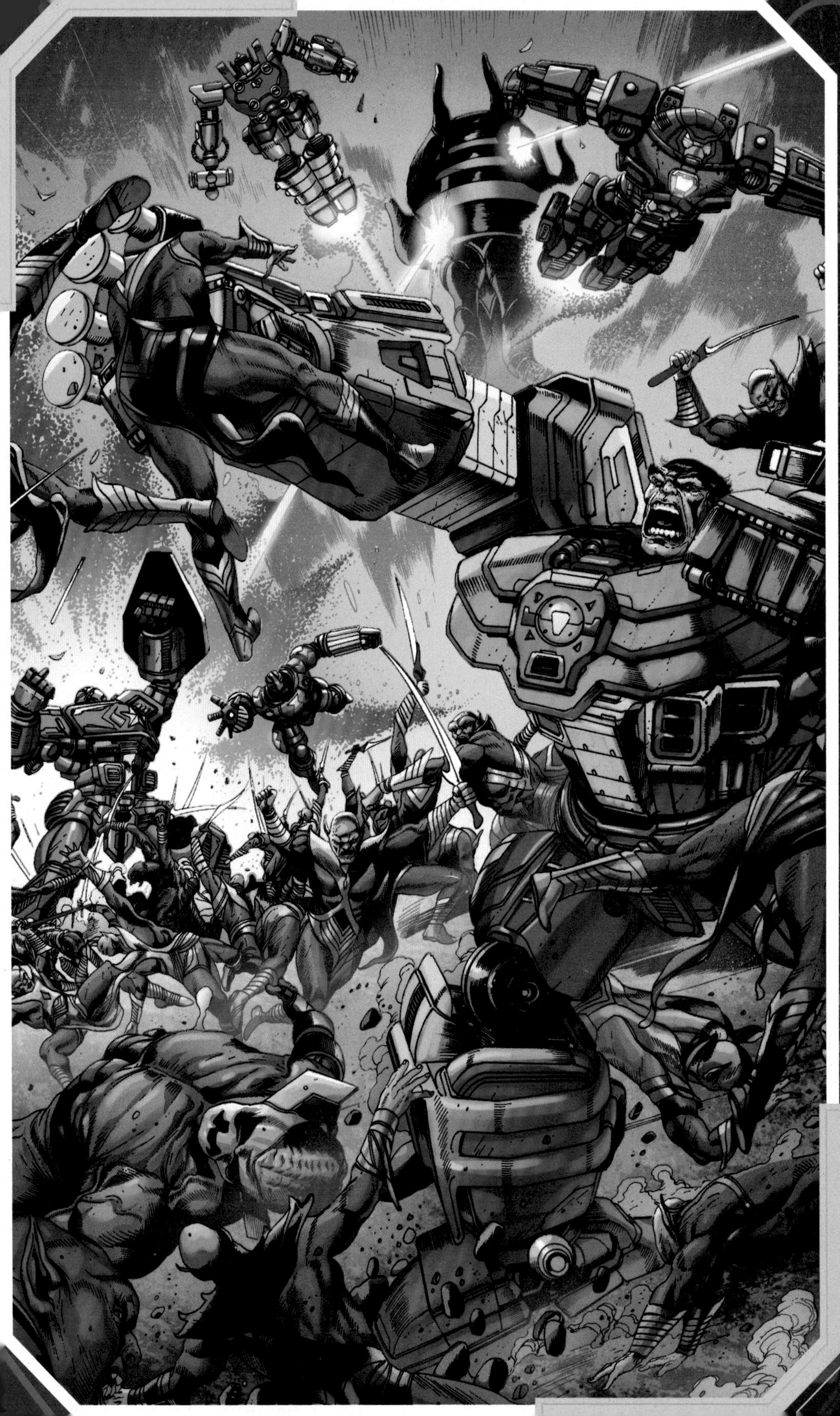

And there came a day, a day unlike any other, when Earth's mightiest heroes found themselves united against a common threat. On that day, the Avengers were born. To fight the foes no single super hero could withstand.

AVENGERS
MECH STRIKE

Jed MacKay
WRITER

Carlos Magno
ARTIST

Guru-eFX
COLOR ARTIST

VC's Cory Petit
LETTERER

Kei Zama & Guru-eFX
COVER ART

Martin Biro
ASSISTANT EDITOR

Alanna Smith
ASSOCIATE EDITOR

Tom Brevoort
EDITOR

Avengers CREATED BY Stan Lee & Jack Kirby

Jennifer Grünwald
COLLECTION EDITOR

Jeff Youngquist
VP PRODUCTION & SPECIAL PROJECTS

Daniel Kirchhoffer
ASSISTANT EDITOR

Adam Del Re
BOOK DESIGNER

Maia Loy
ASSISTANT MANAGING EDITOR

David Gabriel
SVP PRINT, SALES & MARKETING

Lisa Montalbano
ASSISTANT MANAGING EDITOR

C.B. Cebulski
EDITOR IN CHIEF

AVENGERS MECH STRIKE. Contains material originally published in magazine form as AVENGERS MECH STRIKE (2021) #1-5. First printing 2021. ISBN 978-1-302-92788-2. Published by MARVEL WORLDWIDE, INC., a subsidiary of MARVEL ENTERTAINMENT, LLC. OFFICE OF PUBLICATION: 1290 Avenue of the Americas, New York, NY 10104. © 2021 MARVEL. No similarity between any of the names, characters, persons, and/or institutions in this magazine with those of any living or dead person or institution is intended, and any such similarity which may exist is purely coincidental. **Printed in Canada.** KEVIN FEIGE, Chief Creative Officer; DAN BUCKLEY, President, Marvel Entertainment; JOE QUESADA, EVP & Creative Director; DAVID BOGART, Associate Publisher & SVP of Talent Affairs; TOM BREVOORT, VP, Executive Editor; NICK LOWE, Executive Editor, VP of Content, Digital Publishing; DAVID GABRIEL, VP of Print & Digital Publishing; JEFF YOUNGQUIST, VP of Production & Special Projects; ALEX MORALES, Director of Publishing Operations; DAN EDINGTON, Managing Editor; RICKEY PURDIN, Director of Talent Relations; JENNIFER GRÜNWALD, Senior Editor, Special Projects; SUSAN CRESPI, Production Manager; STAN LEE, Chairman Emeritus. For information regarding advertising in Marvel Comics or on Marvel.com, please contact Vit DeBellis, Custom Solutions & Integrated Advertising Manager, at vdebellis@marvel.com. For Marvel subscription inquiries, please call 888-511-5480. **Manufactured between 7/30/2021 and**

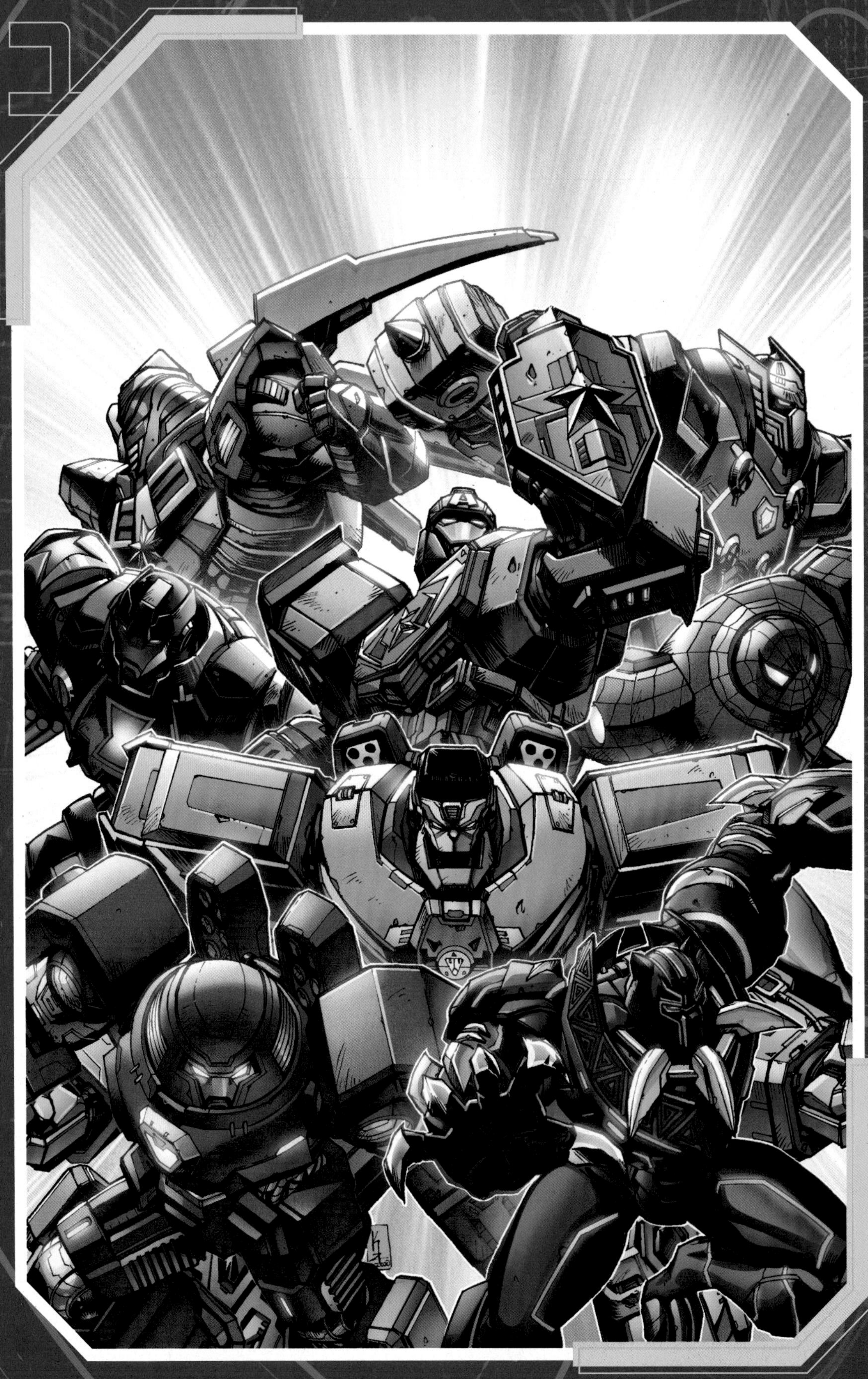

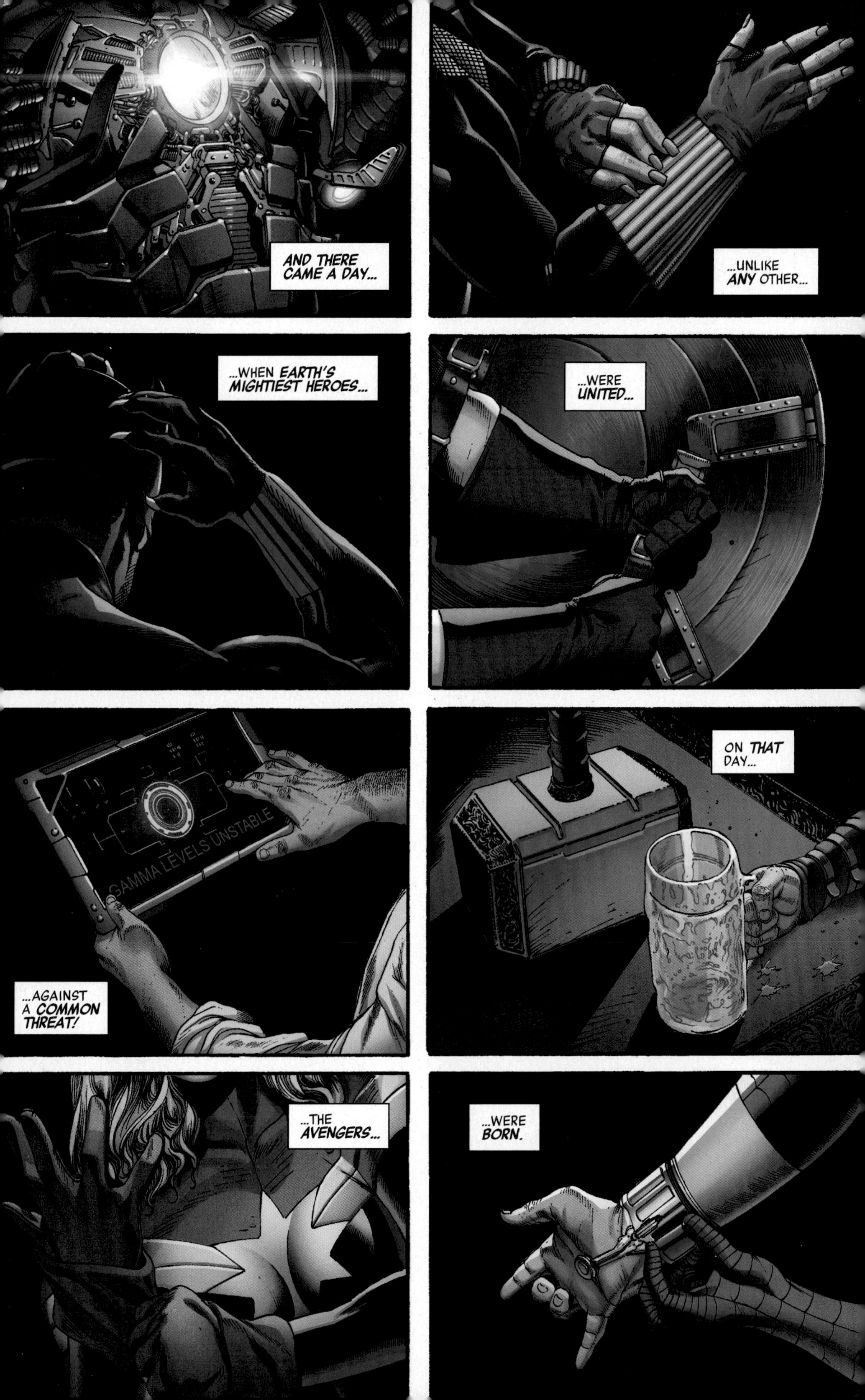
AND THERE CAME A DAY...
...UNLIKE ANY OTHER...
...WHEN EARTH'S MIGHTIEST HEROES...
...WERE UNITED...
GAMMA LEVELS UNSTABLE
...AGAINST A COMMON THREAT!
ON THAT DAY...
...THE AVENGERS...
...WERE BORN.

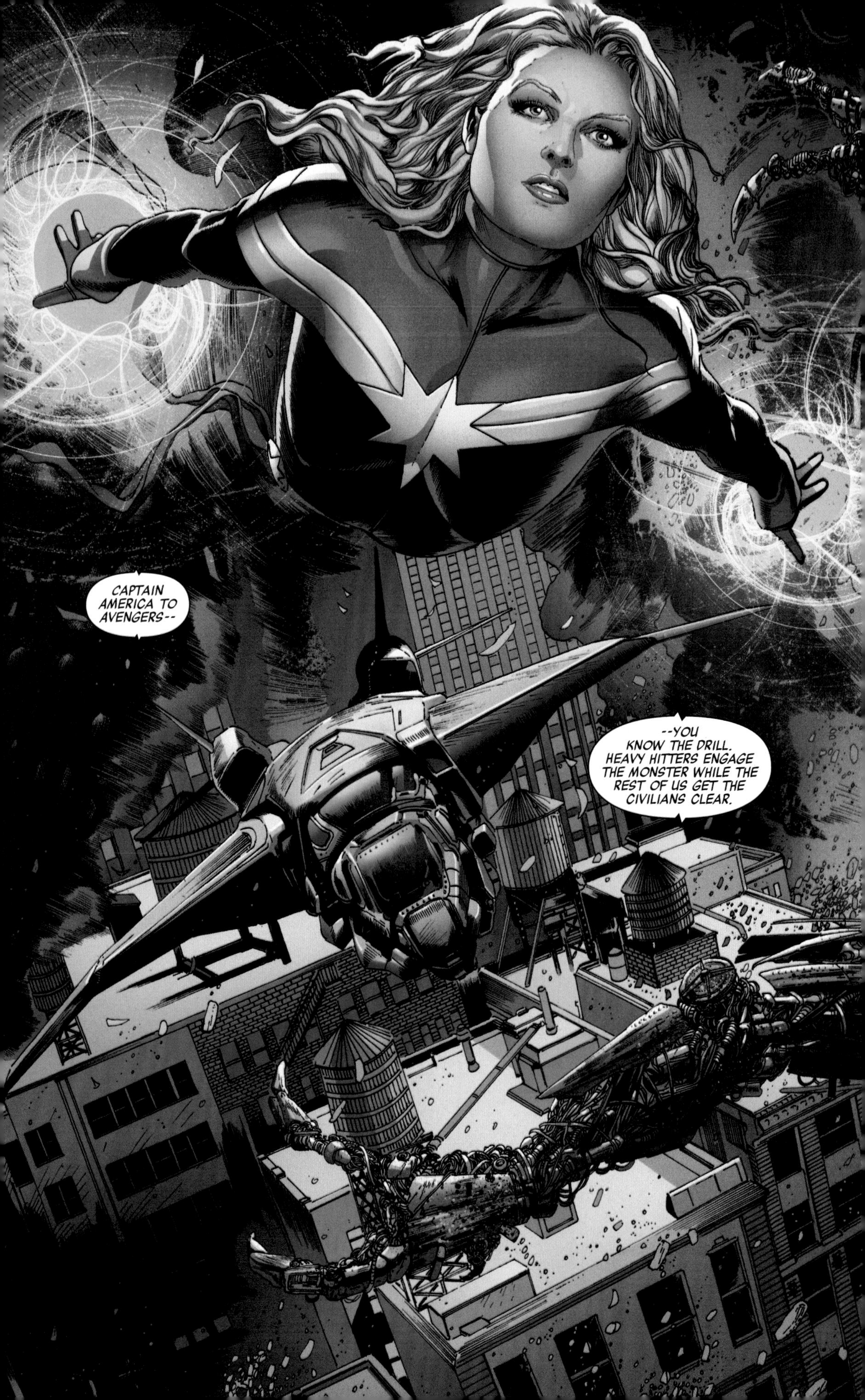
CAPTAIN AMERICA TO AVENGERS--
--YOU KNOW THE DRILL. HEAVY HITTERS ENGAGE THE MONSTER WHILE THE REST OF US GET THE CIVILIANS CLEAR.

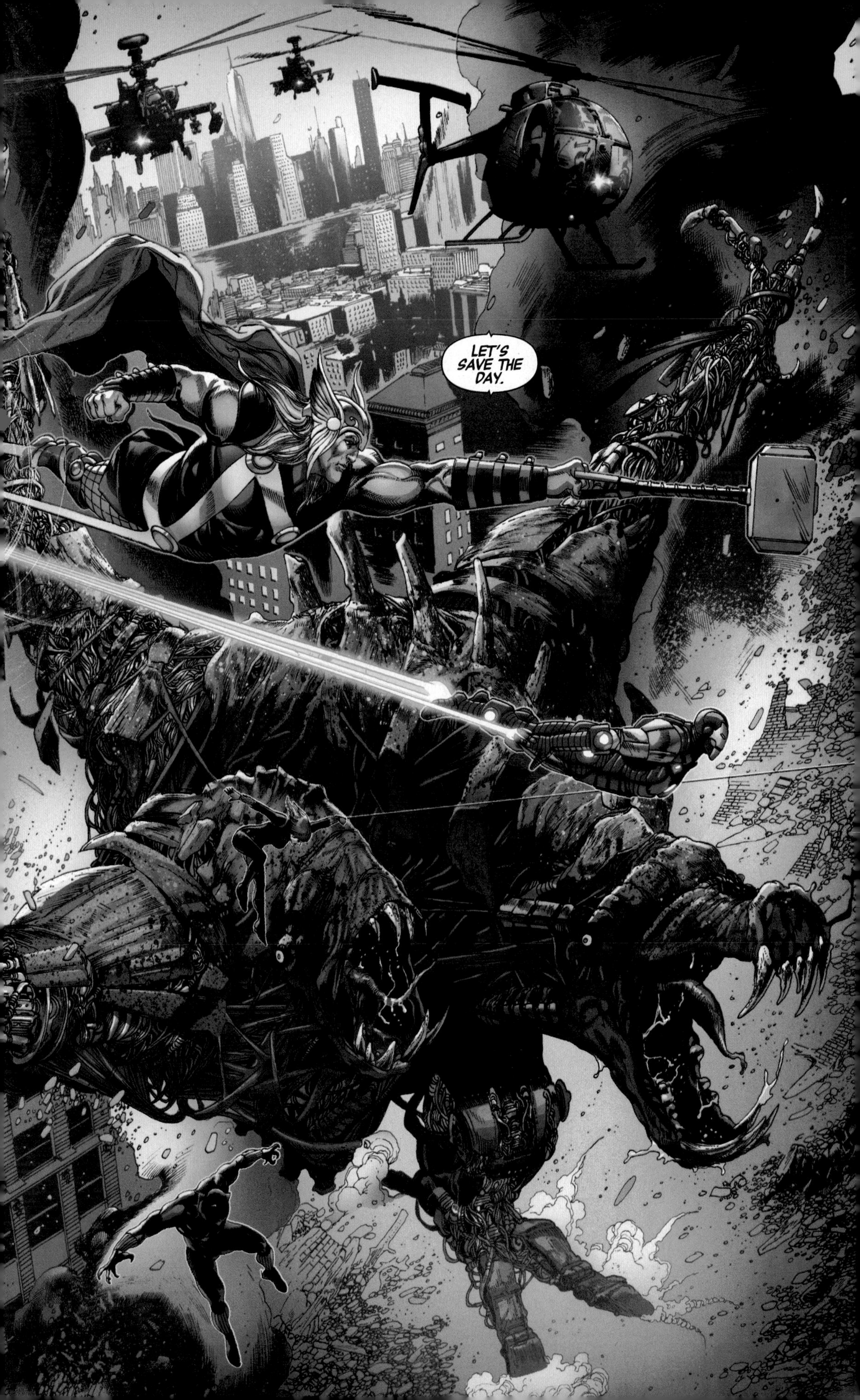
LET'S SAVE THE DAY.

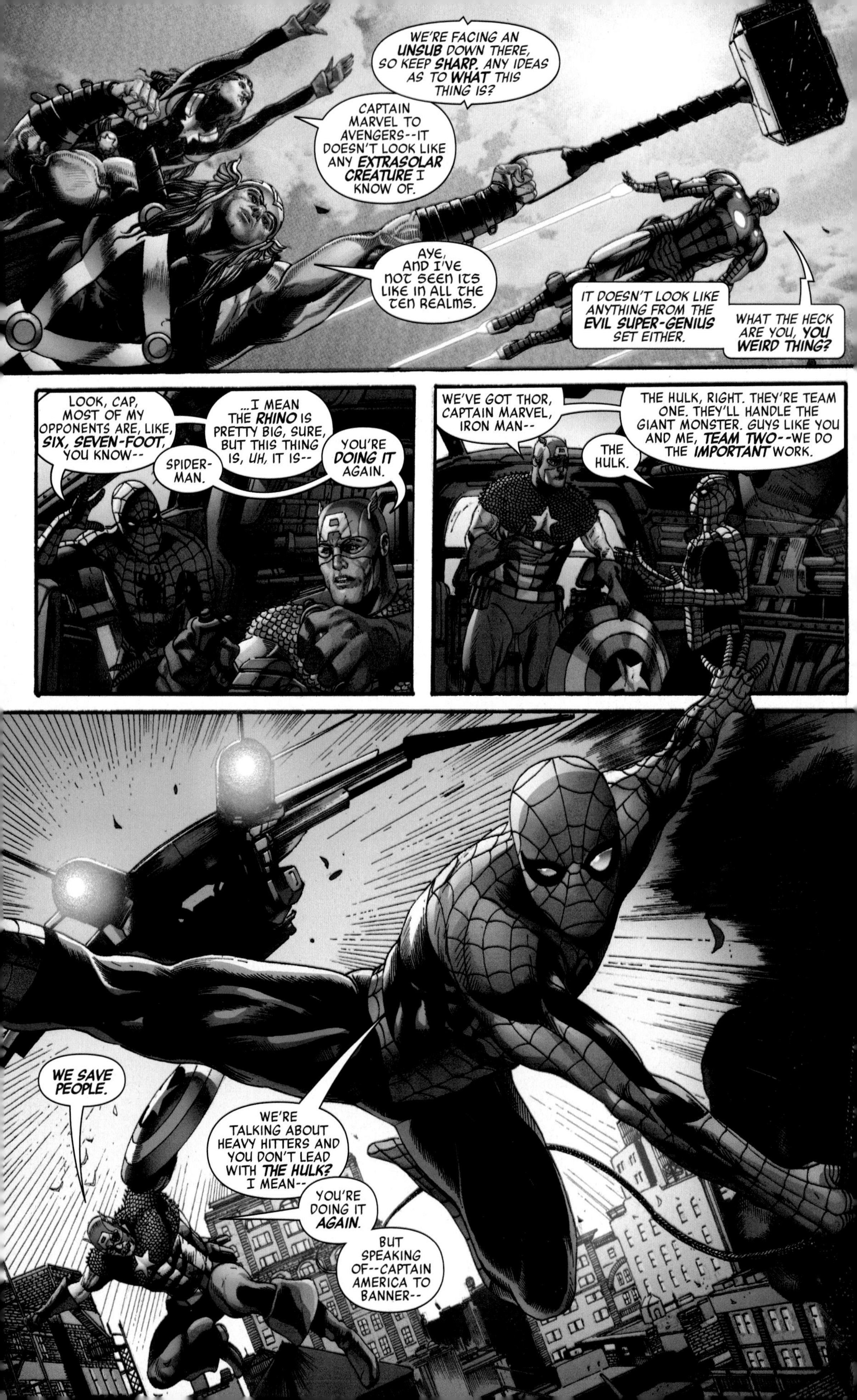
WE'RE FACING AN UNSUB DOWN THERE, SO KEEP SHARP. ANY IDEAS AS TO WHAT THIS THING IS?
CAPTAIN MARVEL TO AVENGERS--IT DOESN'T LOOK LIKE ANY EXTRASOLAR CREATURE I KNOW OF.
AYE, AND I'VE NOT SEEN ITS LIKE IN ALL THE TEN REALMS.
IT DOESN'T LOOK LIKE ANYTHING FROM THE EVIL SUPER-GENIUS SET EITHER.
WHAT THE HECK ARE YOU, YOU WEIRD THING?
LOOK, CAP, MOST OF MY OPPONENTS ARE, LIKE, SIX, SEVEN-FOOT, YOU KNOW--
...I MEAN THE RHINO IS PRETTY BIG, SURE, BUT THIS THING IS, UH, IT IS--
SPIDER-MAN.
YOU'RE DOING IT AGAIN.
WE'VE GOT THOR, CAPTAIN MARVEL, IRON MAN--
THE HULK.
THE HULK, RIGHT. THEY'RE TEAM ONE. THEY'LL HANDLE THE GIANT MONSTER. GUYS LIKE YOU AND ME, TEAM TWO--WE DO THE IMPORTANT WORK.
WE SAVE PEOPLE.
WE'RE TALKING ABOUT HEAVY HITTERS AND YOU DON'T LEAD WITH THE HULK? I MEAN--
YOU'RE DOING IT AGAIN.
BUT SPEAKING OF--CAPTAIN AMERICA TO BANNER--

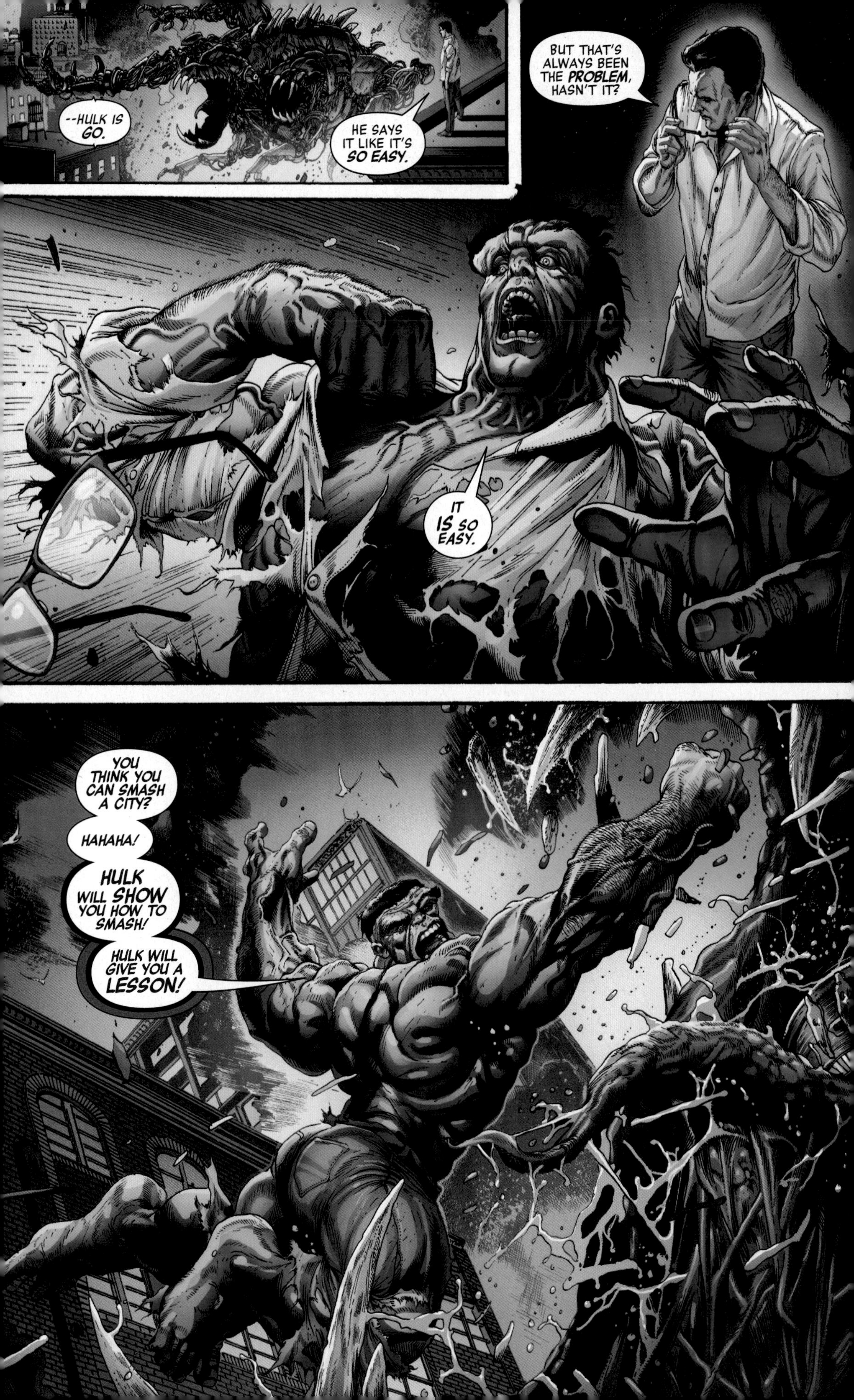
--HULK IS GO.
HE SAYS IT LIKE IT'S SO EASY.
BUT THAT'S ALWAYS BEEN THE PROBLEM, HASN'T IT?
IT IS SO EASY.
YOU THINK YOU CAN SMASH A CITY?
HAHAHA!
HULK WILL SHOW YOU HOW TO SMASH!
HULK WILL GIVE YOU A LESSON!

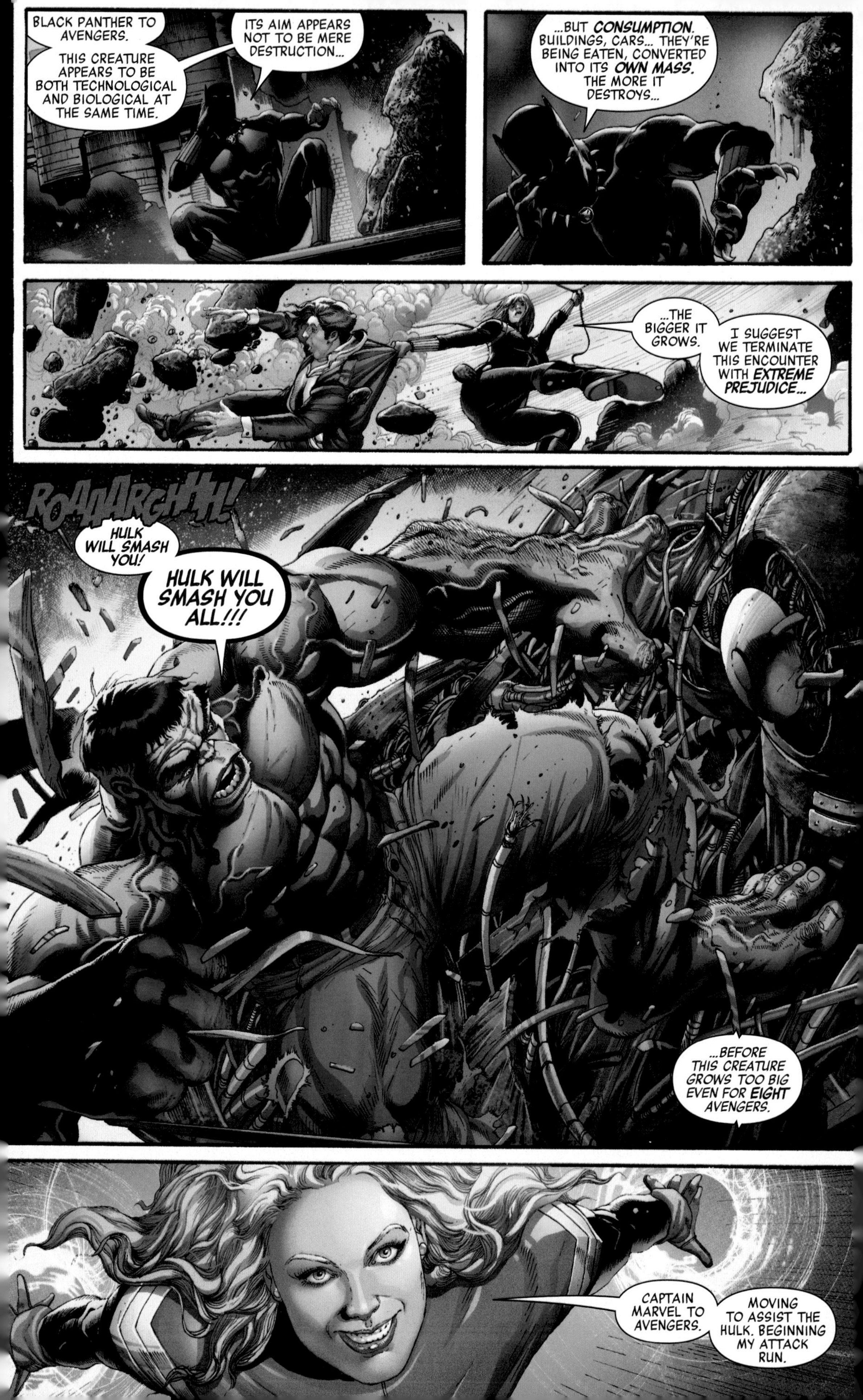

BLACK PANTHER TO AVENGERS.
THIS CREATURE APPEARS TO BE BOTH TECHNOLOGICAL AND BIOLOGICAL AT THE SAME TIME.
ITS AIM APPEARS NOT TO BE MERE DESTRUCTION...
...BUT CONSUMPTION. BUILDINGS, CARS... THEY'RE BEING EATEN, CONVERTED INTO ITS OWN MASS. THE MORE IT DESTROYS...
...THE BIGGER IT GROWS.
I SUGGEST WE TERMINATE THIS ENCOUNTER WITH EXTREME PREJUDICE...
ROAAARGHHH!
HULK WILL SMASH YOU!
HULK WILL SMASH YOU ALL!!!
...BEFORE THIS CREATURE GROWS TOO BIG EVEN FOR EIGHT AVENGERS.
CAPTAIN MARVEL TO AVENGERS.
MOVING TO ASSIST THE HULK. BEGINNING MY ATTACK RUN.

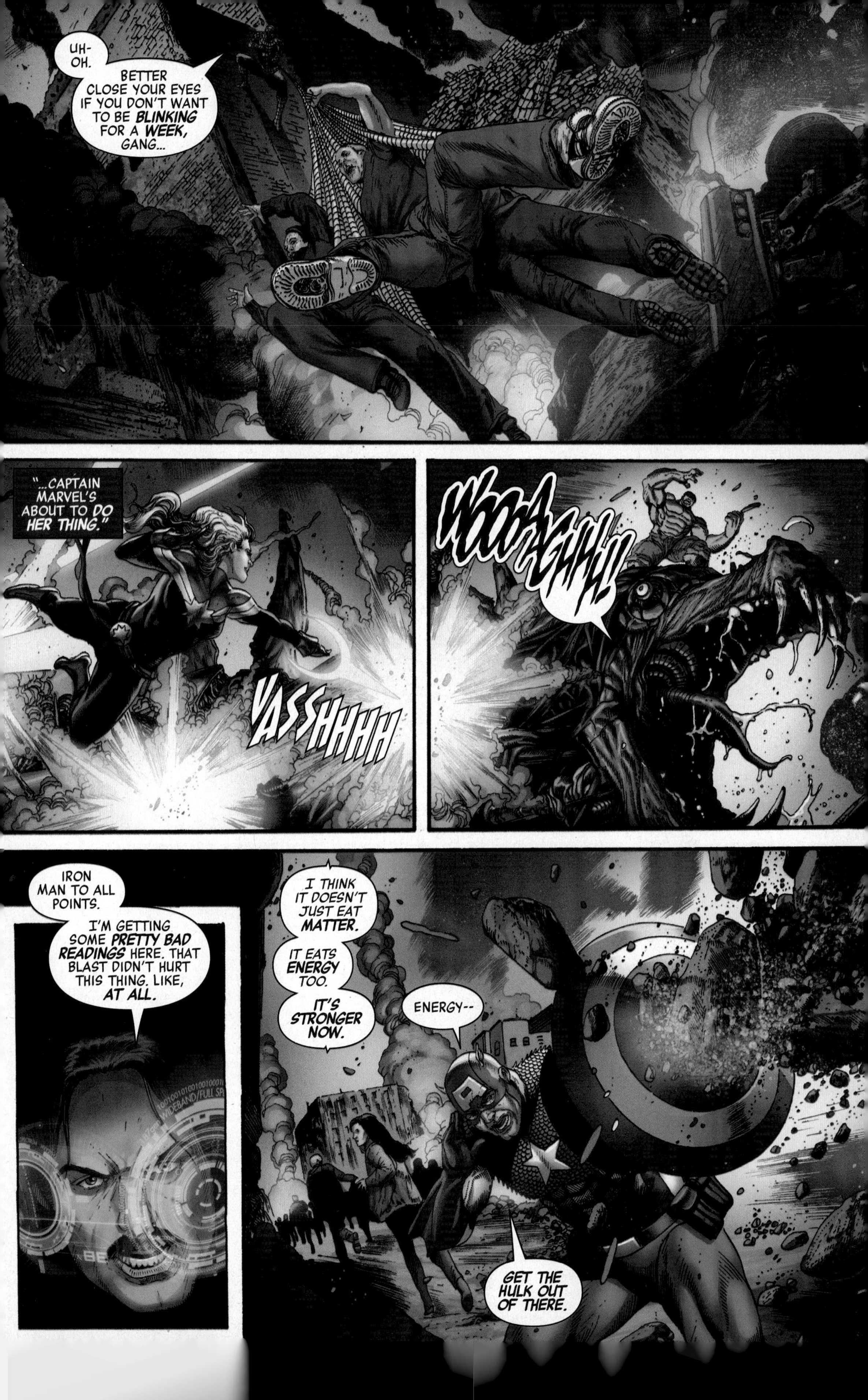
UH-OH.
BETTER CLOSE YOUR EYES IF YOU DON'T WANT TO BE BLINKING FOR A WEEK, GANG...
"...CAPTAIN MARVEL'S ABOUT TO DO HER THING."
VASSHHHH
WOOOAGHHH!!
IRON MAN TO ALL POINTS.
I'M GETTING SOME PRETTY BAD READINGS HERE. THAT BLAST DIDN'T HURT THIS THING. LIKE, AT ALL.
I THINK IT DOESN'T JUST EAT MATTER.
IT EATS ENERGY TOO.
IT'S STRONGER NOW.
ENERGY--
GET THE HULK OUT OF THERE.

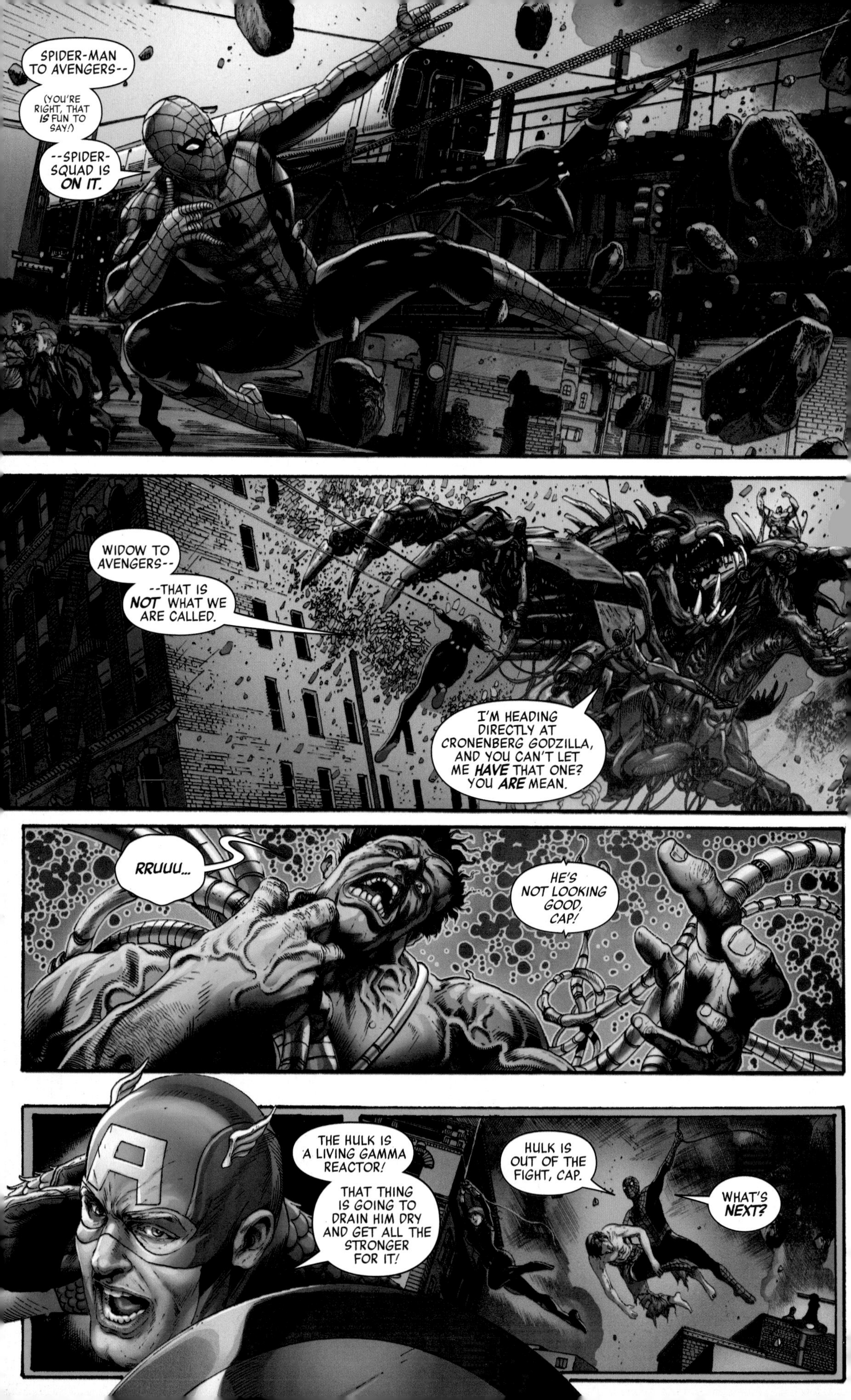
SPIDER-MAN TO AVENGERS--
(YOU'RE RIGHT, THAT IS FUN TO SAY!)
--SPIDER-SQUAD IS ON IT.
WIDOW TO AVENGERS--
--THAT IS NOT WHAT WE ARE CALLED.
I'M HEADING DIRECTLY AT CRONENBERG GODZILLA, AND YOU CAN'T LET ME HAVE THAT ONE? YOU ARE MEAN.
RRUUU...
HE'S NOT LOOKING GOOD, CAP!
THE HULK IS A LIVING GAMMA REACTOR!
THAT THING IS GOING TO DRAIN HIM DRY AND GET ALL THE STRONGER FOR IT!
HULK IS OUT OF THE FIGHT, CAP.
WHAT'S NEXT?

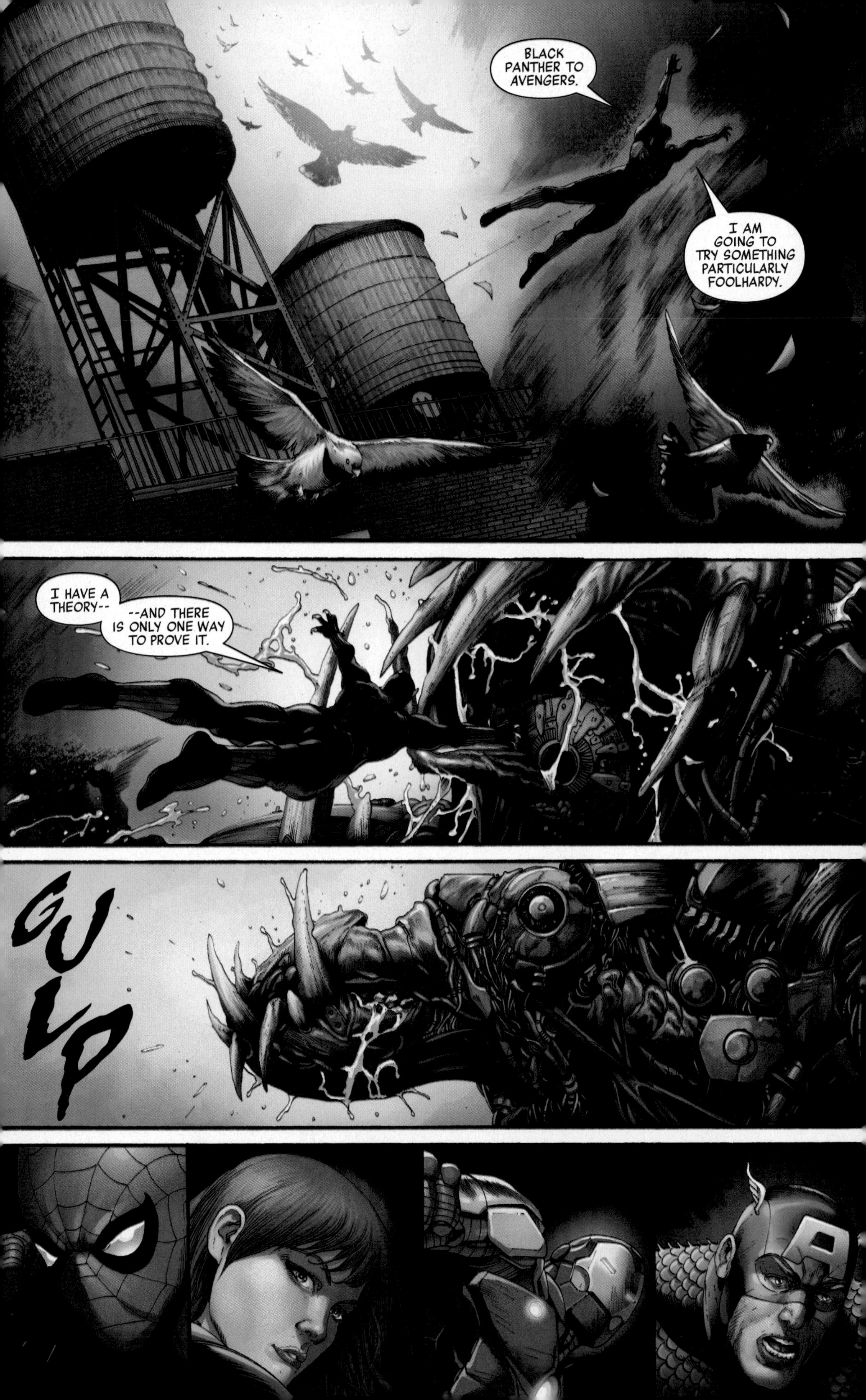
BLACK PANTHER TO AVENGERS.
I AM GOING TO TRY SOMETHING PARTICULARLY FOOLHARDY.
I HAVE A THEORY--
--AND THERE IS ONLY ONE WAY TO PROVE IT.
GULP

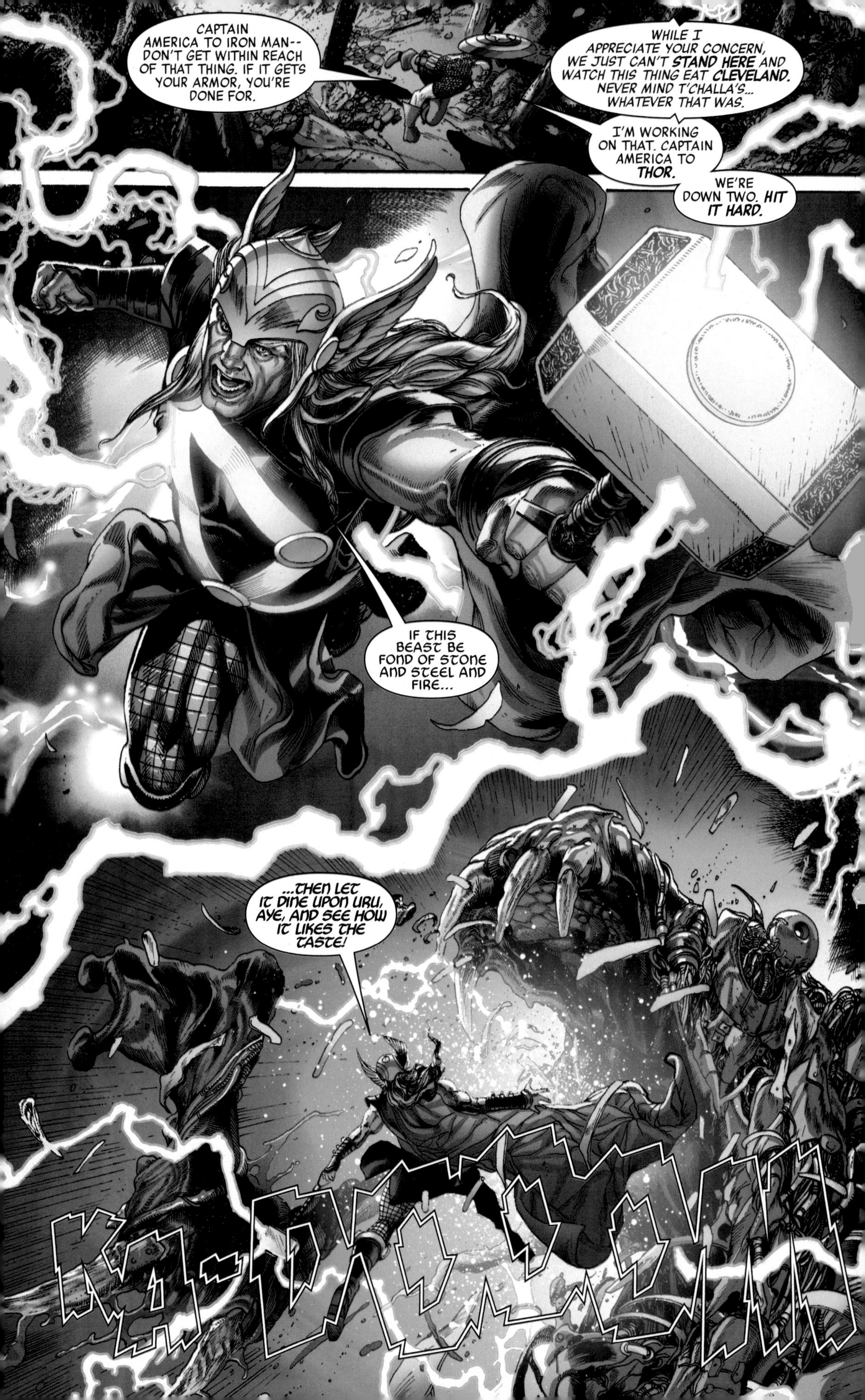
CAPTAIN AMERICA TO IRON MAN-- DON'T GET WITHIN REACH OF THAT THING. IF IT GETS YOUR ARMOR, YOU'RE DONE FOR.
WHILE I APPRECIATE YOUR CONCERN, WE JUST CAN'T STAND HERE AND WATCH THIS THING EAT CLEVELAND. NEVER MIND T'CHALLA'S... WHATEVER THAT WAS.
I'M WORKING ON THAT. CAPTAIN AMERICA TO THOR.
WE'RE DOWN TWO. HIT IT HARD.
IF THIS BEAST BE FOND OF STONE AND STEEL AND FIRE...
...THEN LET IT DINE UPON URU, AYE, AND SEE HOW IT LIKES THE TASTE!
KA-DOOOOM

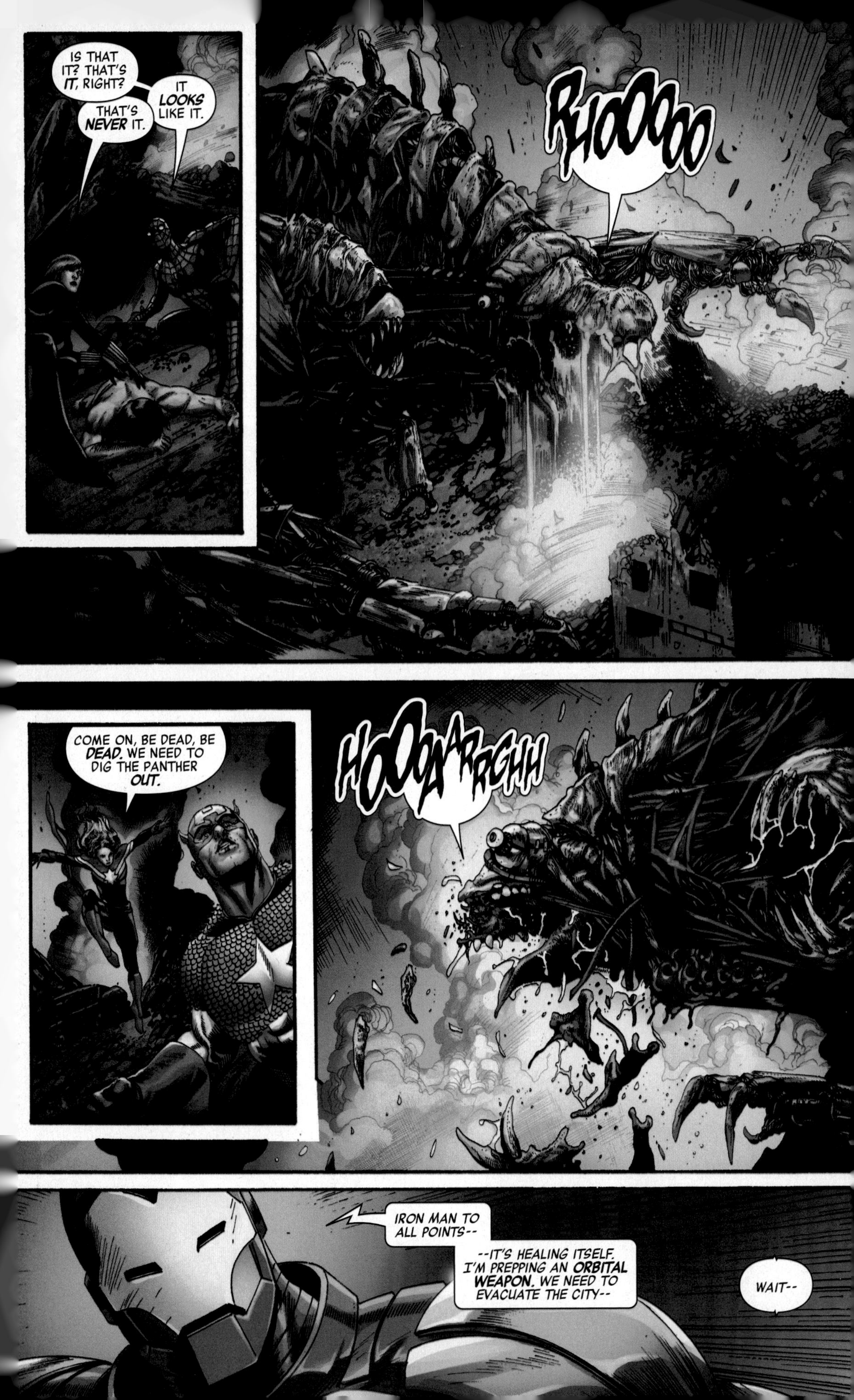

IS THAT IT? THAT'S IT, RIGHT?
IT LOOKS LIKE IT.
THAT'S NEVER IT.
RHOOOOO
COME ON, BE DEAD, BE DEAD. WE NEED TO DIG THE PANTHER OUT.
HOOOAARRGHH
IRON MAN TO ALL POINTS--
--IT'S HEALING ITSELF. I'M PREPPING AN ORBITAL WEAPON. WE NEED TO EVACUATE THE CITY--
WAIT--

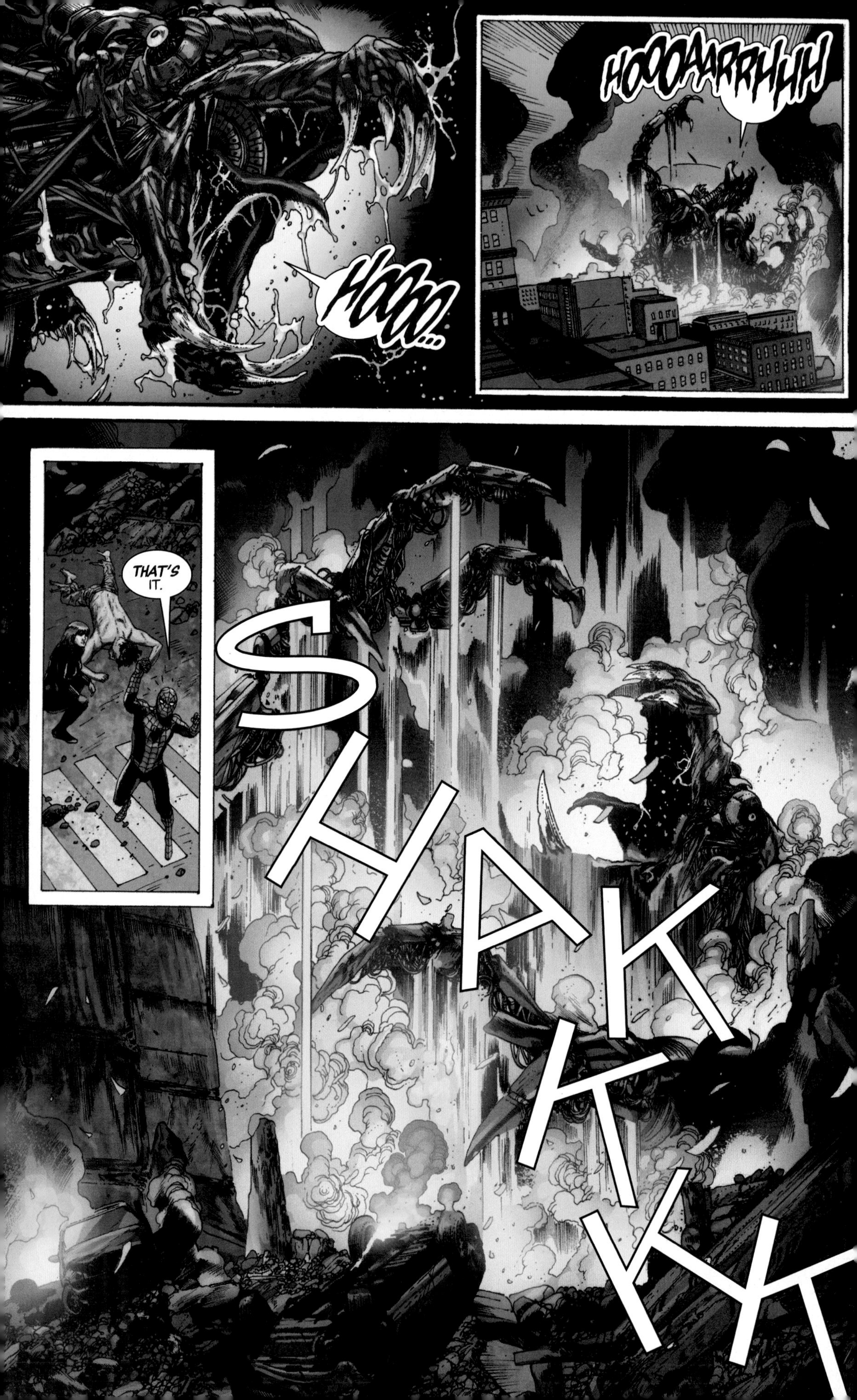
HOOO...
HOOOAARRHHH
THAT'S IT.
SHAKTKYT

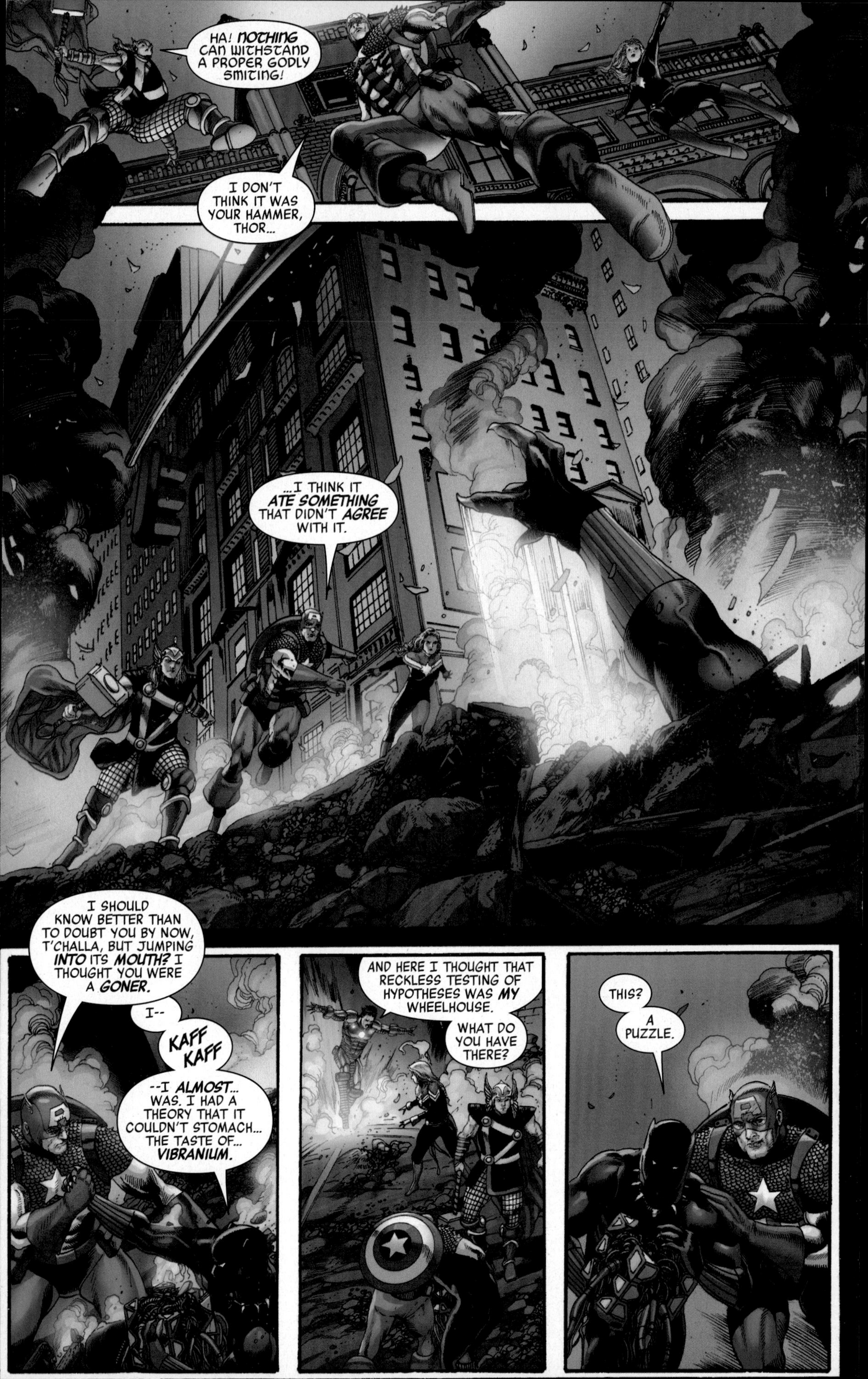
HA! NOTHING CAN WITHSTAND A PROPER GODLY SMITING!
I DON'T THINK IT WAS YOUR HAMMER, THOR...
...I THINK IT ATE SOMETHING THAT DIDN'T AGREE WITH IT.
I SHOULD KNOW BETTER THAN TO DOUBT YOU BY NOW, T'CHALLA, BUT JUMPING INTO ITS MOUTH? I THOUGHT YOU WERE A GONER.
I--
KAFF KAFF
--I ALMOST... WAS. I HAD A THEORY THAT IT COULDN'T STOMACH... THE TASTE OF... VIBRANIUM.
AND HERE I THOUGHT THAT RECKLESS TESTING OF HYPOTHESES WAS MY WHEELHOUSE.
WHAT DO YOU HAVE THERE?
THIS?
A PUZZLE.

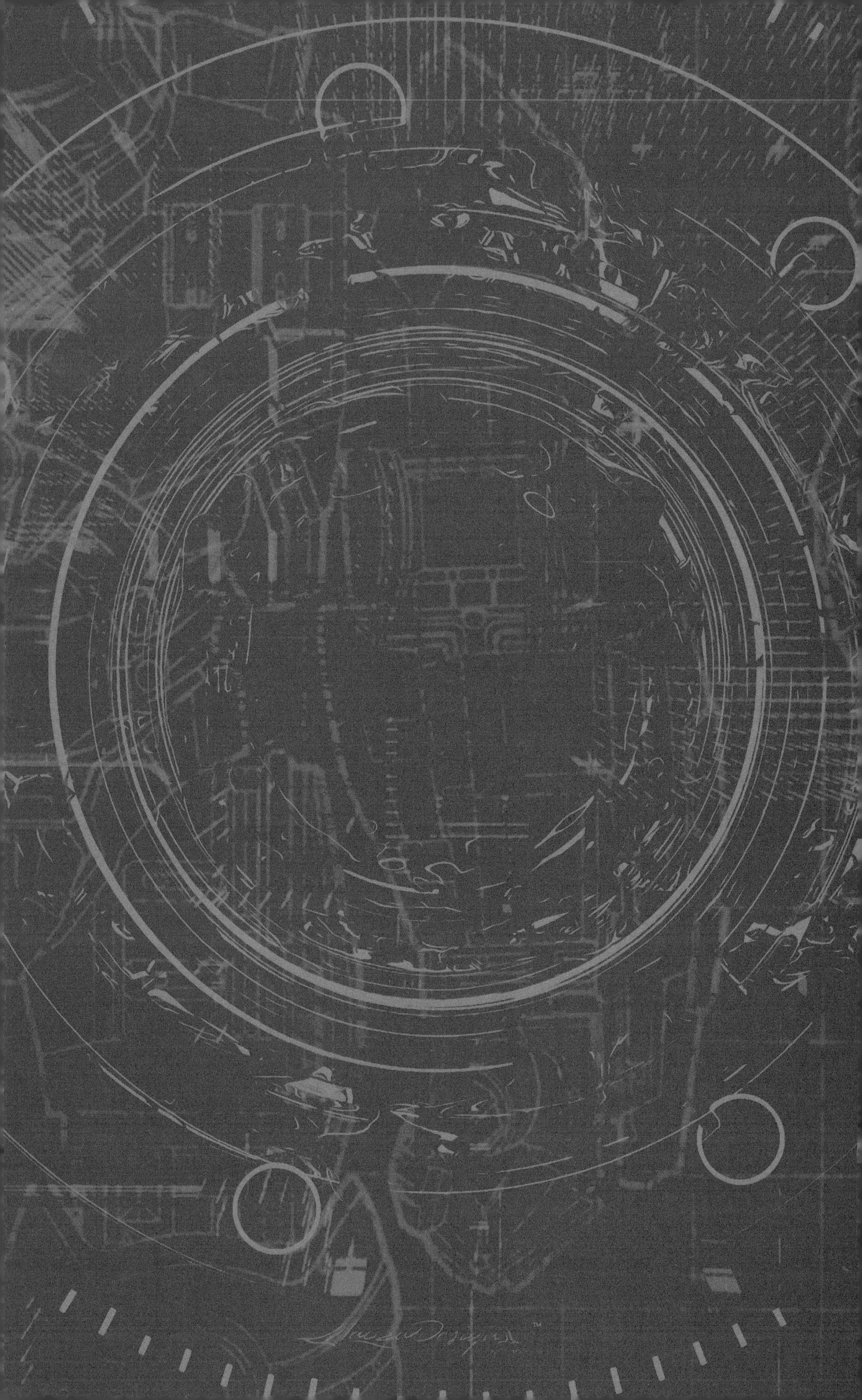

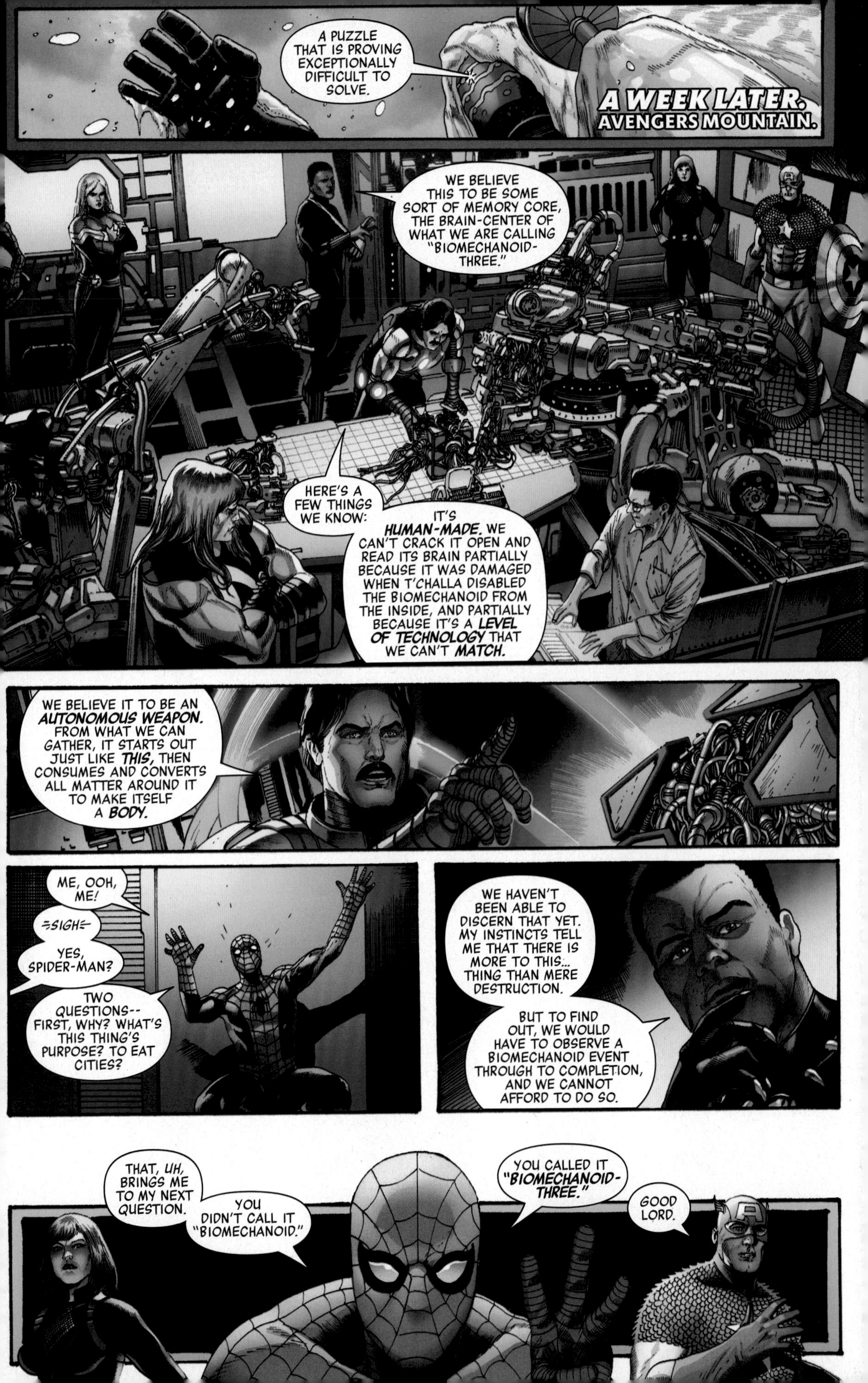
A PUZZLE THAT IS PROVING EXCEPTIONALLY DIFFICULT TO SOLVE.
A WEEK LATER. AVENGERS MOUNTAIN.
WE BELIEVE THIS TO BE SOME SORT OF MEMORY CORE, THE BRAIN-CENTER OF WHAT WE ARE CALLING "BIOMECHANOID-THREE."
HERE'S A FEW THINGS WE KNOW:
IT'S HUMAN-MADE. WE CAN'T CRACK IT OPEN AND READ ITS BRAIN PARTIALLY BECAUSE IT WAS DAMAGED WHEN T'CHALLA DISABLED THE BIOMECHANOID FROM THE INSIDE, AND PARTIALLY BECAUSE IT'S A LEVEL OF TECHNOLOGY THAT WE CAN'T MATCH.
WE BELIEVE IT TO BE AN AUTONOMOUS WEAPON. FROM WHAT WE CAN GATHER, IT STARTS OUT JUST LIKE THIS, THEN CONSUMES AND CONVERTS ALL MATTER AROUND IT TO MAKE ITSELF A BODY.
ME, OOH, ME!
=SIGH=
YES, SPIDER-MAN?
TWO QUESTIONS-- FIRST, WHY? WHAT'S THIS THING'S PURPOSE? TO EAT CITIES?
WE HAVEN'T BEEN ABLE TO DISCERN THAT YET. MY INSTINCTS TELL ME THAT THERE IS MORE TO THIS... THING THAN MERE DESTRUCTION.
BUT TO FIND OUT, WE WOULD HAVE TO OBSERVE A BIOMECHANOID EVENT THROUGH TO COMPLETION, AND WE CANNOT AFFORD TO DO SO.
THAT, UH, BRINGS ME TO MY NEXT QUESTION.
YOU DIDN'T CALL IT "BIOMECHANOID."
YOU CALLED IT "BIOMECHANOID-THREE."
GOOD LORD.

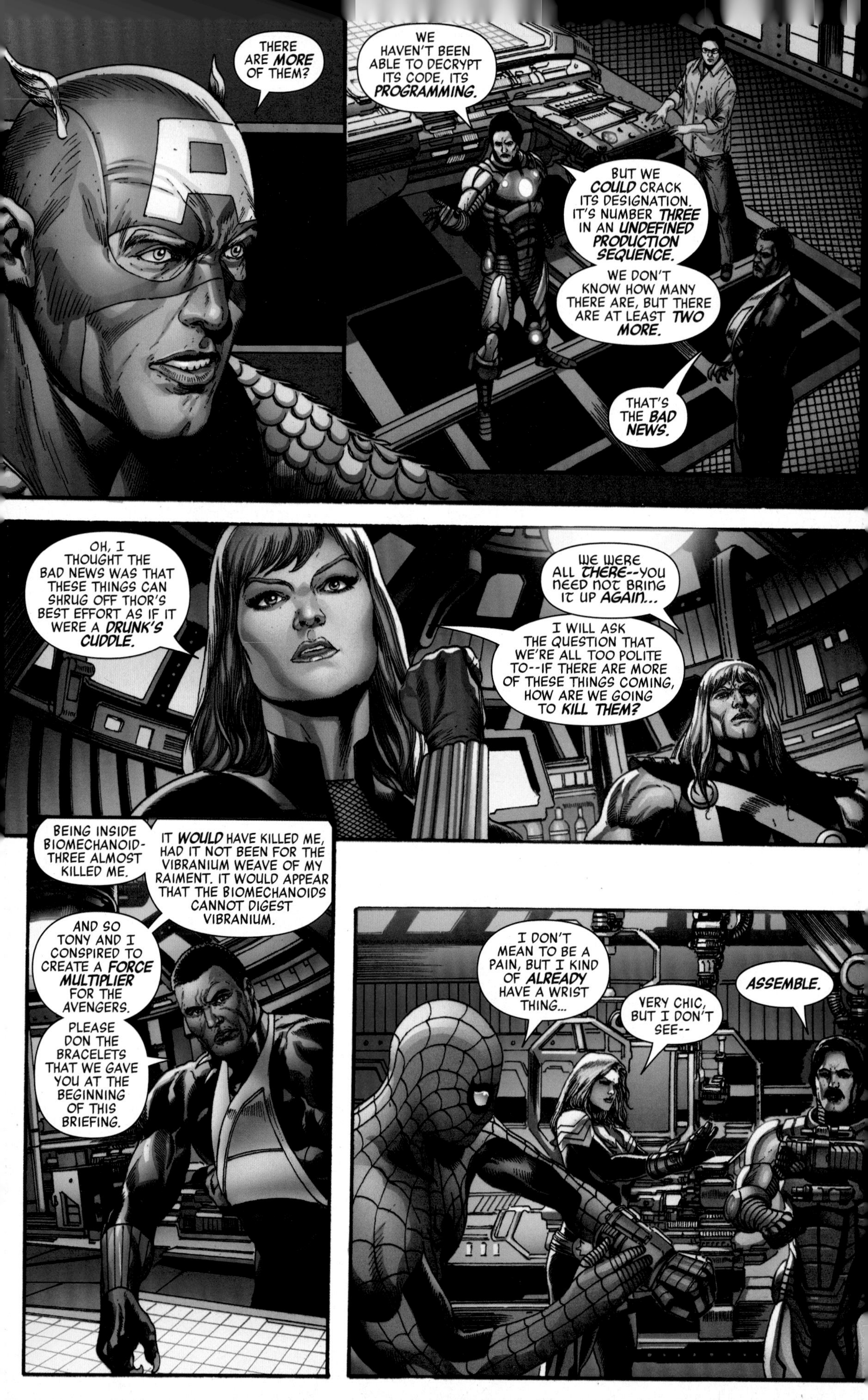
THERE ARE MORE OF THEM?
WE HAVEN'T BEEN ABLE TO DECRYPT ITS CODE, ITS PROGRAMMING.
BUT WE COULD CRACK ITS DESIGNATION. IT'S NUMBER THREE IN AN UNDEFINED PRODUCTION SEQUENCE.
WE DON'T KNOW HOW MANY THERE ARE, BUT THERE ARE AT LEAST TWO MORE.
THAT'S THE BAD NEWS.
OH, I THOUGHT THE BAD NEWS WAS THAT THESE THINGS CAN SHRUG OFF THOR'S BEST EFFORT AS IF IT WERE A DRUNK'S CUDDLE.
WE WERE ALL THERE--YOU NEED NOT BRING IT UP AGAIN...
I WILL ASK THE QUESTION THAT WE'RE ALL TOO POLITE TO--IF THERE ARE MORE OF THESE THINGS COMING, HOW ARE WE GOING TO KILL THEM?
BEING INSIDE BIOMECHANOID-THREE ALMOST KILLED ME.
IT WOULD HAVE KILLED ME, HAD IT NOT BEEN FOR THE VIBRANIUM WEAVE OF MY RAIMENT. IT WOULD APPEAR THAT THE BIOMECHANOIDS CANNOT DIGEST VIBRANIUM.
AND SO TONY AND I CONSPIRED TO CREATE A FORCE MULTIPLIER FOR THE AVENGERS.
PLEASE DON THE BRACELETS THAT WE GAVE YOU AT THE BEGINNING OF THIS BRIEFING.
I DON'T MEAN TO BE A PAIN, BUT I KIND OF ALREADY HAVE A WRIST THING...
VERY CHIC, BUT I DON'T SEE--
ASSEMBLE.

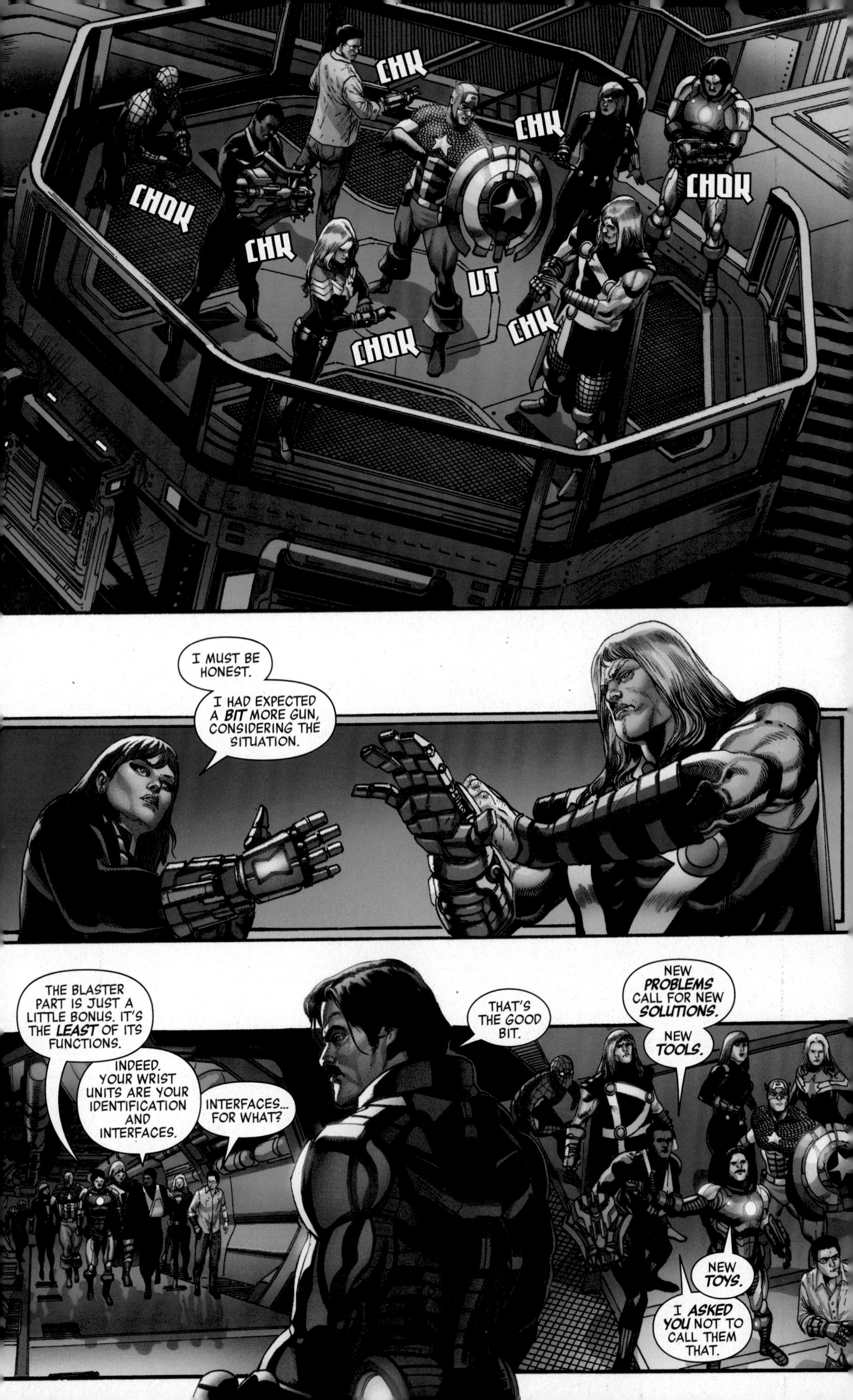

CHK
CHOK
CHK
CHK
VT
CHOK
CHK
CHOK
I MUST BE HONEST.
I HAD EXPECTED A BIT MORE GUN, CONSIDERING THE SITUATION.
THE BLASTER PART IS JUST A LITTLE BONUS. IT'S THE LEAST OF ITS FUNCTIONS.
INDEED. YOUR WRIST UNITS ARE YOUR IDENTIFICATION AND INTERFACES.
INTERFACES... FOR WHAT?
THAT'S THE GOOD BIT.
NEW PROBLEMS CALL FOR NEW SOLUTIONS.
NEW TOOLS.
NEW TOYS.
I ASKED YOU NOT TO CALL THEM THAT.

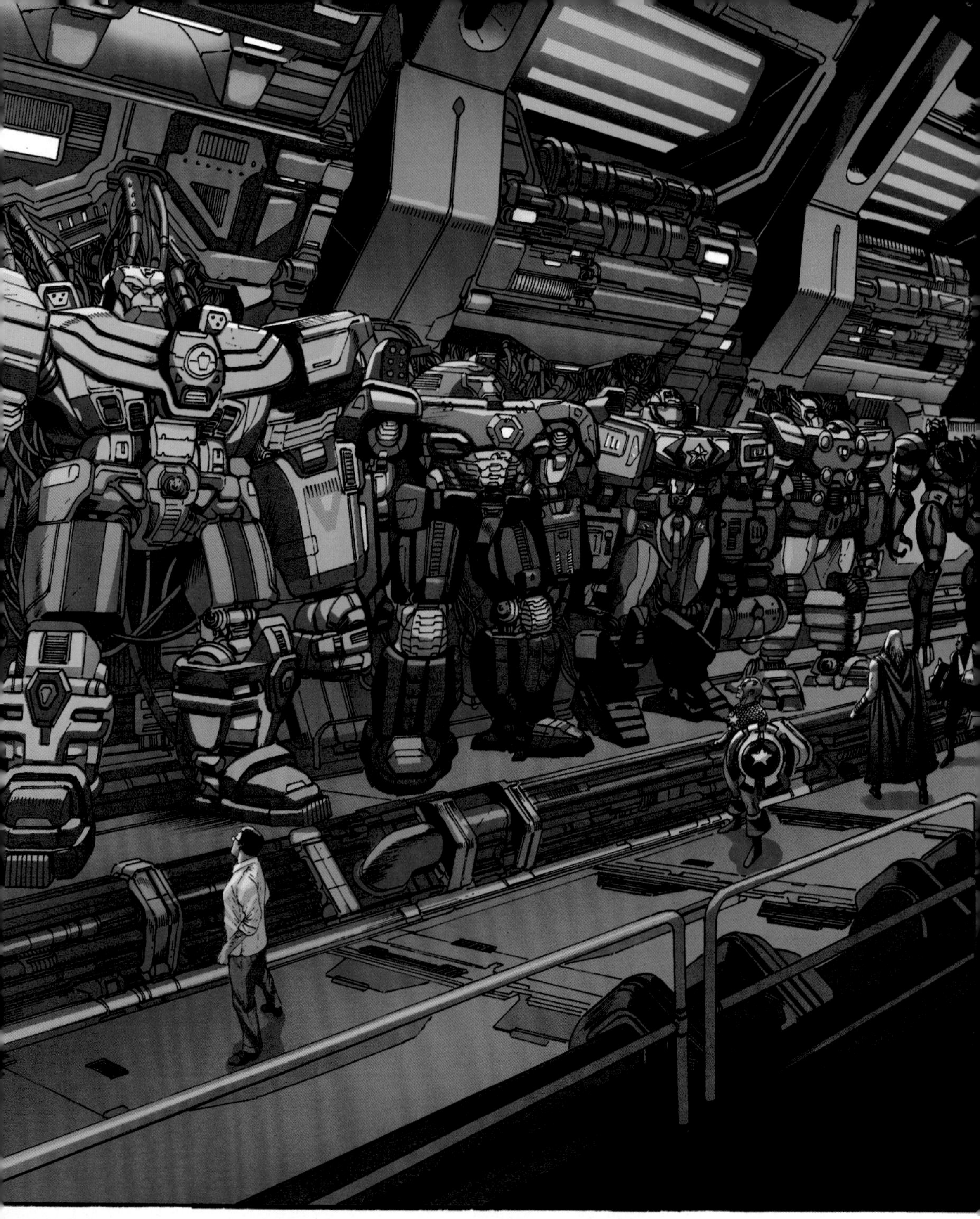

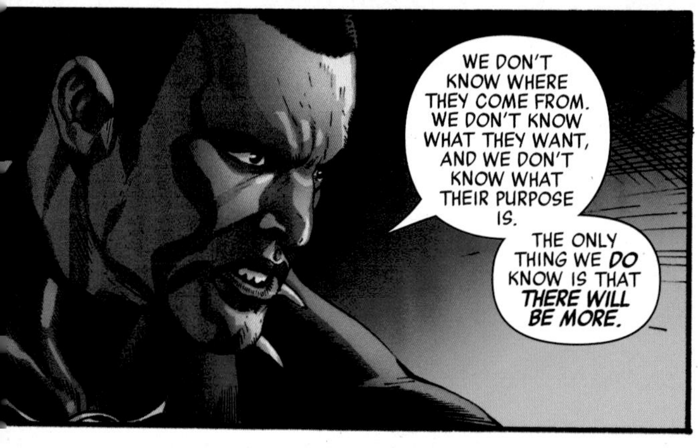

WE DON'T KNOW WHERE THEY COME FROM. WE DON'T KNOW WHAT THEY WANT, AND WE DON'T KNOW WHAT THEIR PURPOSE IS.
THE ONLY THING WE *DO* KNOW IS THAT ***THERE WILL BE MORE.***

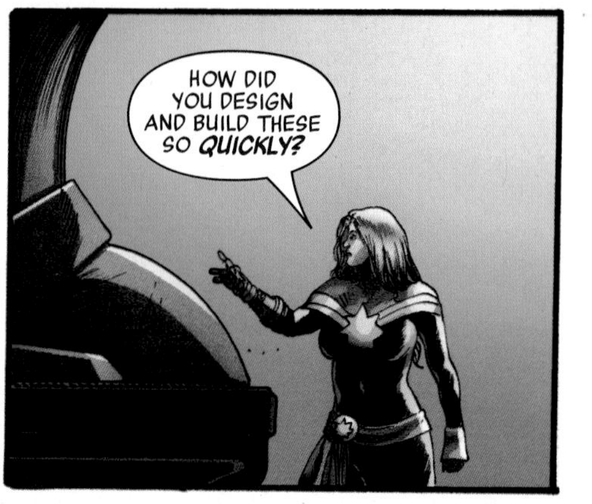

HOW DID YOU DESIGN AND BUILD THESE SO ***QUICKLY?***

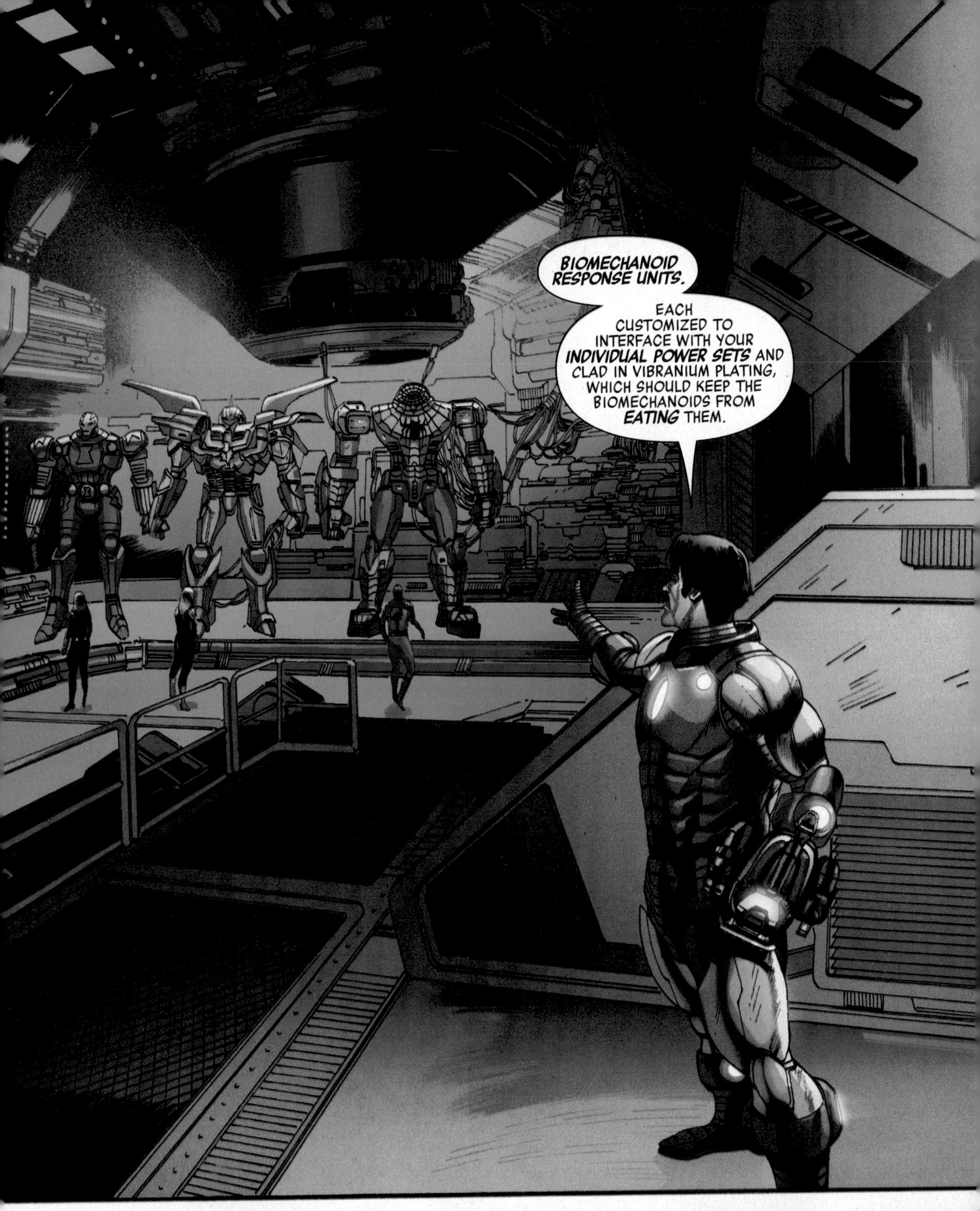
BIOMECHANOID RESPONSE UNITS.
EACH CUSTOMIZED TO INTERFACE WITH YOUR INDIVIDUAL POWER SETS AND CLAD IN VIBRANIUM PLATING, WHICH SHOULD KEEP THE BIOMECHANOIDS FROM EATING THEM.

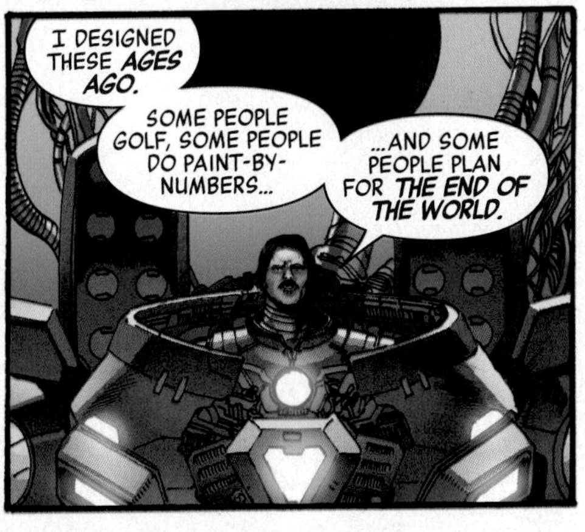
I DESIGNED THESE AGES AGO.
SOME PEOPLE GOLF, SOME PEOPLE DO PAINT-BY-NUMBERS...
...AND SOME PEOPLE PLAN FOR THE END OF THE WORLD.

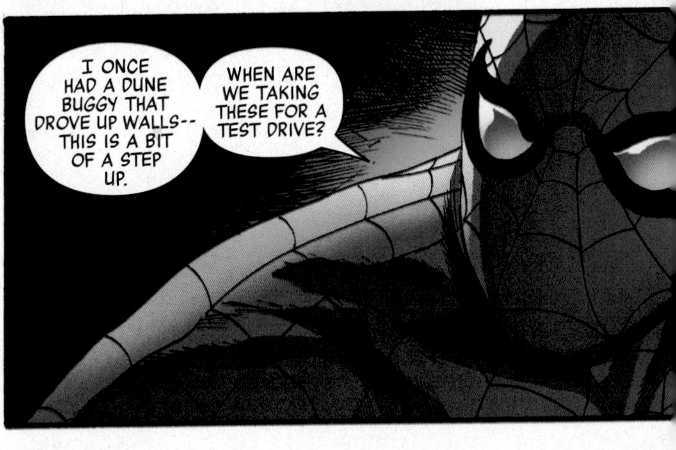
I ONCE HAD A DUNE BUGGY THAT DROVE UP WALLS-- THIS IS A BIT OF A STEP UP.
WHEN ARE WE TAKING THESE FOR A TEST DRIVE?

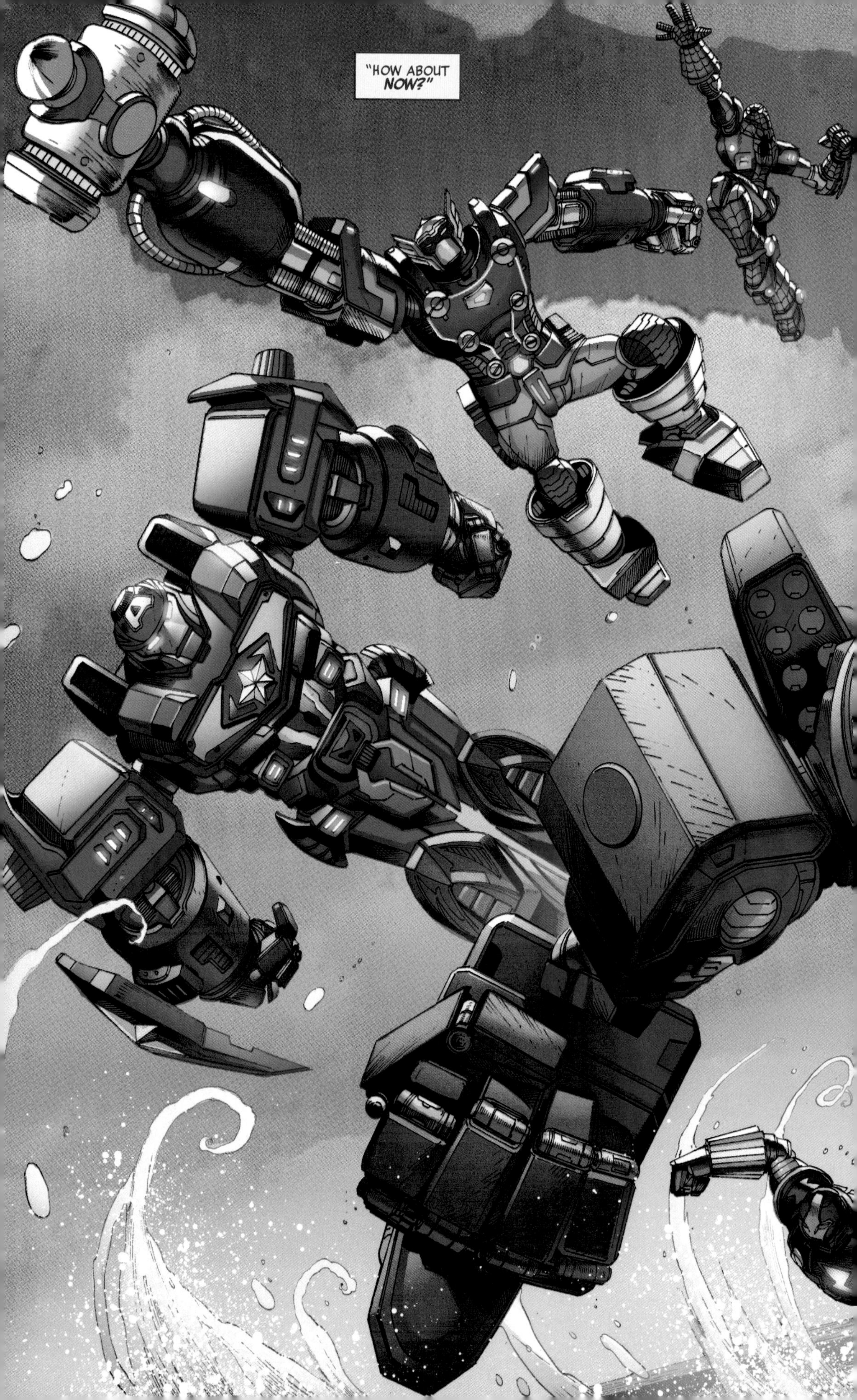
"HOW ABOUT NOW?"

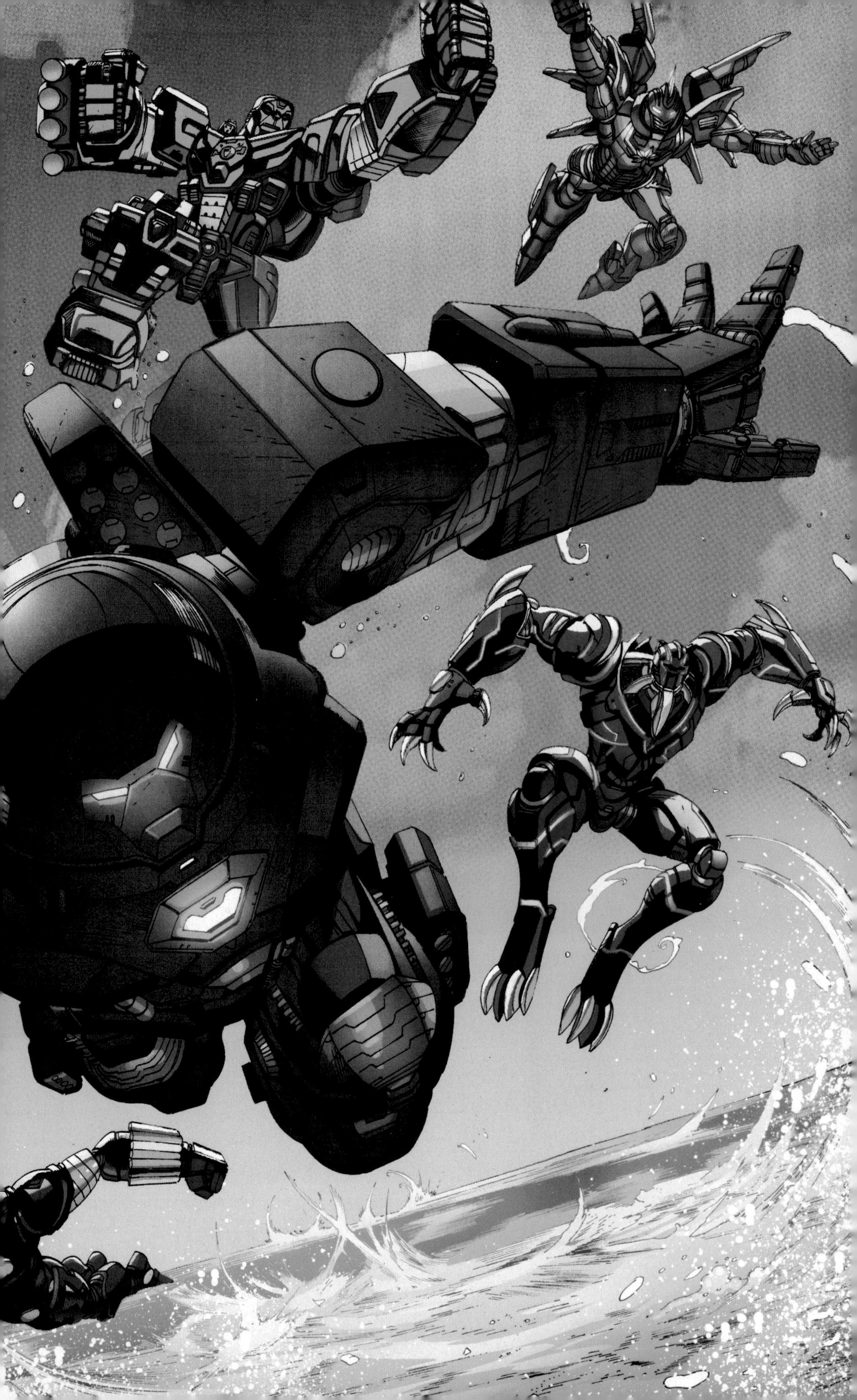

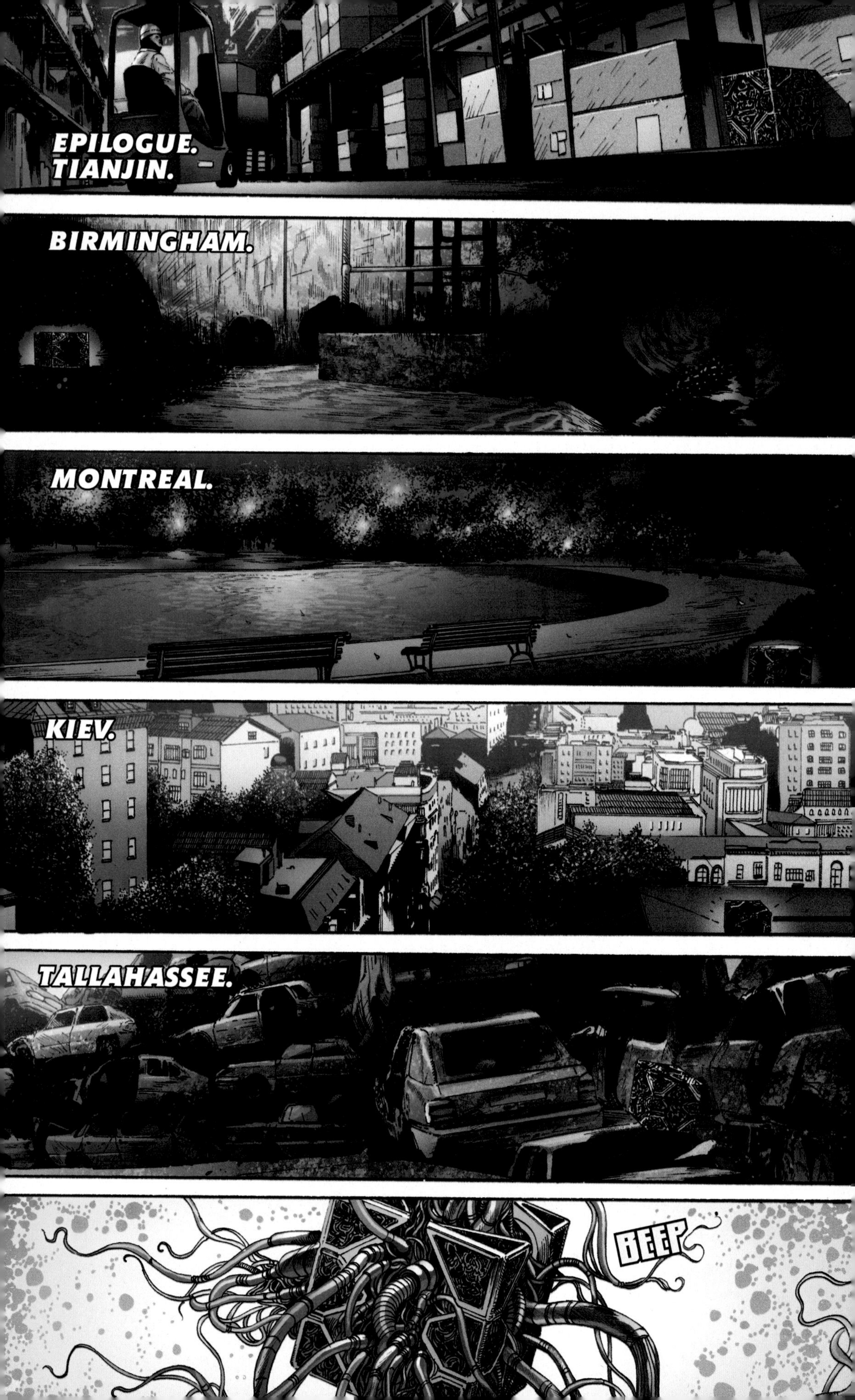
EPILOGUE.
TIANJIN.
BIRMINGHAM.
MONTREAL.
KIEV.
TALLAHASSEE.
BEEP

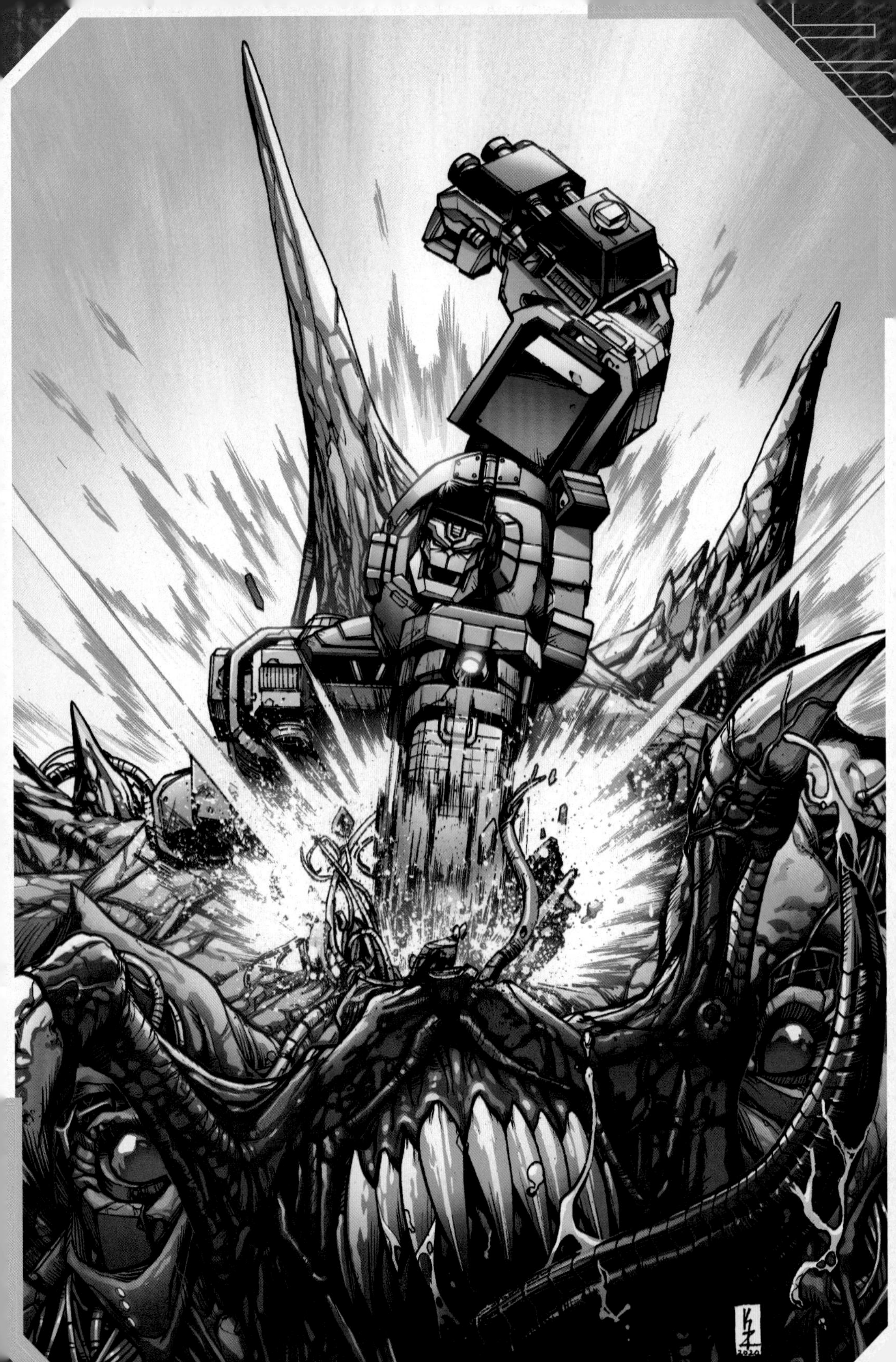

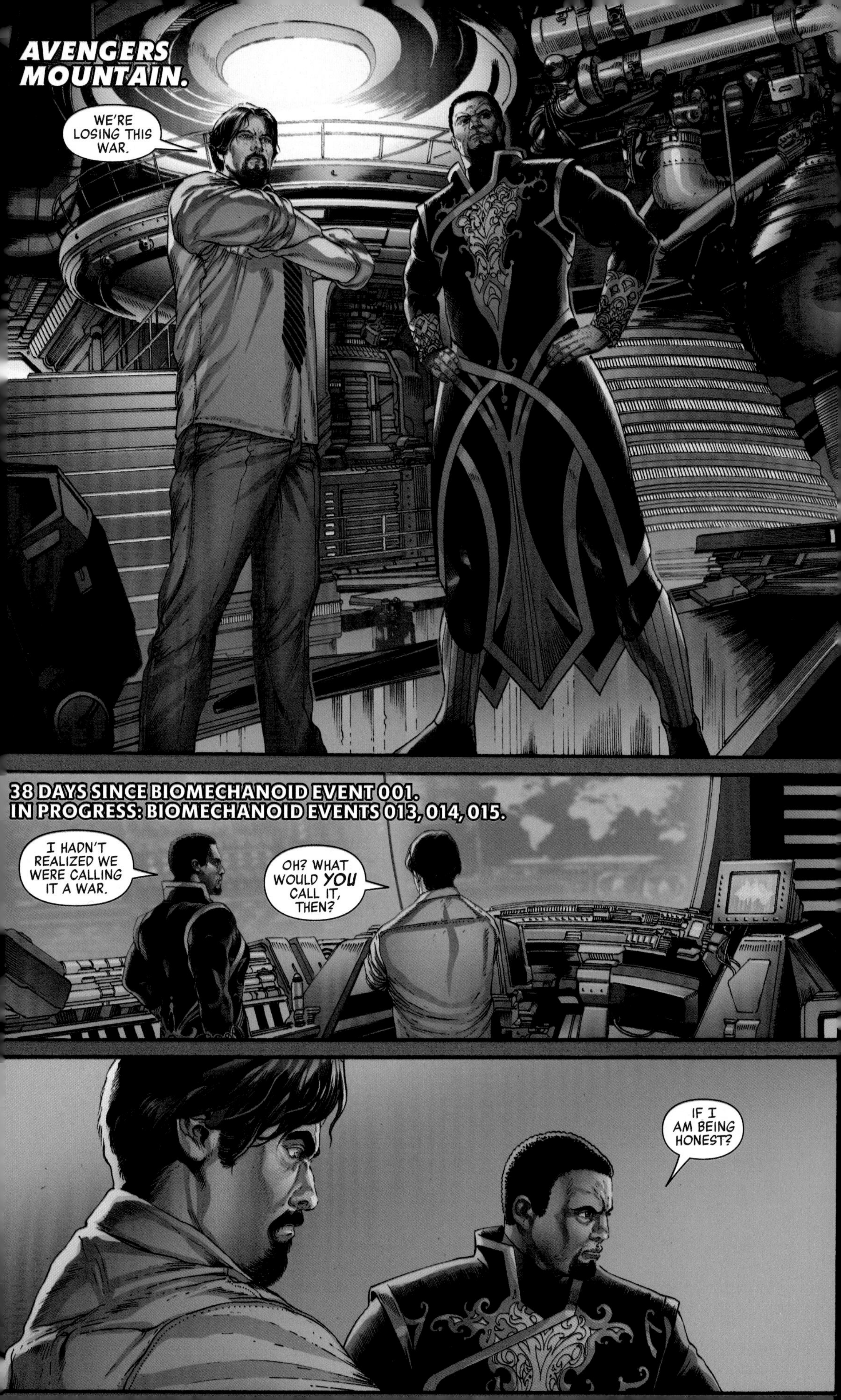
AVENGERS MOUNTAIN.
WE'RE LOSING THIS WAR.
38 DAYS SINCE BIOMECHANOID EVENT 001.
IN PROGRESS: BIOMECHANOID EVENTS 013, 014, 015.
I HADN'T REALIZED WE WERE CALLING IT A WAR.
OH? WHAT WOULD YOU CALL IT, THEN?
IF I AM BEING HONEST?

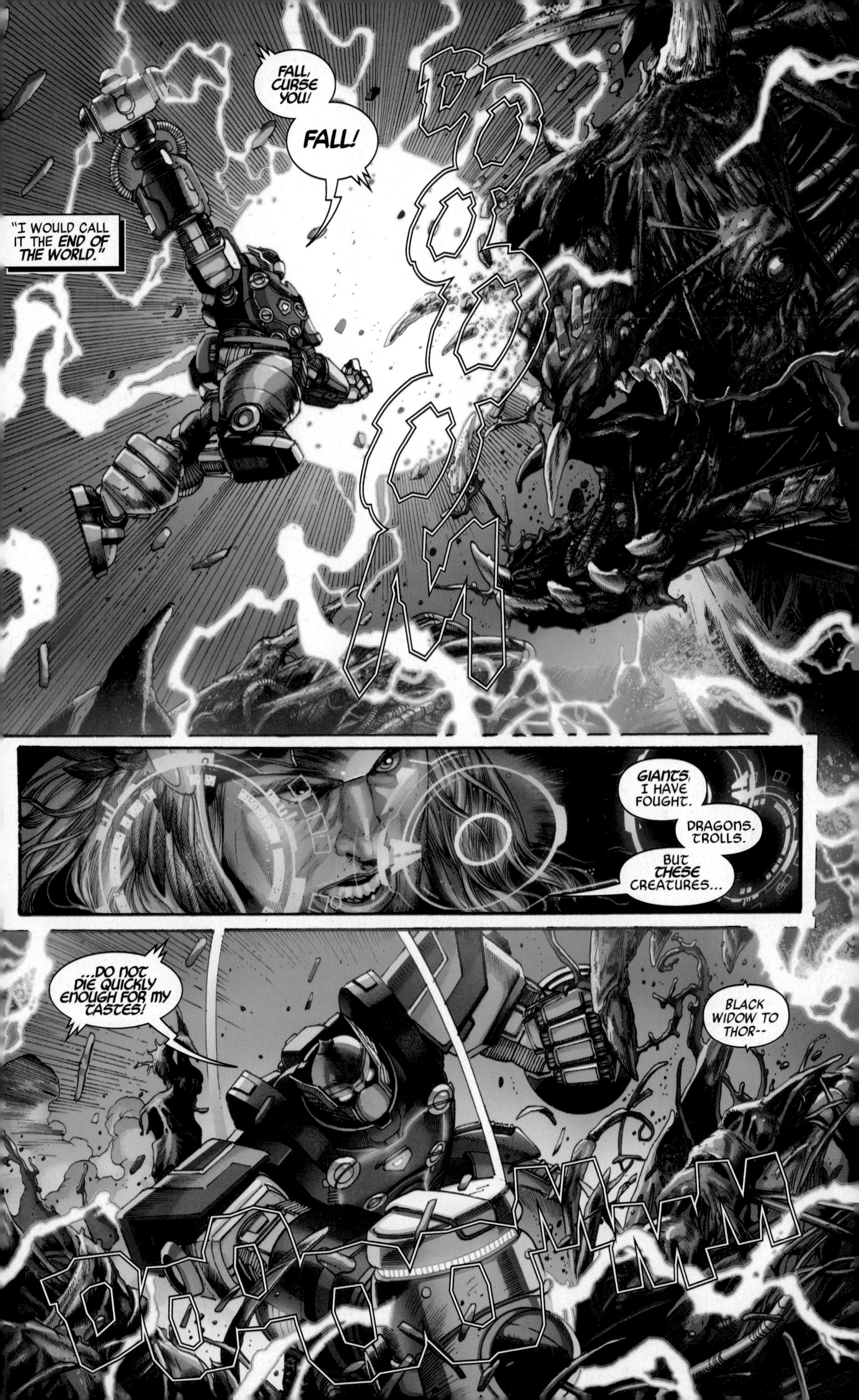
FALL, CURSE YOU!
FALL!
"I WOULD CALL IT THE END OF THE WORLD."
DOOOOOM
GIANTS, I HAVE FOUGHT.
DRAGONS. TROLLS.
BUT THESE CREATURES...
...DO NOT DIE QUICKLY ENOUGH FOR MY TASTES!
BLACK WIDOW TO THOR--
DOOOOOMMM

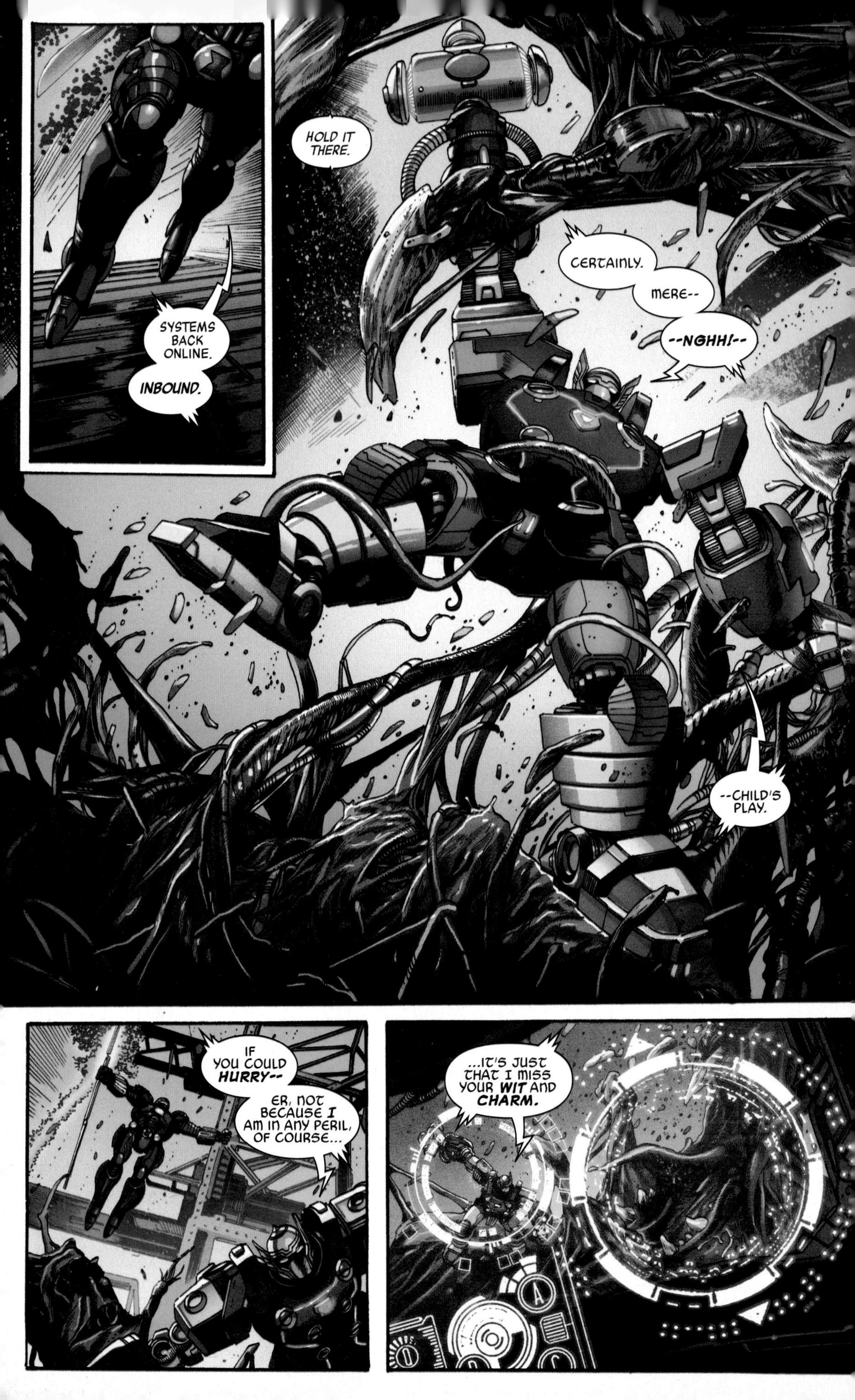
HOLD IT THERE.
SYSTEMS BACK ONLINE.
INBOUND.
CERTAINLY.
MERE--
--NGHH!--
--CHILD'S PLAY.
IF YOU COULD HURRY--
ER, NOT BECAUSE I AM IN ANY PERIL, OF COURSE...
...IT'S JUST THAT I MISS YOUR WIT AND CHARM.

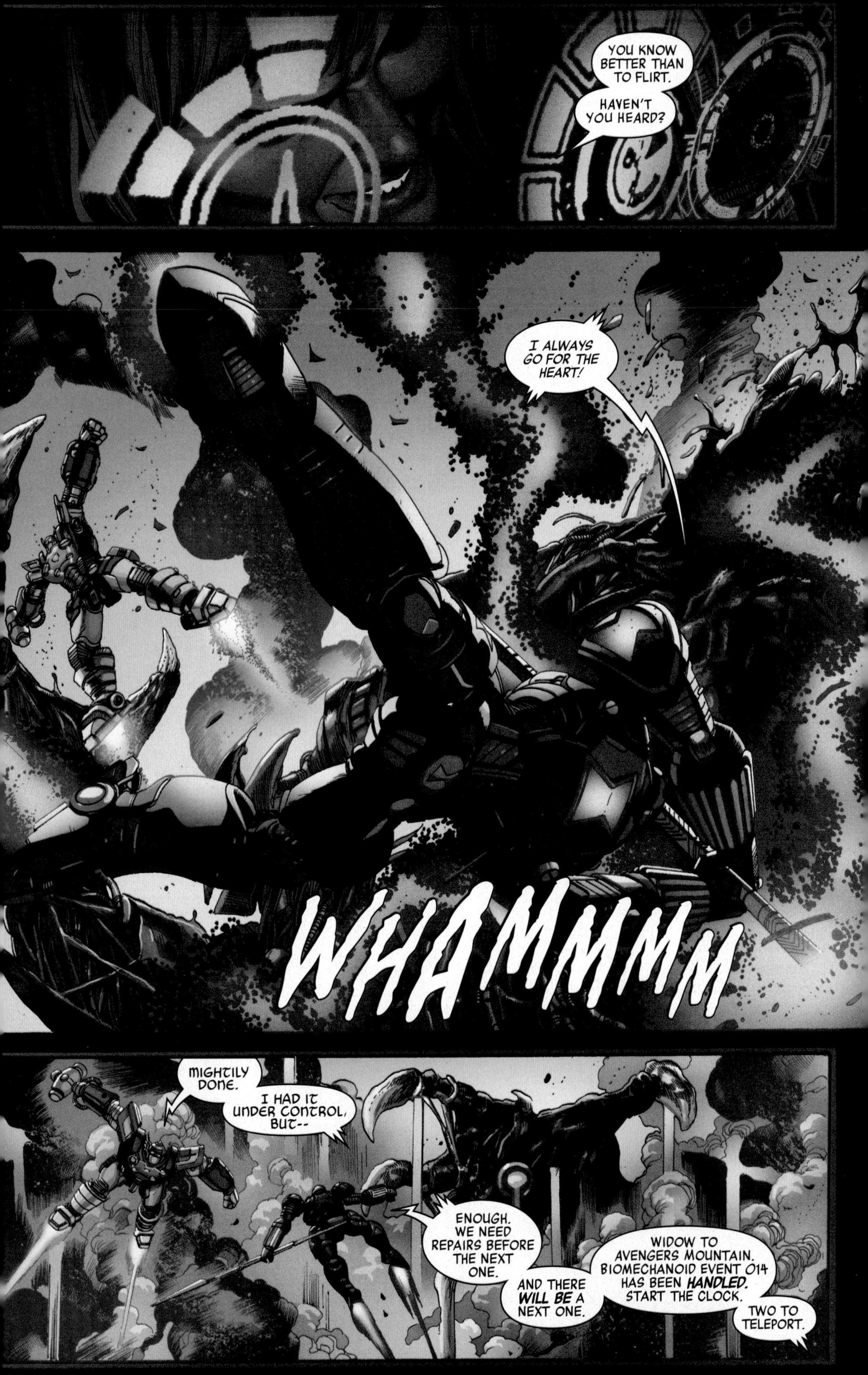
YOU KNOW BETTER THAN TO FLIRT.
HAVEN'T YOU HEARD?
I ALWAYS GO FOR THE HEART!
WHAMMMMM
MIGHTILY DONE.
I HAD IT UNDER CONTROL, BUT--
ENOUGH. WE NEED REPAIRS BEFORE THE NEXT ONE.
AND THERE WILL BE A NEXT ONE.
WIDOW TO AVENGERS MOUNTAIN. BIOMECHANOID EVENT 014 HAS BEEN HANDLED. START THE CLOCK.
TWO TO TELEPORT.

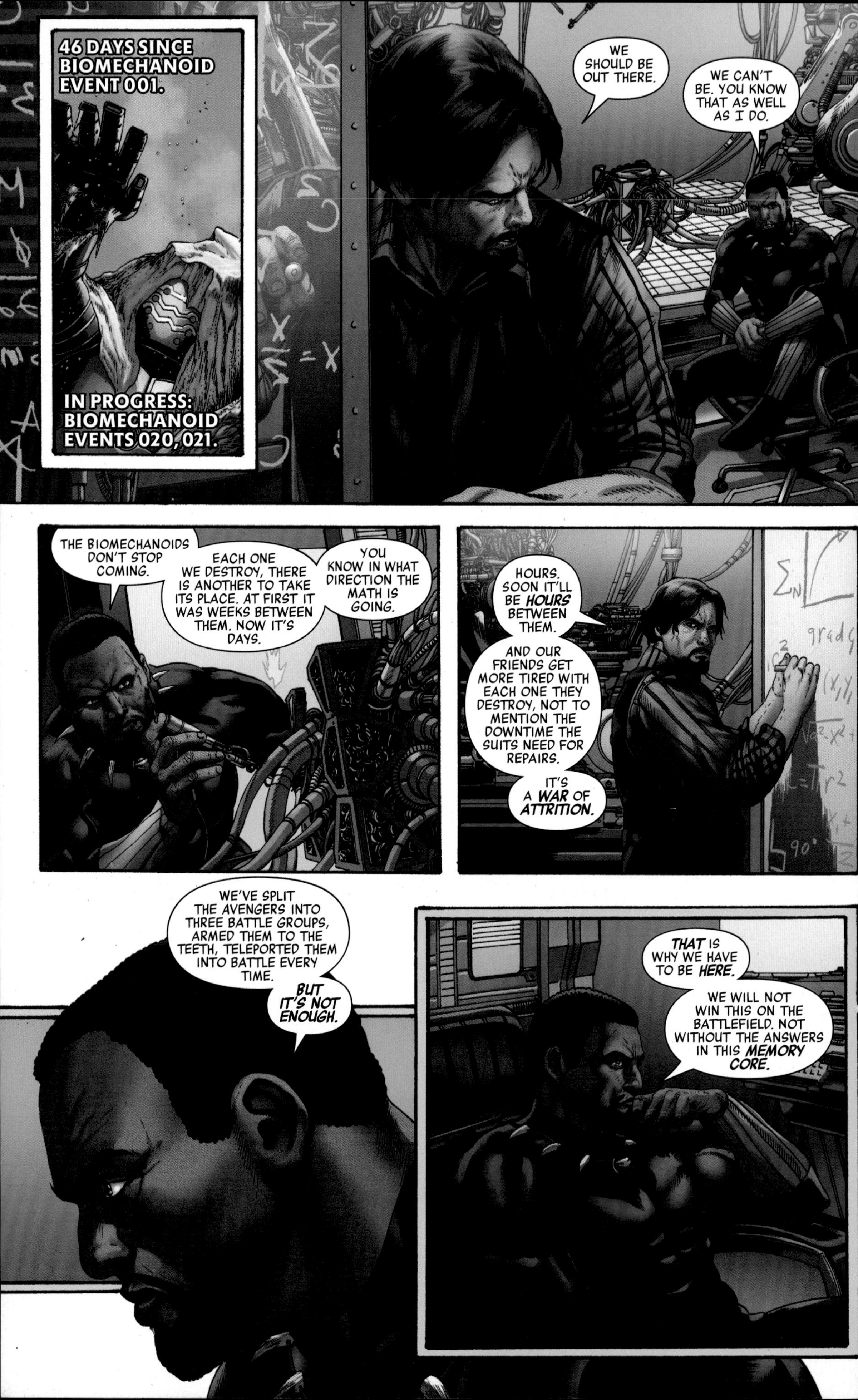

46 DAYS SINCE BIOMECHANOID EVENT 001.
IN PROGRESS: BIOMECHANOID EVENTS 020, 021.
WE SHOULD BE OUT THERE.
WE CAN'T BE. YOU KNOW THAT AS WELL AS I DO.
THE BIOMECHANOIDS DON'T STOP COMING.
EACH ONE WE DESTROY, THERE IS ANOTHER TO TAKE ITS PLACE. AT FIRST IT WAS WEEKS BETWEEN THEM. NOW IT'S DAYS.
YOU KNOW IN WHAT DIRECTION THE MATH IS GOING.
HOURS. SOON IT'LL BE HOURS BETWEEN THEM.
AND OUR FRIENDS GET MORE TIRED WITH EACH ONE THEY DESTROY, NOT TO MENTION THE DOWNTIME THE SUITS NEED FOR REPAIRS.
IT'S A WAR OF ATTRITION.
WE'VE SPLIT THE AVENGERS INTO THREE BATTLE GROUPS, ARMED THEM TO THE TEETH, TELEPORTED THEM INTO BATTLE EVERY TIME.
BUT IT'S NOT ENOUGH.
THAT IS WHY WE HAVE TO BE HERE.
WE WILL NOT WIN THIS ON THE BATTLEFIELD. NOT WITHOUT THE ANSWERS IN THIS MEMORY CORE.

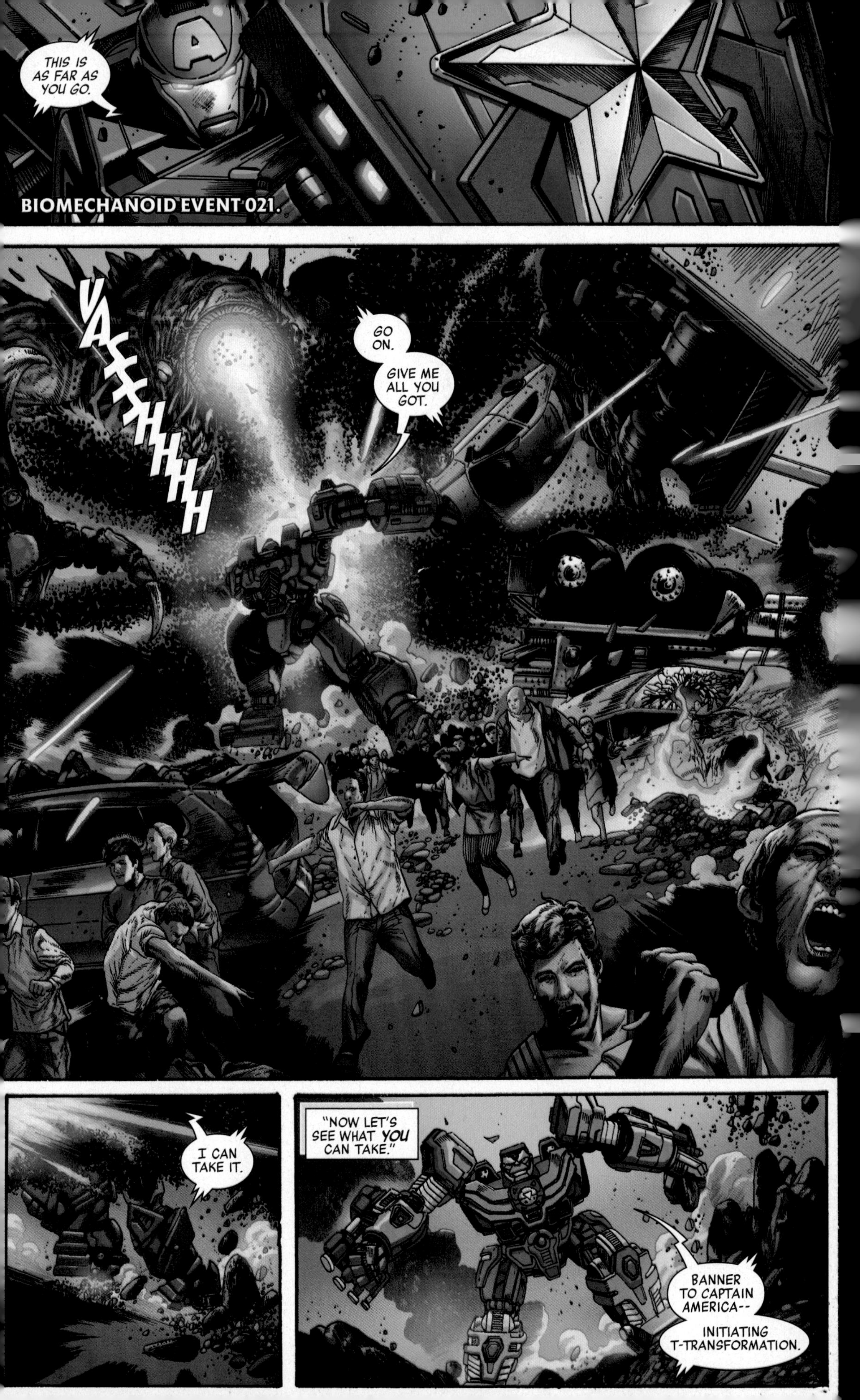
THIS IS AS FAR AS YOU GO.
BIOMECHANOID EVENT 021.
VASSSHHHHH
GO ON.
GIVE ME ALL YOU GOT.
I CAN TAKE IT.
"NOW LET'S SEE WHAT YOU CAN TAKE."
BANNER TO CAPTAIN AMERICA--
INITIATING T-TRANSFORMATION.

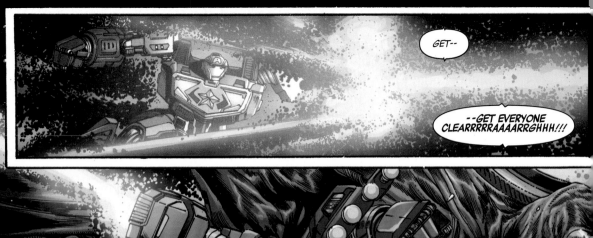

GET--

--GET EVERYONE CLEARRRRAAAARRGHHH!!!

HUR.

HUR HUR HUR.

ABOUT TIME...

...YOU CLOSED YOUR BIG MOUTH.

APPRECIATE THE ASSIST, DR. BANNER.

HULK!

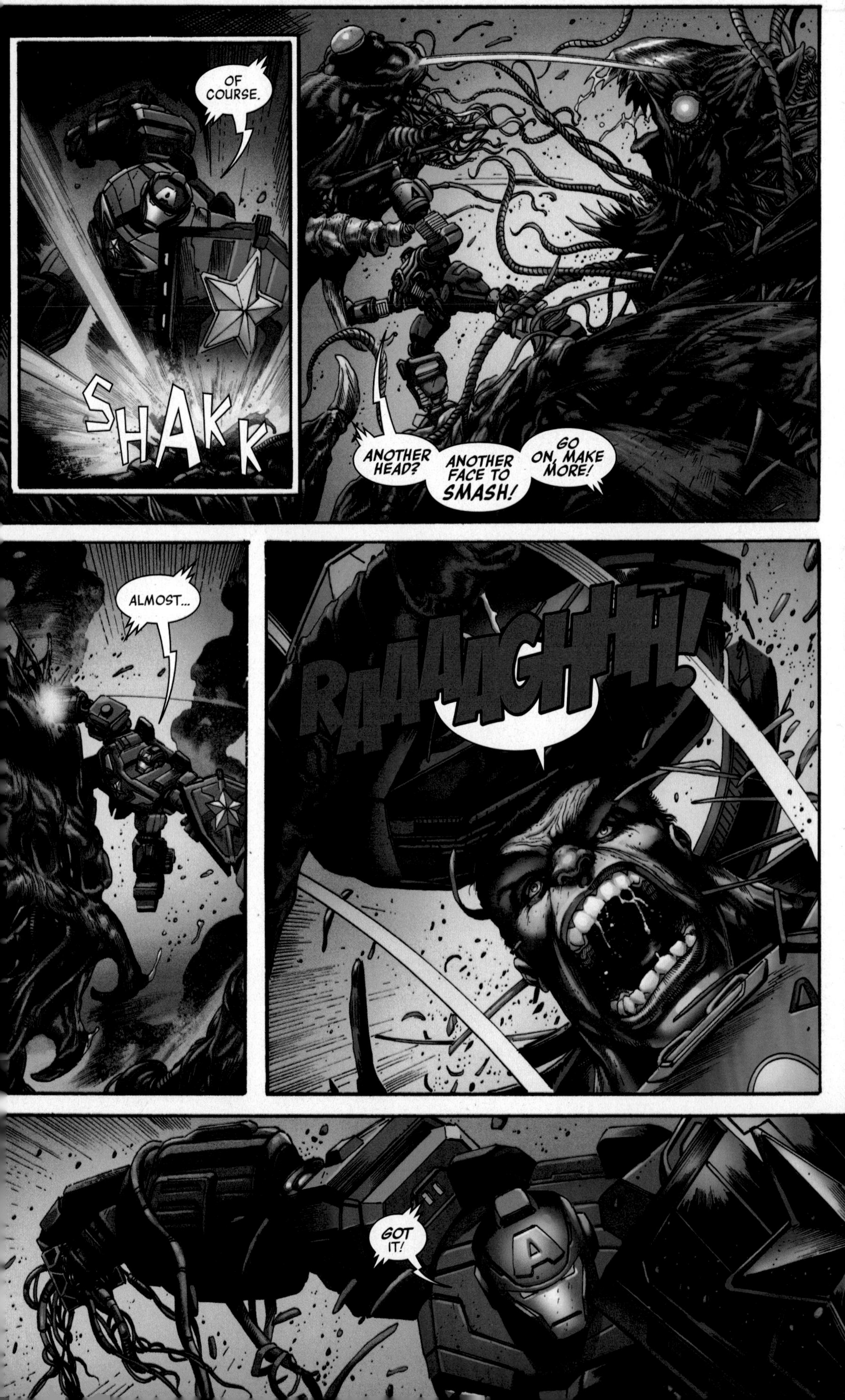
OF COURSE.
SHAKK
ANOTHER HEAD?
ANOTHER FACE TO SMASH!
GO ON, MAKE MORE!
ALMOST...
RAAAAGHHH!
GOT IT!

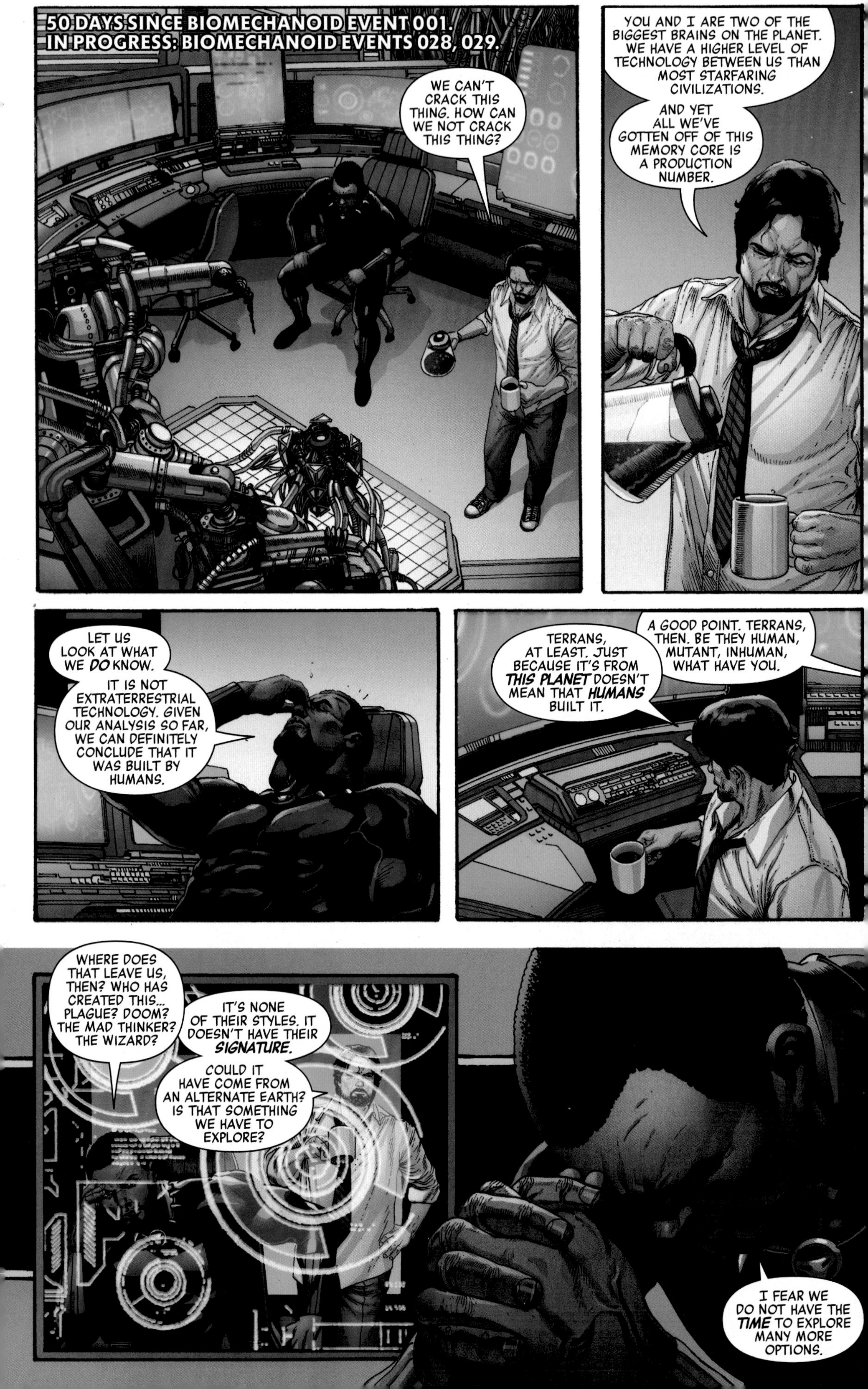
50 DAYS SINCE BIOMECHANOID EVENT 001.
IN PROGRESS: BIOMECHANOID EVENTS 028, 029.
WE CAN'T CRACK THIS THING. HOW CAN WE NOT CRACK THIS THING?
YOU AND I ARE TWO OF THE BIGGEST BRAINS ON THE PLANET. WE HAVE A HIGHER LEVEL OF TECHNOLOGY BETWEEN US THAN MOST STARFARING CIVILIZATIONS.
AND YET ALL WE'VE GOTTEN OFF OF THIS MEMORY CORE IS A PRODUCTION NUMBER.
LET US LOOK AT WHAT WE *DO* KNOW.
IT IS NOT EXTRATERRESTRIAL TECHNOLOGY. GIVEN OUR ANALYSIS SO FAR, WE CAN DEFINITELY CONCLUDE THAT IT WAS BUILT BY HUMANS.
TERRANS, AT LEAST. JUST BECAUSE IT'S FROM *THIS PLANET* DOESN'T MEAN THAT *HUMANS* BUILT IT.
A GOOD POINT. TERRANS, THEN. BE THEY HUMAN, MUTANT, INHUMAN, WHAT HAVE YOU.
WHERE DOES THAT LEAVE US, THEN? WHO HAS CREATED THIS... PLAGUE? DOOM? THE MAD THINKER? THE WIZARD?
IT'S NONE OF THEIR STYLES. IT DOESN'T HAVE THEIR *SIGNATURE.*
COULD IT HAVE COME FROM AN ALTERNATE EARTH? IS THAT SOMETHING WE HAVE TO EXPLORE?
I FEAR WE DO NOT HAVE THE *TIME* TO EXPLORE MANY MORE OPTIONS.

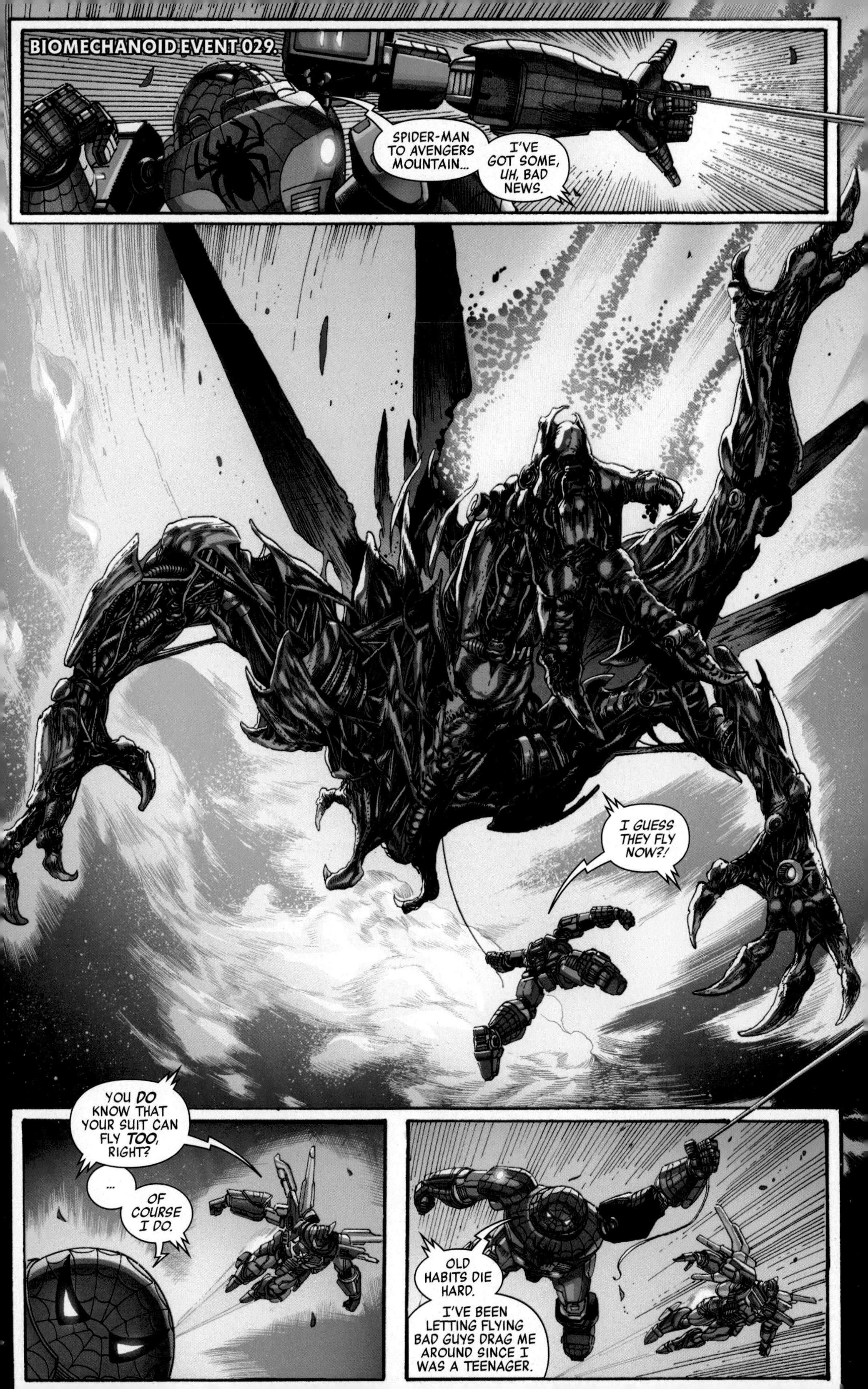
BIOMECHANOID EVENT 029.
SPIDER-MAN TO AVENGERS MOUNTAIN...
I'VE GOT SOME, UH, BAD NEWS.
I GUESS THEY FLY NOW?!
YOU DO KNOW THAT YOUR SUIT CAN FLY TOO, RIGHT?
...
OF COURSE I DO.
OLD HABITS DIE HARD.
I'VE BEEN LETTING FLYING BAD GUYS DRAG ME AROUND SINCE I WAS A TEENAGER.

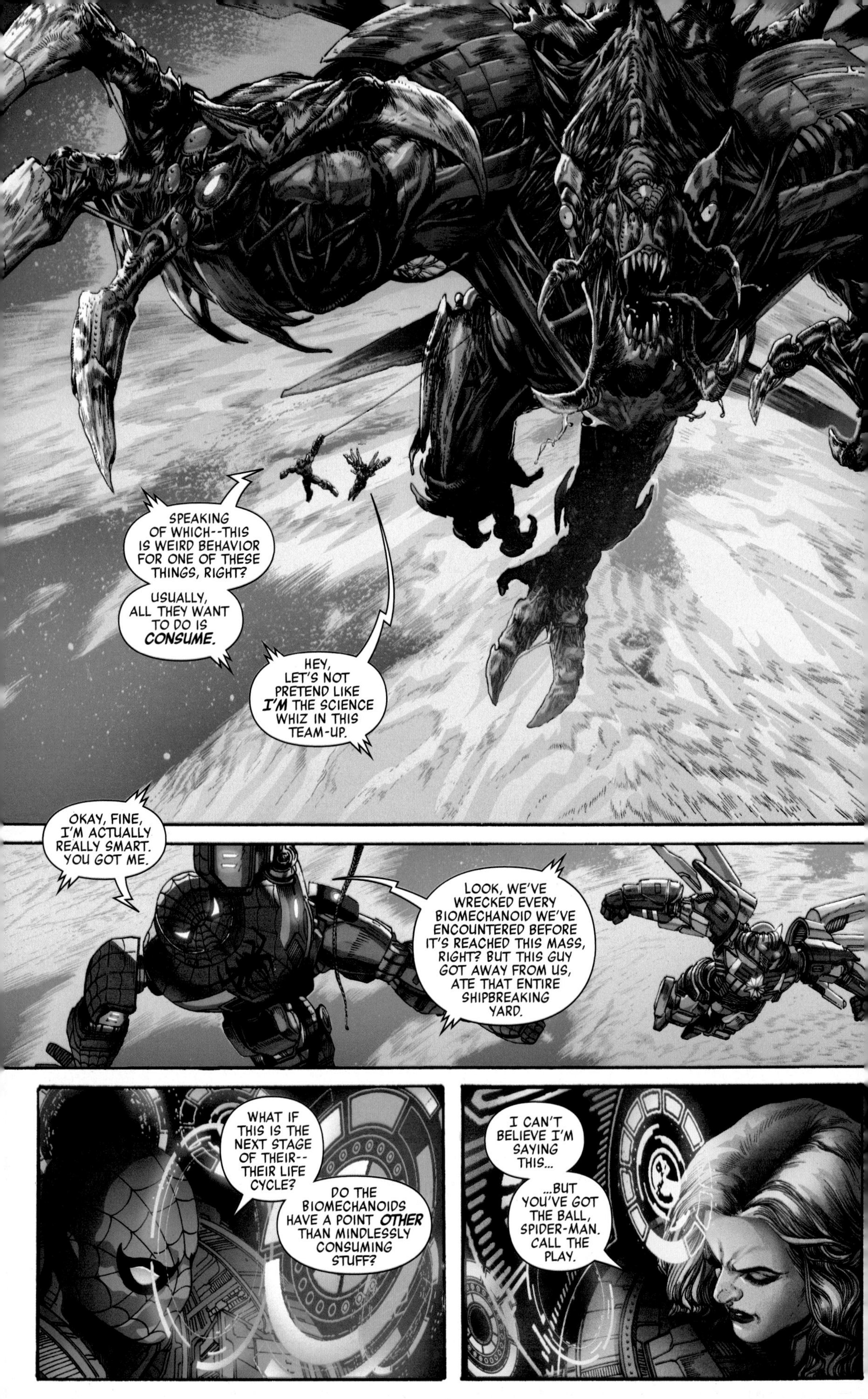
SPEAKING OF WHICH--THIS IS WEIRD BEHAVIOR FOR ONE OF THESE THINGS, RIGHT?
USUALLY, ALL THEY WANT TO DO IS CONSUME.
HEY, LET'S NOT PRETEND LIKE I'M THE SCIENCE WHIZ IN THIS TEAM-UP.
OKAY, FINE, I'M ACTUALLY REALLY SMART. YOU GOT ME.
LOOK, WE'VE WRECKED EVERY BIOMECHANOID WE'VE ENCOUNTERED BEFORE IT'S REACHED THIS MASS, RIGHT? BUT THIS GUY GOT AWAY FROM US, ATE THAT ENTIRE SHIPBREAKING YARD.
WHAT IF THIS IS THE NEXT STAGE OF THEIR--THEIR LIFE CYCLE?
DO THE BIOMECHANOIDS HAVE A POINT OTHER THAN MINDLESSLY CONSUMING STUFF?
I CAN'T BELIEVE I'M SAYING THIS...
...BUT YOU'VE GOT THE BALL, SPIDER-MAN. CALL THE PLAY.

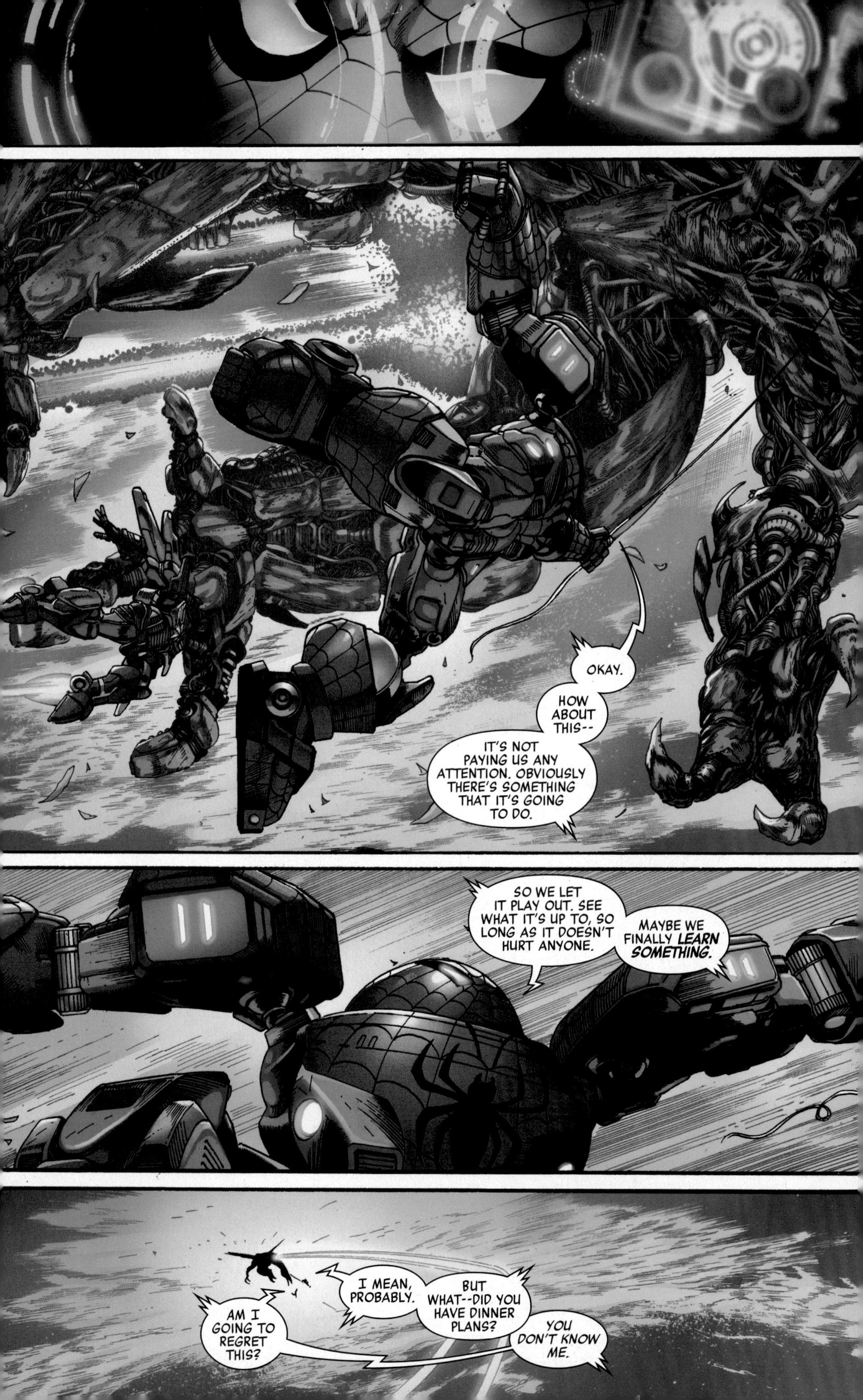
OKAY.
HOW ABOUT THIS--
IT'S NOT PAYING US ANY ATTENTION. OBVIOUSLY THERE'S SOMETHING THAT IT'S GOING TO DO.
SO WE LET IT PLAY OUT. SEE WHAT IT'S UP TO, SO LONG AS IT DOESN'T HURT ANYONE.
MAYBE WE FINALLY LEARN SOMETHING.
AM I GOING TO REGRET THIS?
I MEAN, PROBABLY.
BUT WHAT--DID YOU HAVE DINNER PLANS?
YOU DON'T KNOW ME.

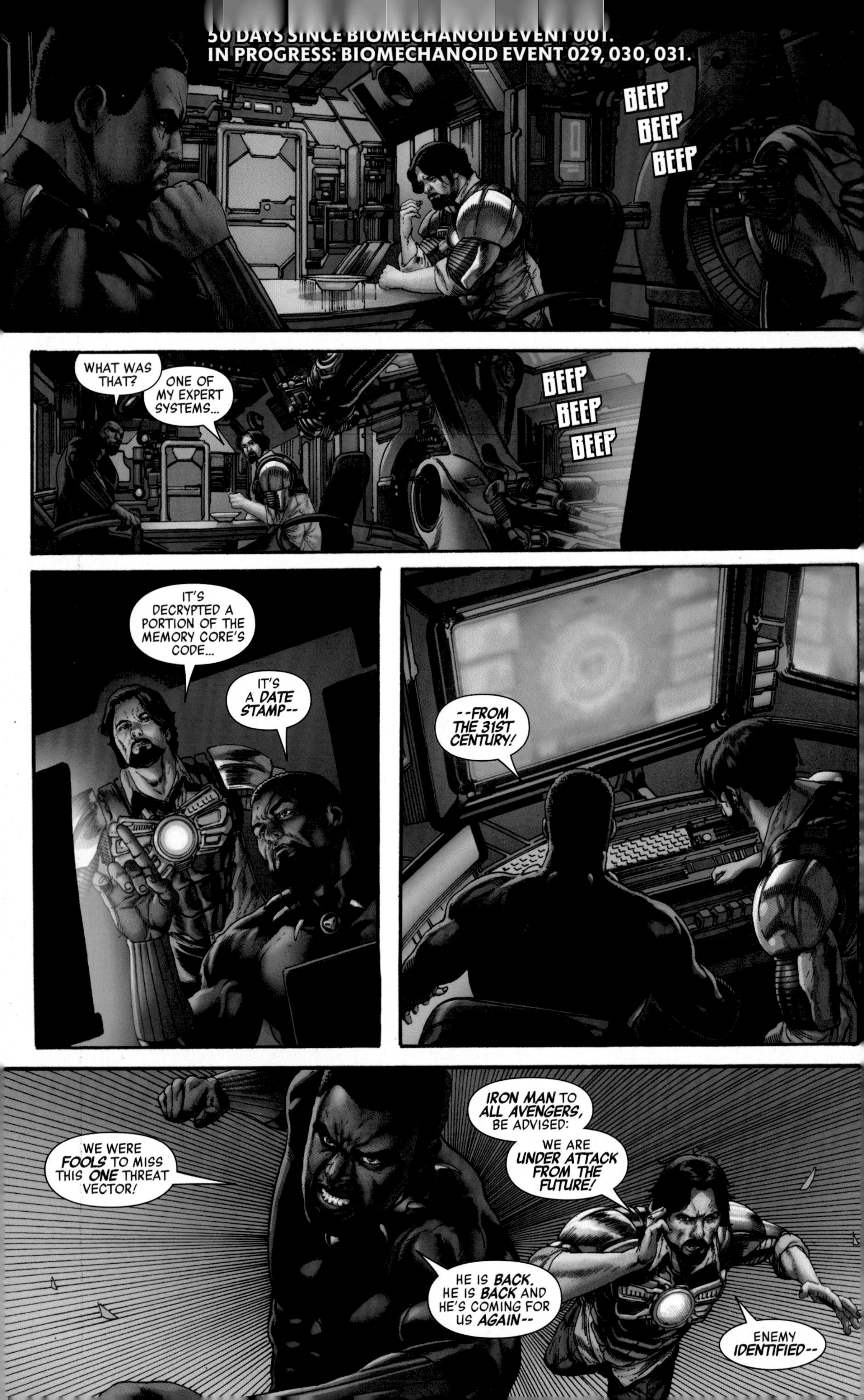

50 DAYS SINCE BIOMECHANOID EVENT 001.
IN PROGRESS: BIOMECHANOID EVENT 029, 030, 031.
BEEP BEEP BEEP
WHAT WAS THAT?
ONE OF MY EXPERT SYSTEMS...
BEEP BEEP BEEP
IT'S DECRYPTED A PORTION OF THE MEMORY CORE'S CODE...
IT'S A DATE STAMP--
--FROM THE 31ST CENTURY!
WE WERE FOOLS TO MISS THIS ONE THREAT VECTOR!
IRON MAN TO ALL AVENGERS, BE ADVISED:
WE ARE UNDER ATTACK FROM THE FUTURE!
HE IS BACK. HE IS BACK AND HE'S COMING FOR US AGAIN--
ENEMY IDENTIFIED--

KANG THE CONQUEROR.

NORMALLY AT THIS JUNCTURE I WOULD SAY "VERY GOOD" AND PERHAPS OFFER SOME IRONIC APPLAUSE.

BUT IN TRUTH...

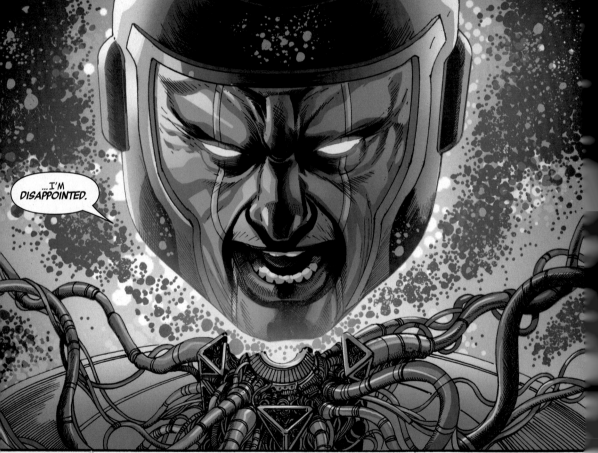

...I'M DISAPPOINTED.

I TOOK GREAT PAINS TO ENCRYPT MY CODING, TO HIDE THE ORIGINS OF MY BIOMECHANOID WEAPONS, DERIVED AS THEY WERE FROM MY GROWING MAN TECHNOLOGY...

...BUT STILL. YOU ARE ALL SUPPOSED TO BE THE AVENGERS.

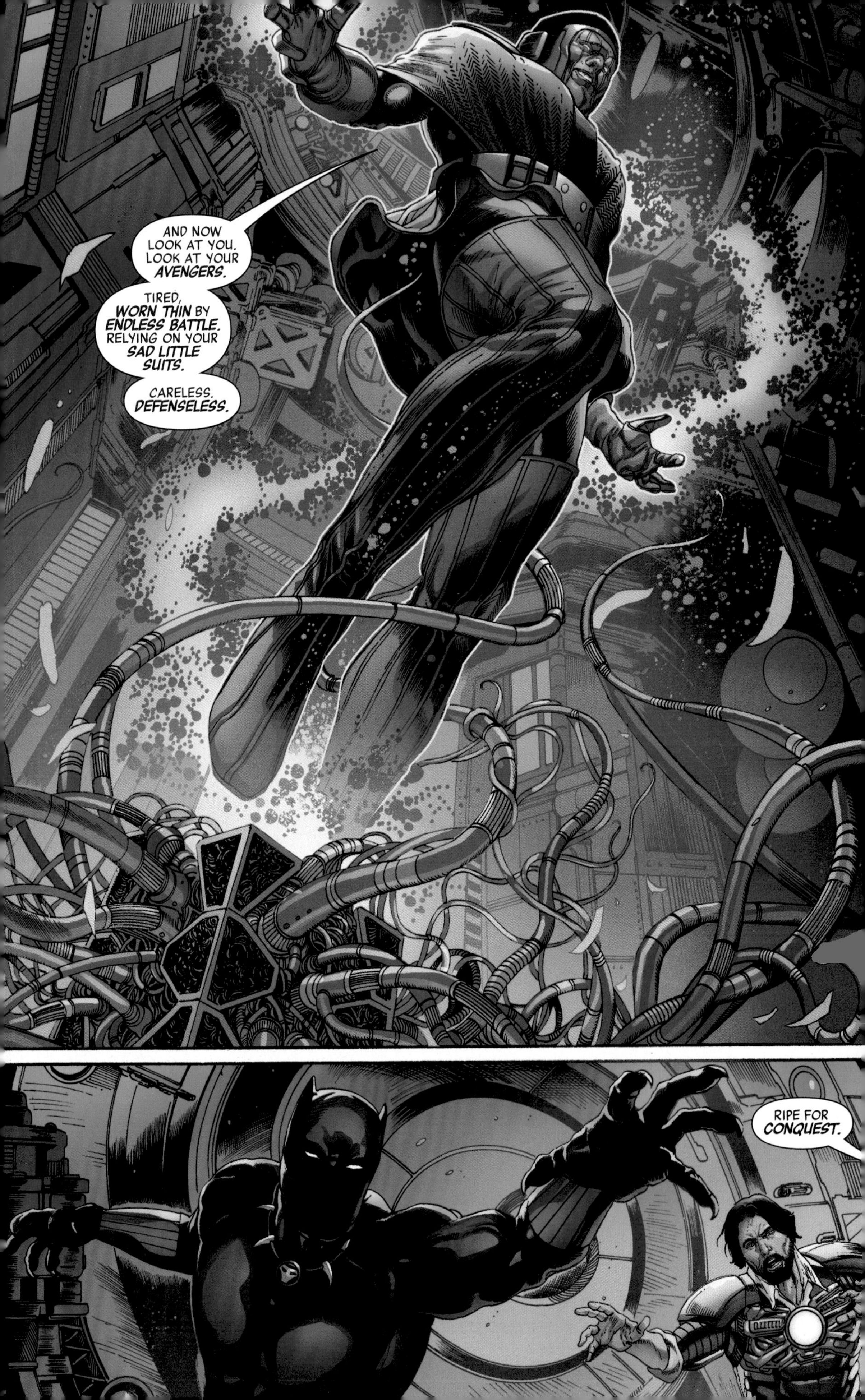
AND NOW LOOK AT YOU. LOOK AT YOUR AVENGERS.
TIRED, WORN THIN BY ENDLESS BATTLE. RELYING ON YOUR SAD LITTLE SUITS.
CARELESS. DEFENSELESS.
RIPE FOR CONQUEST.

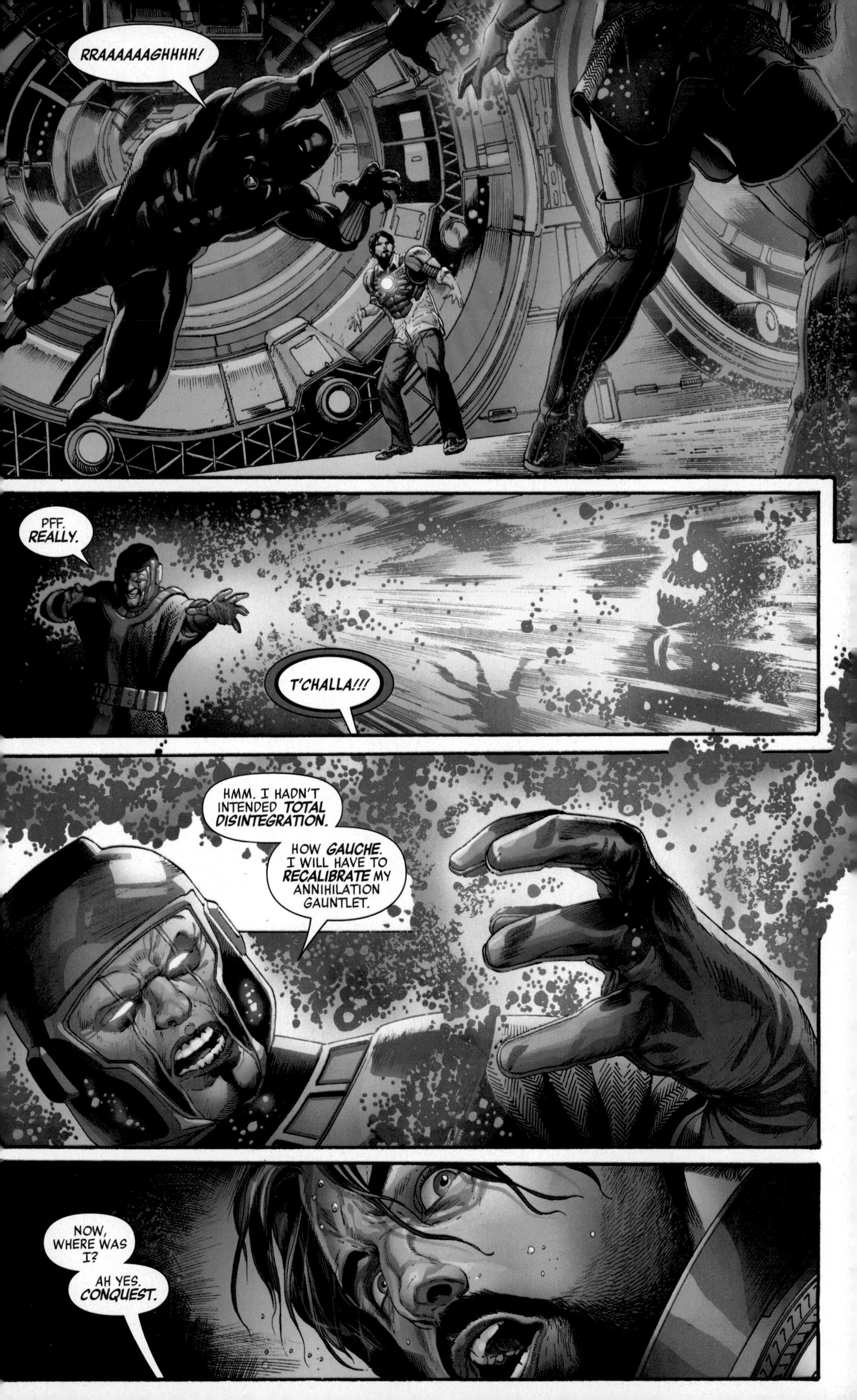
RRAAAAAAGHHHH!
PFF. REALLY.
T'CHALLA!!!
HMM. I HADN'T INTENDED TOTAL DISINTEGRATION.
HOW GAUCHE. I WILL HAVE TO RECALIBRATE MY ANNIHILATION GAUNTLET.
NOW, WHERE WAS I?
AH YES. CONQUEST.

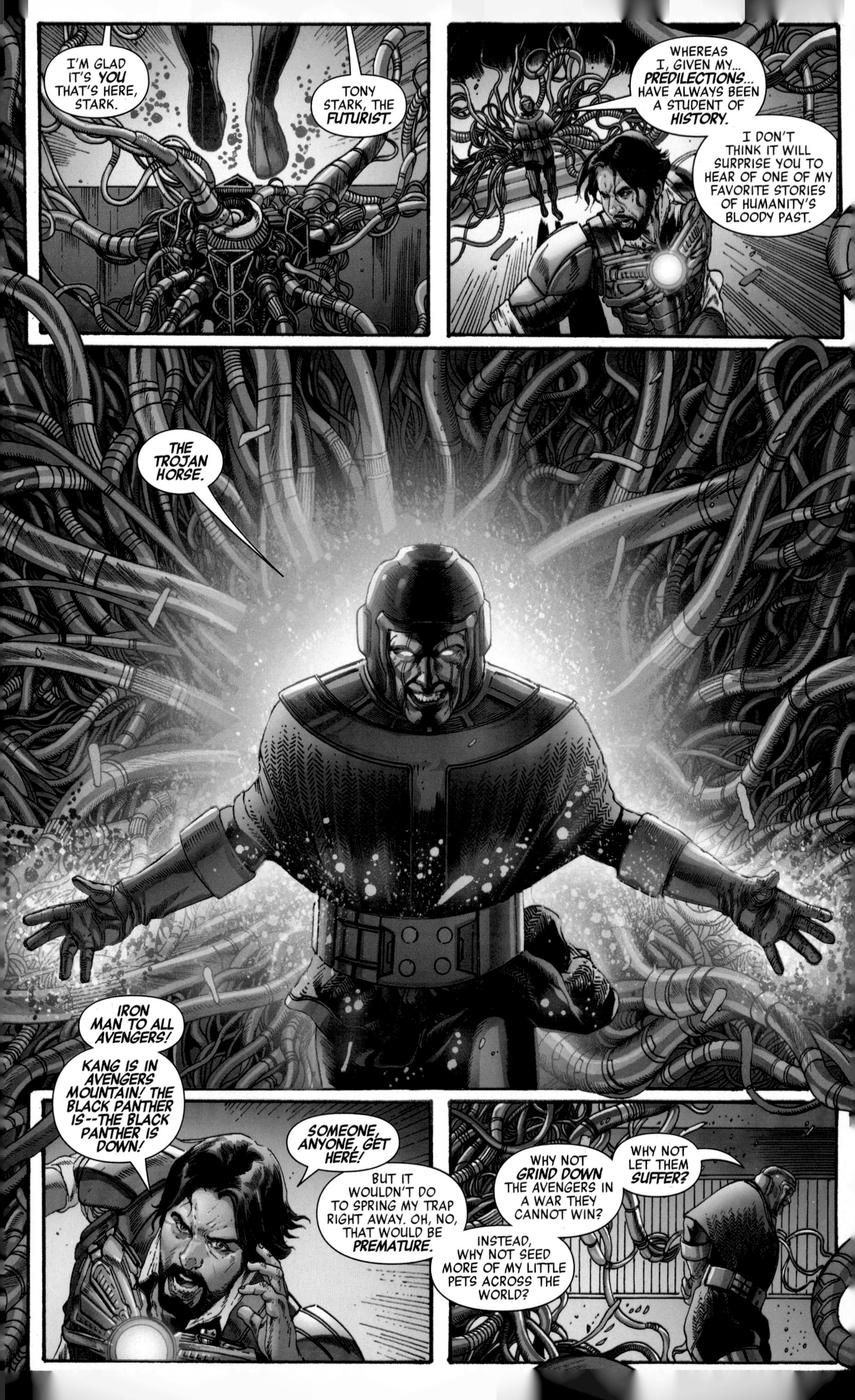
I'M GLAD IT'S YOU THAT'S HERE, STARK.
TONY STARK, THE FUTURIST.
WHEREAS I, GIVEN MY... PREDILECTIONS... HAVE ALWAYS BEEN A STUDENT OF HISTORY.
I DON'T THINK IT WILL SURPRISE YOU TO HEAR OF ONE OF MY FAVORITE STORIES OF HUMANITY'S BLOODY PAST.
THE TROJAN HORSE.
IRON MAN TO ALL AVENGERS!
KANG IS IN AVENGERS MOUNTAIN! THE BLACK PANTHER IS--THE BLACK PANTHER IS DOWN!
SOMEONE, ANYONE, GET HERE!
BUT IT WOULDN'T DO TO SPRING MY TRAP RIGHT AWAY. OH, NO, THAT WOULD BE PREMATURE.
WHY NOT GRIND DOWN THE AVENGERS IN A WAR THEY CANNOT WIN?
WHY NOT LET THEM SUFFER?
INSTEAD, WHY NOT SEED MORE OF MY LITTLE PETS ACROSS THE WORLD?

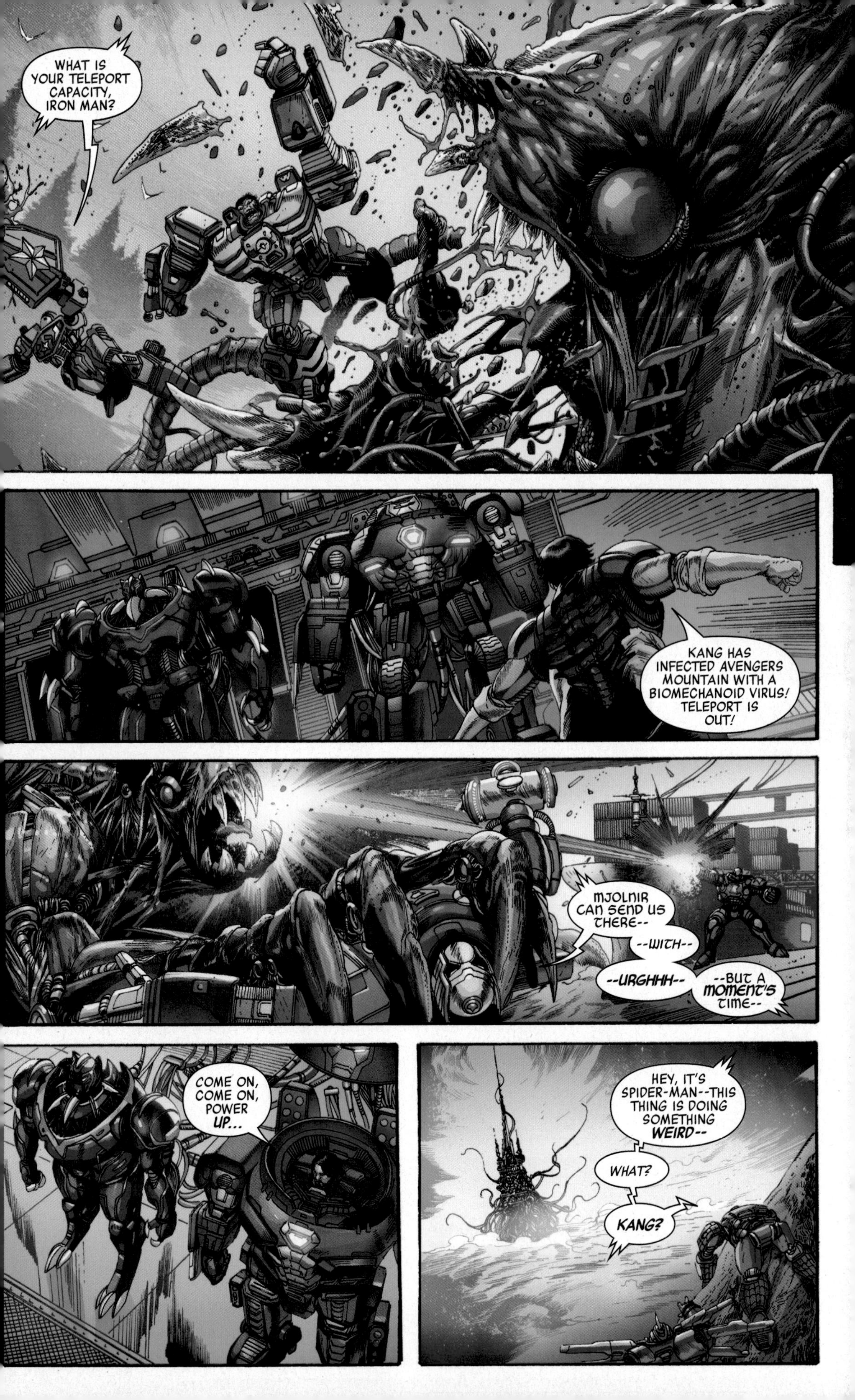
WHAT IS YOUR TELEPORT CAPACITY, IRON MAN?
KANG HAS INFECTED AVENGERS MOUNTAIN WITH A BIOMECHANOID VIRUS! TELEPORT IS OUT!
MJOLNIR CAN SEND US THERE--
--WITH--
--URGHHH--
--BUT A MOMENT'S TIME--
COME ON, COME ON, POWER UP...
HEY, IT'S SPIDER-MAN--THIS THING IS DOING SOMETHING WEIRD--
WHAT?
KANG?

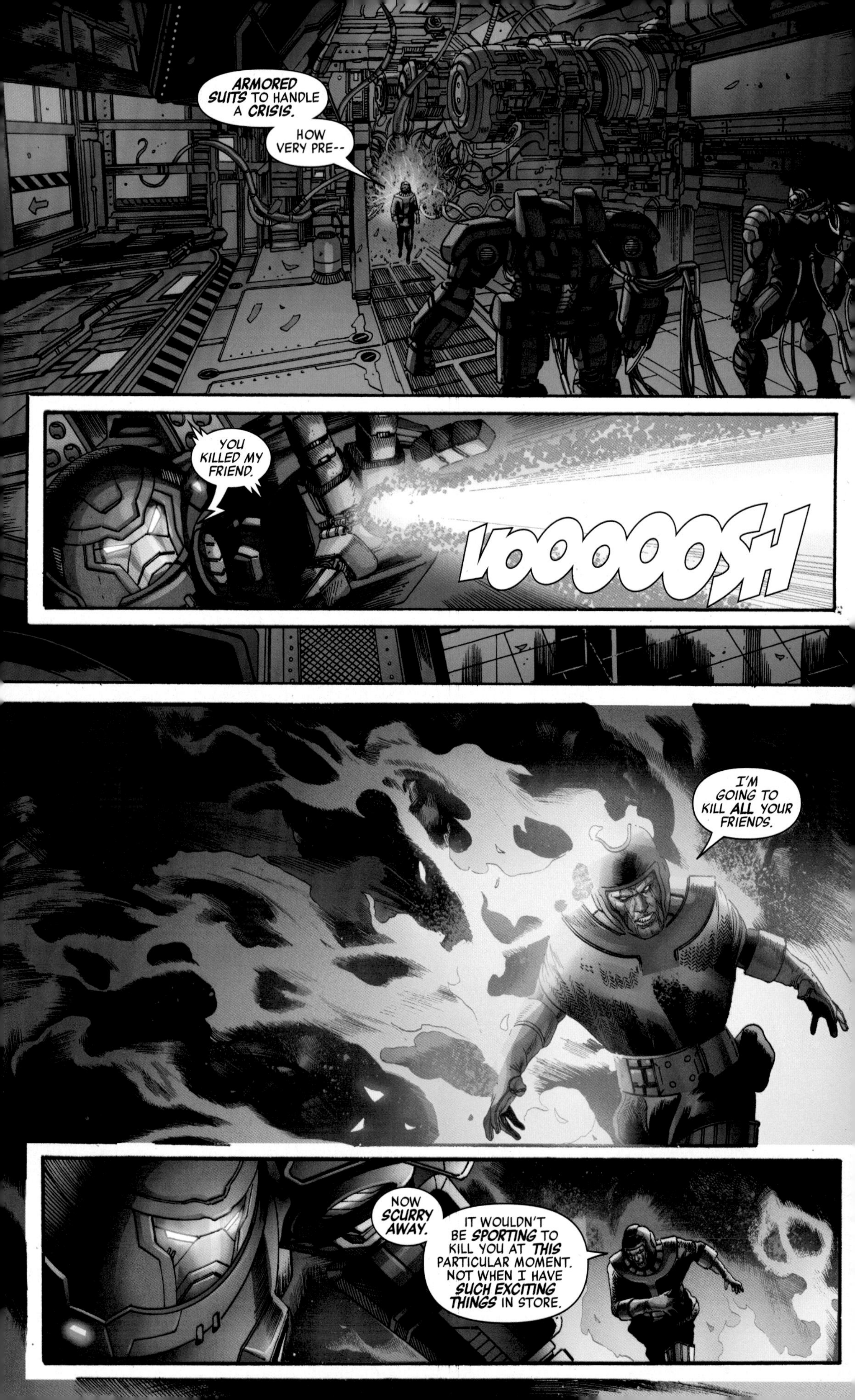
ARMORED SUITS TO HANDLE A CRISIS.
HOW VERY PRE--
YOU KILLED MY FRIEND.
VOOOOOSH
I'M GOING TO KILL ALL YOUR FRIENDS.
NOW SCURRY AWAY.
IT WOULDN'T BE SPORTING TO KILL YOU AT THIS PARTICULAR MOMENT. NOT WHEN I HAVE SUCH EXCITING THINGS IN STORE.

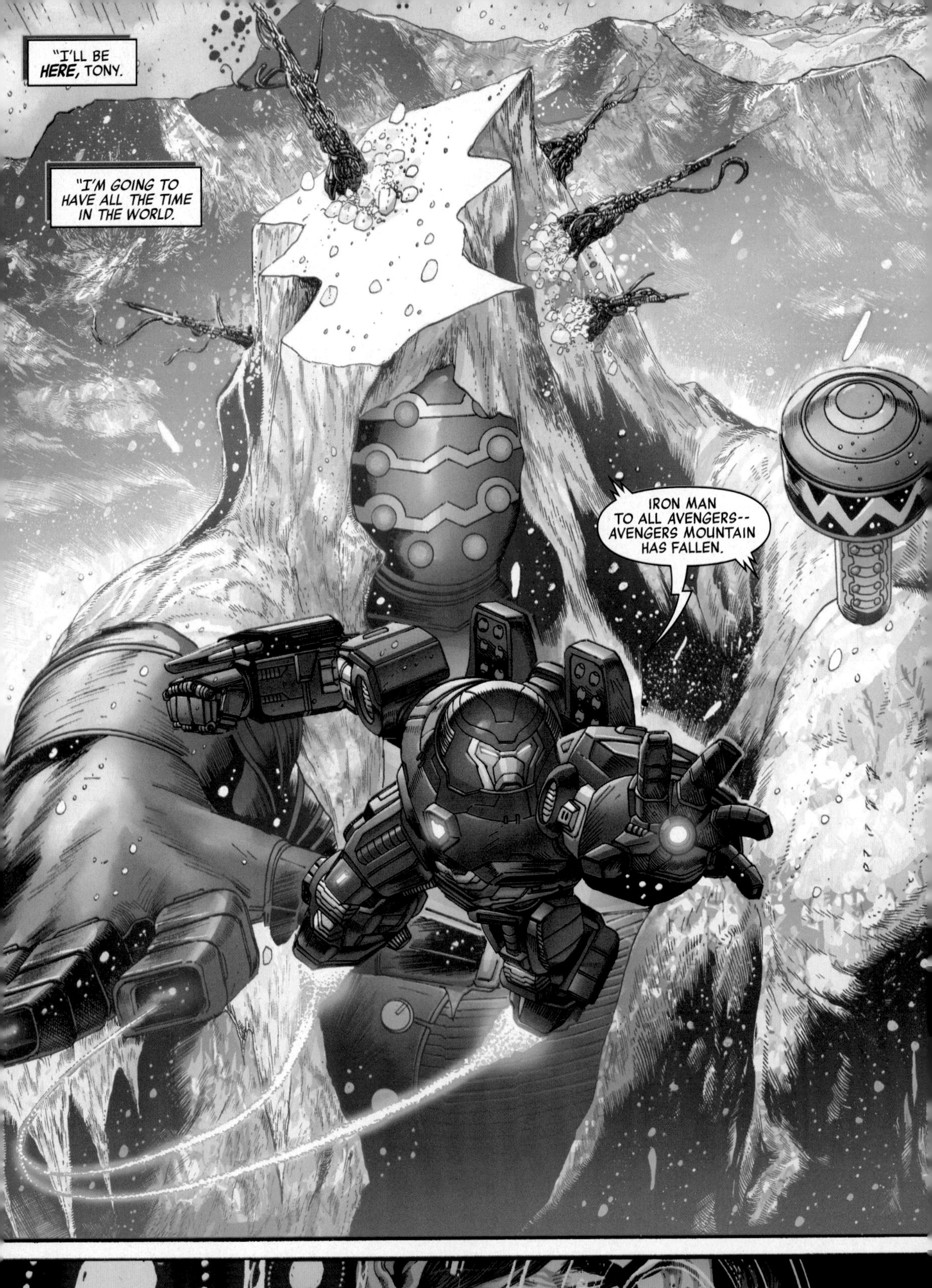
"I'LL BE HERE, TONY.
"I'M GOING TO HAVE ALL THE TIME IN THE WORLD.
IRON MAN TO ALL AVENGERS-- AVENGERS MOUNTAIN HAS FALLEN.

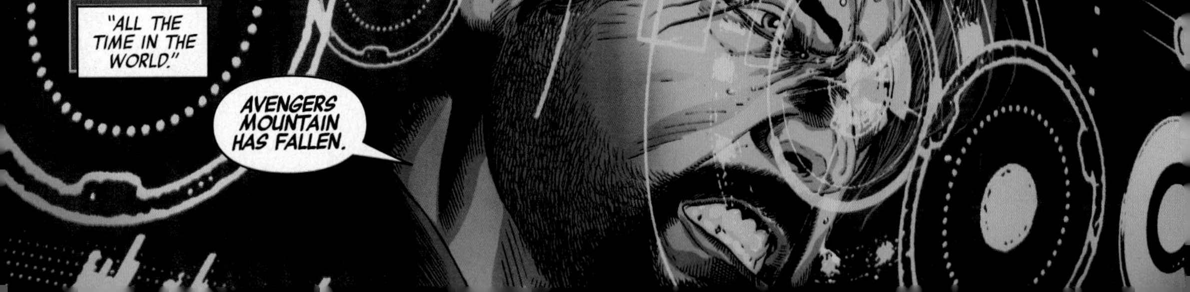
"ALL THE TIME IN THE WORLD."
AVENGERS MOUNTAIN HAS FALLEN.

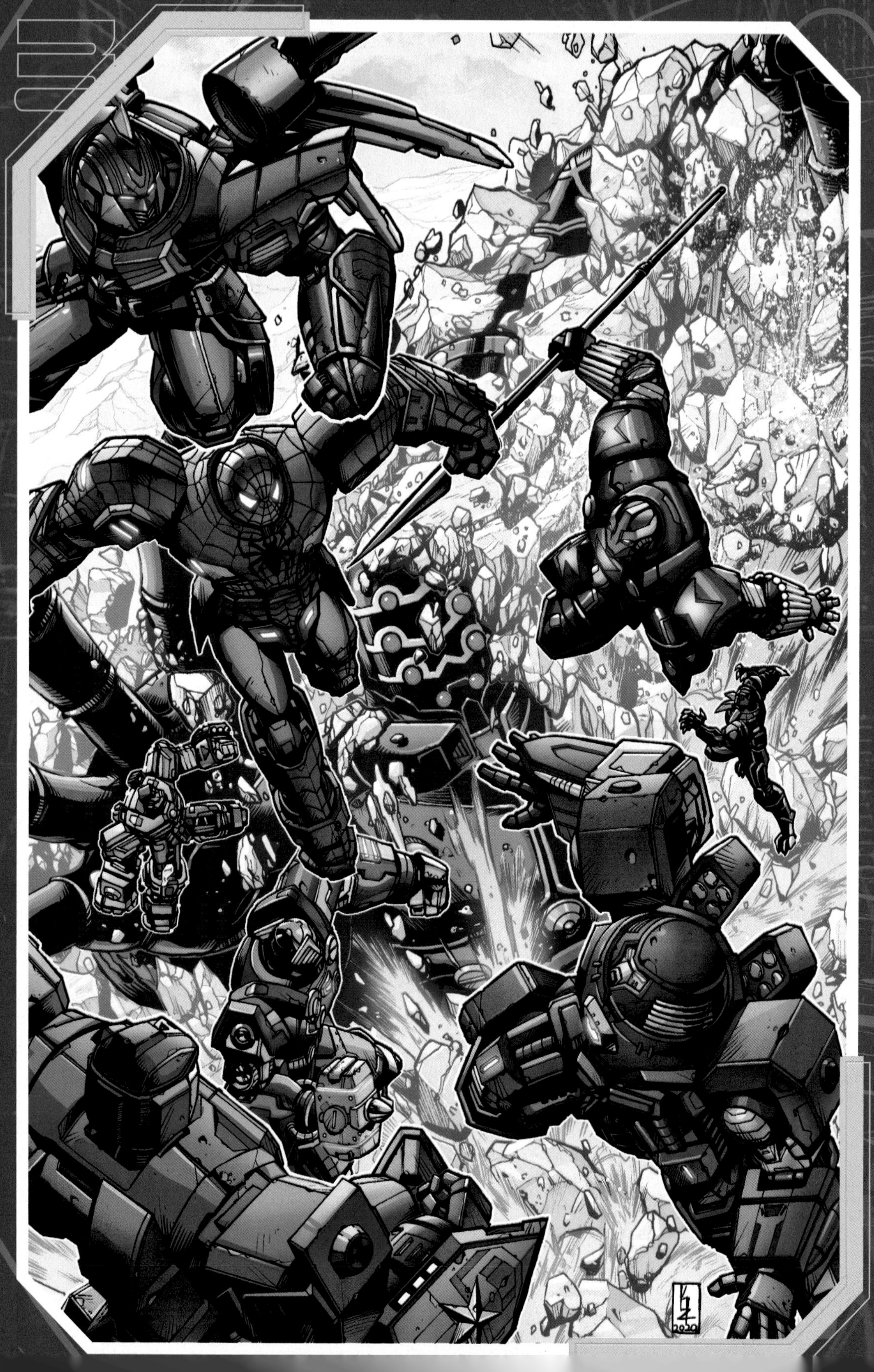

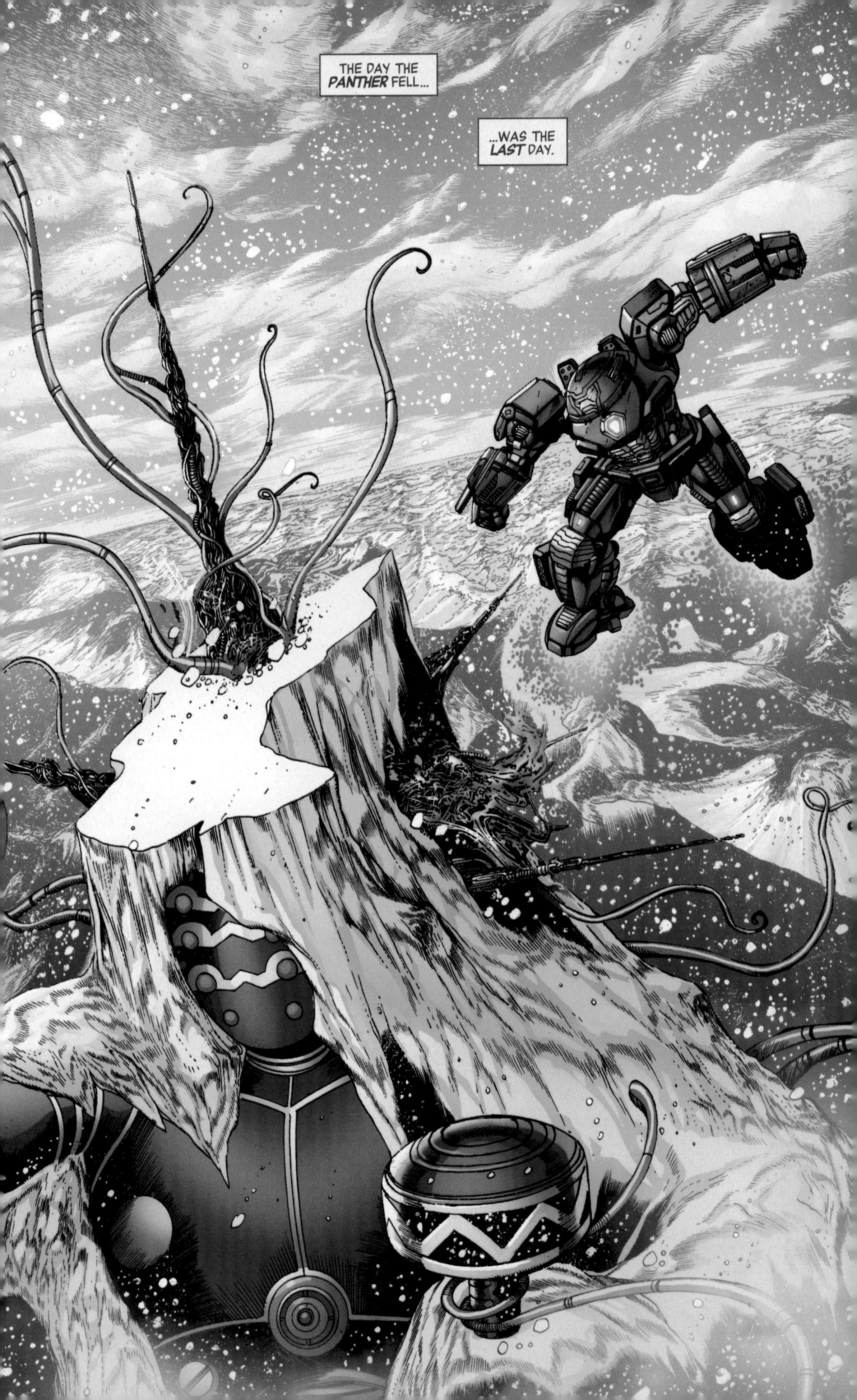
THE DAY THE PANTHER FELL...
...WAS THE LAST DAY.

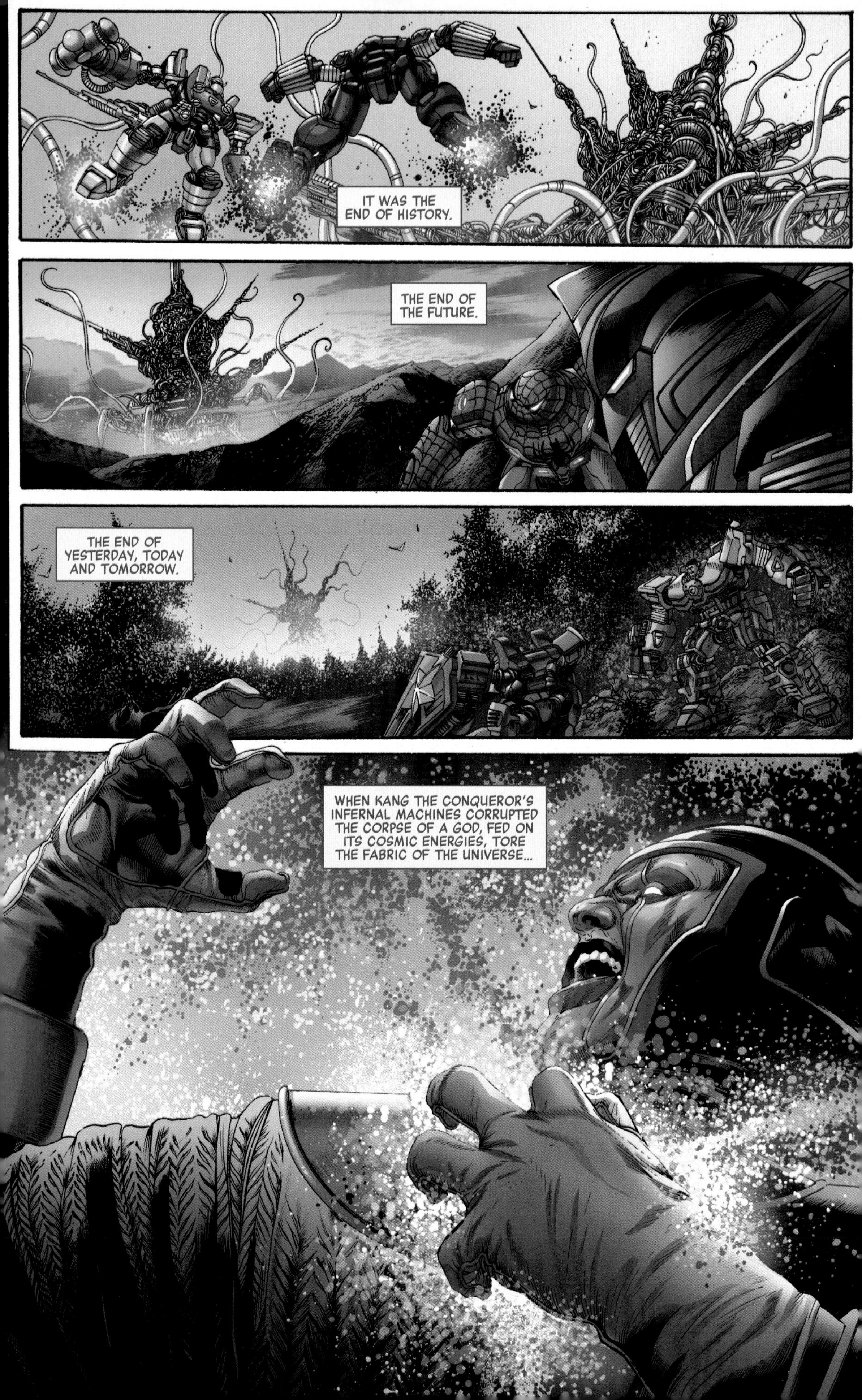
IT WAS THE END OF HISTORY.
THE END OF THE FUTURE.
THE END OF YESTERDAY, TODAY AND TOMORROW.
WHEN KANG THE CONQUEROR'S INFERNAL MACHINES CORRUPTED THE CORPSE OF A GOD, FED ON ITS COSMIC ENERGIES, TORE THE FABRIC OF THE UNIVERSE...

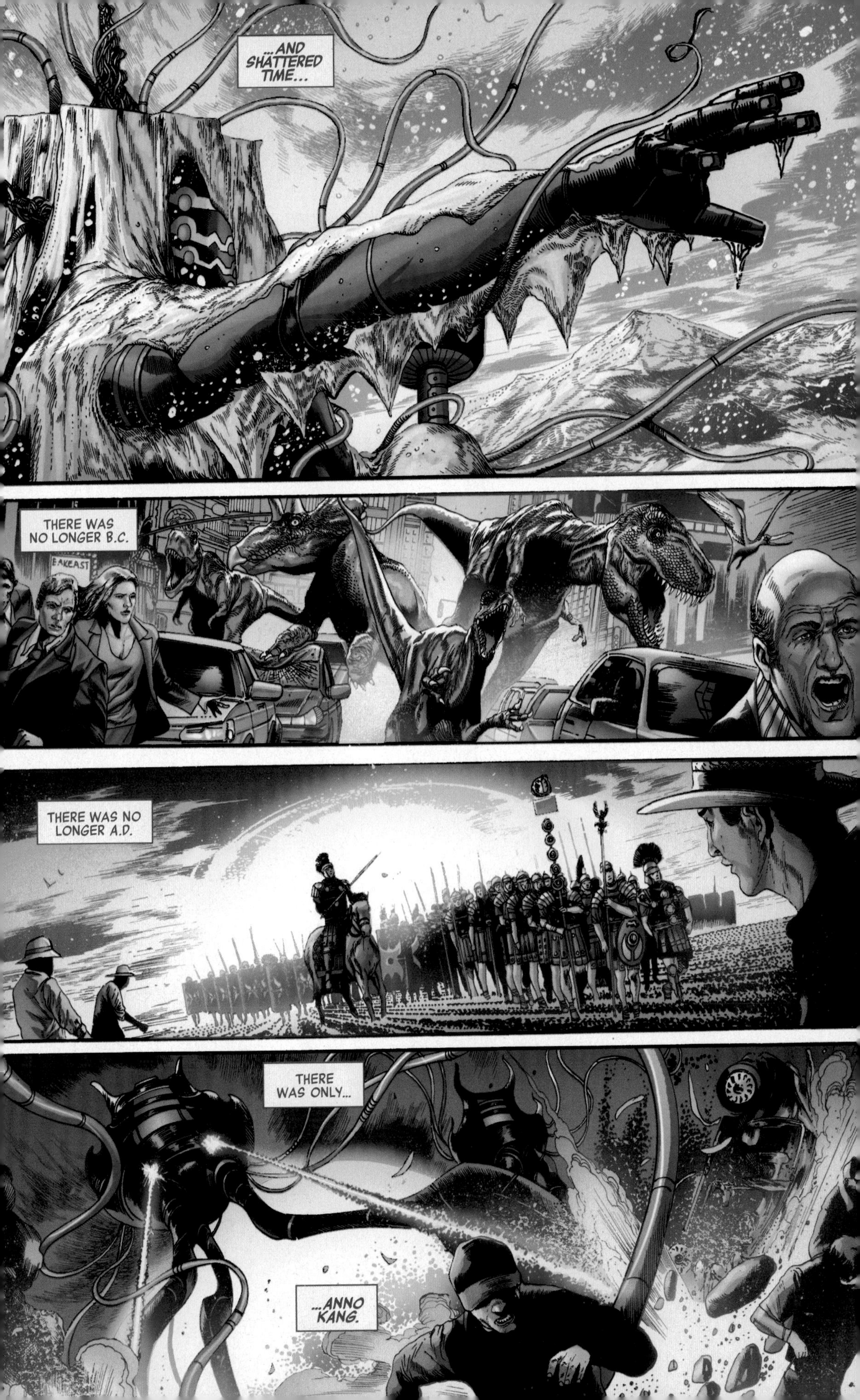
...AND SHATTERED TIME...
THERE WAS NO LONGER B.C.
THERE WAS NO LONGER A.D.
THERE WAS ONLY...
...ANNO KANG.

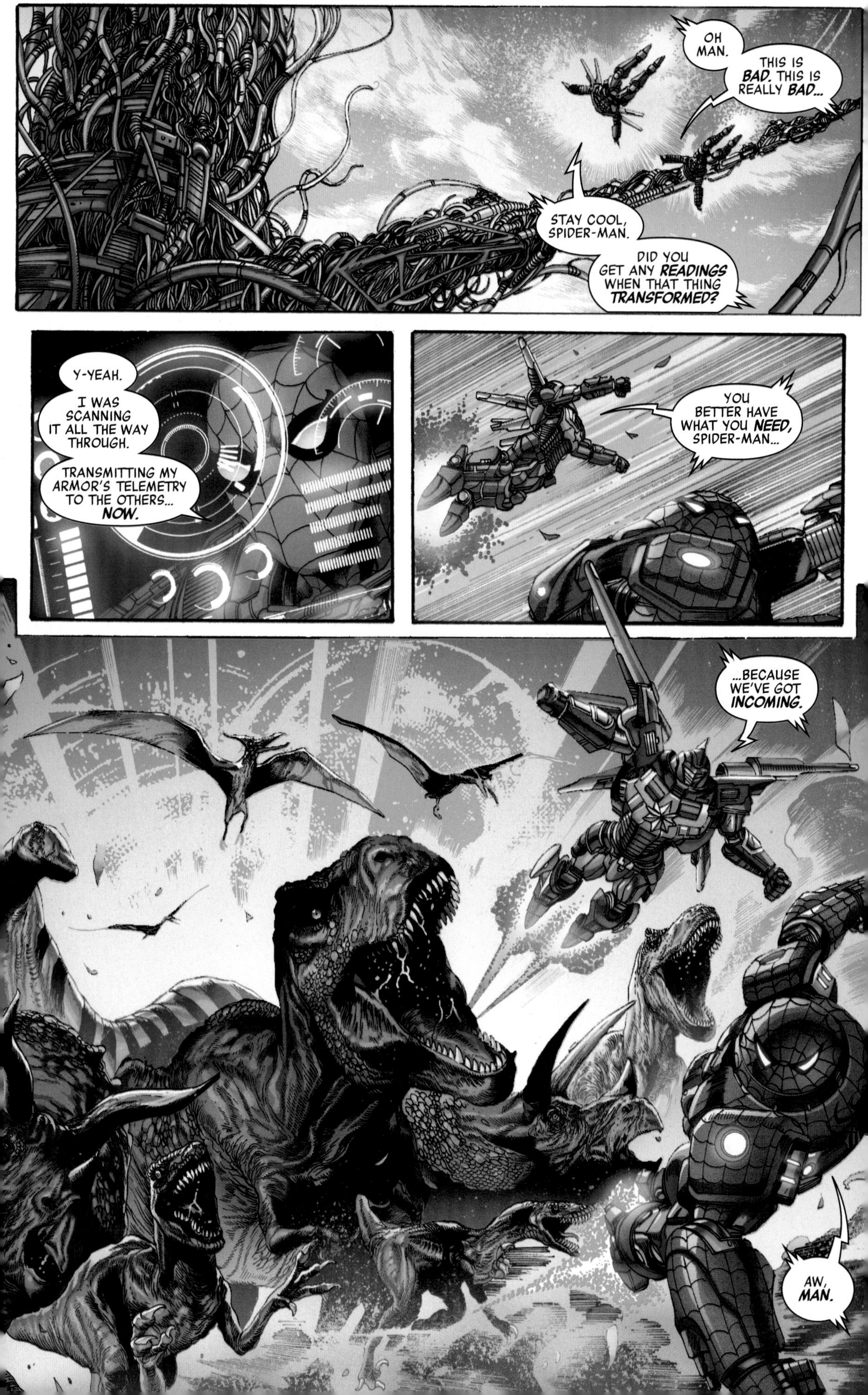
OH MAN.
THIS IS BAD. THIS IS REALLY BAD...
STAY COOL, SPIDER-MAN.
DID YOU GET ANY READINGS WHEN THAT THING TRANSFORMED?
Y-YEAH.
I WAS SCANNING IT ALL THE WAY THROUGH.
TRANSMITTING MY ARMOR'S TELEMETRY TO THE OTHERS... NOW.
YOU BETTER HAVE WHAT YOU NEED, SPIDER-MAN...
...BECAUSE WE'VE GOT INCOMING.
AW, MAN.

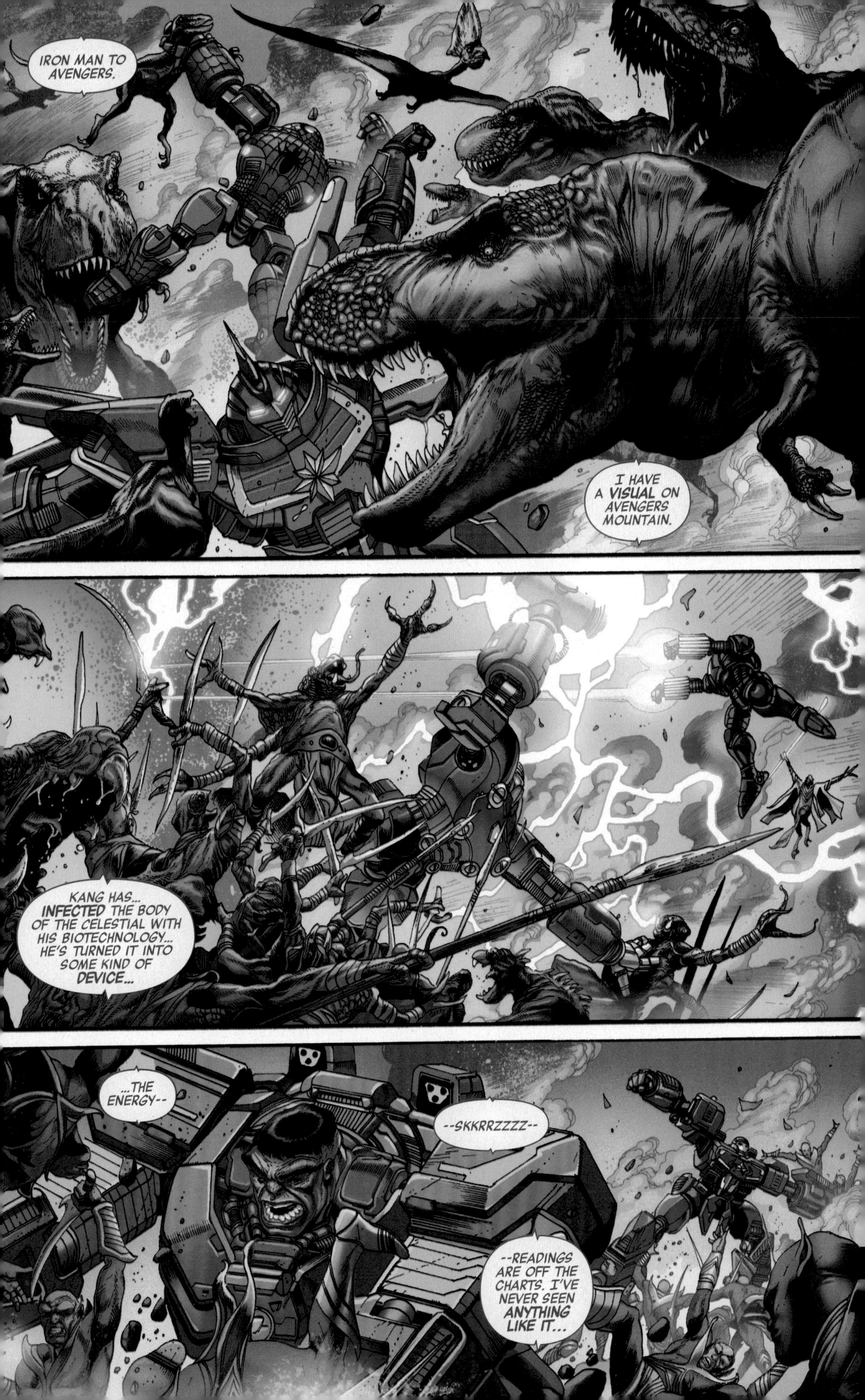
IRON MAN TO AVENGERS.
I HAVE A VISUAL ON AVENGERS MOUNTAIN.
KANG HAS... INFECTED THE BODY OF THE CELESTIAL WITH HIS BIOTECHNOLOGY... HE'S TURNED IT INTO SOME KIND OF DEVICE...
...THE ENERGY--
--SKKRRZZZZ--
--READINGS ARE OFF THE CHARTS. I'VE NEVER SEEN ANYTHING LIKE IT...

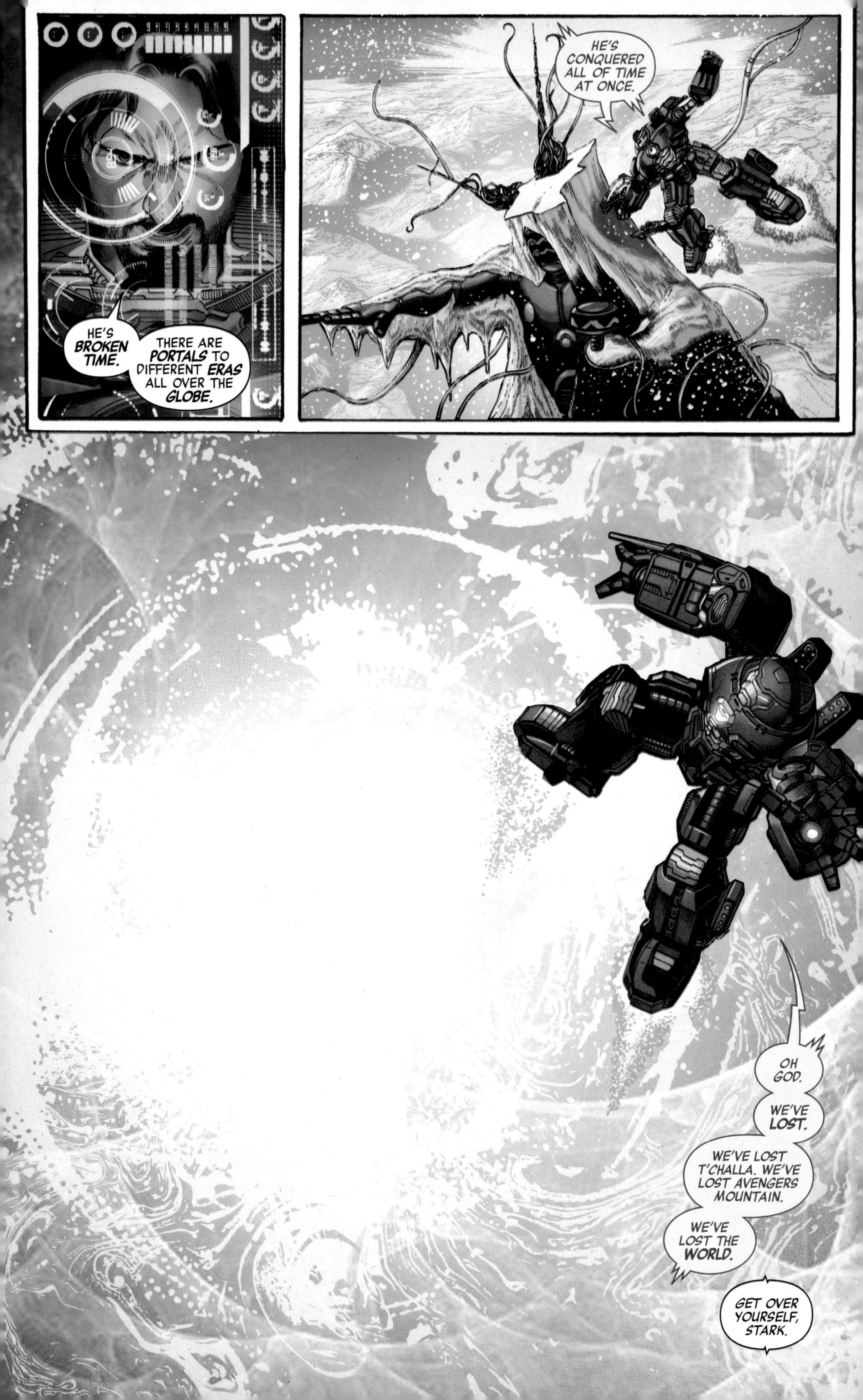
HE'S BROKEN TIME.
THERE ARE PORTALS TO DIFFERENT ERAS ALL OVER THE GLOBE.
HE'S CONQUERED ALL OF TIME AT ONCE.
OH GOD.
WE'VE LOST.
WE'VE LOST T'CHALLA. WE'VE LOST AVENGERS MOUNTAIN.
WE'VE LOST THE WORLD.
GET OVER YOURSELF, STARK.

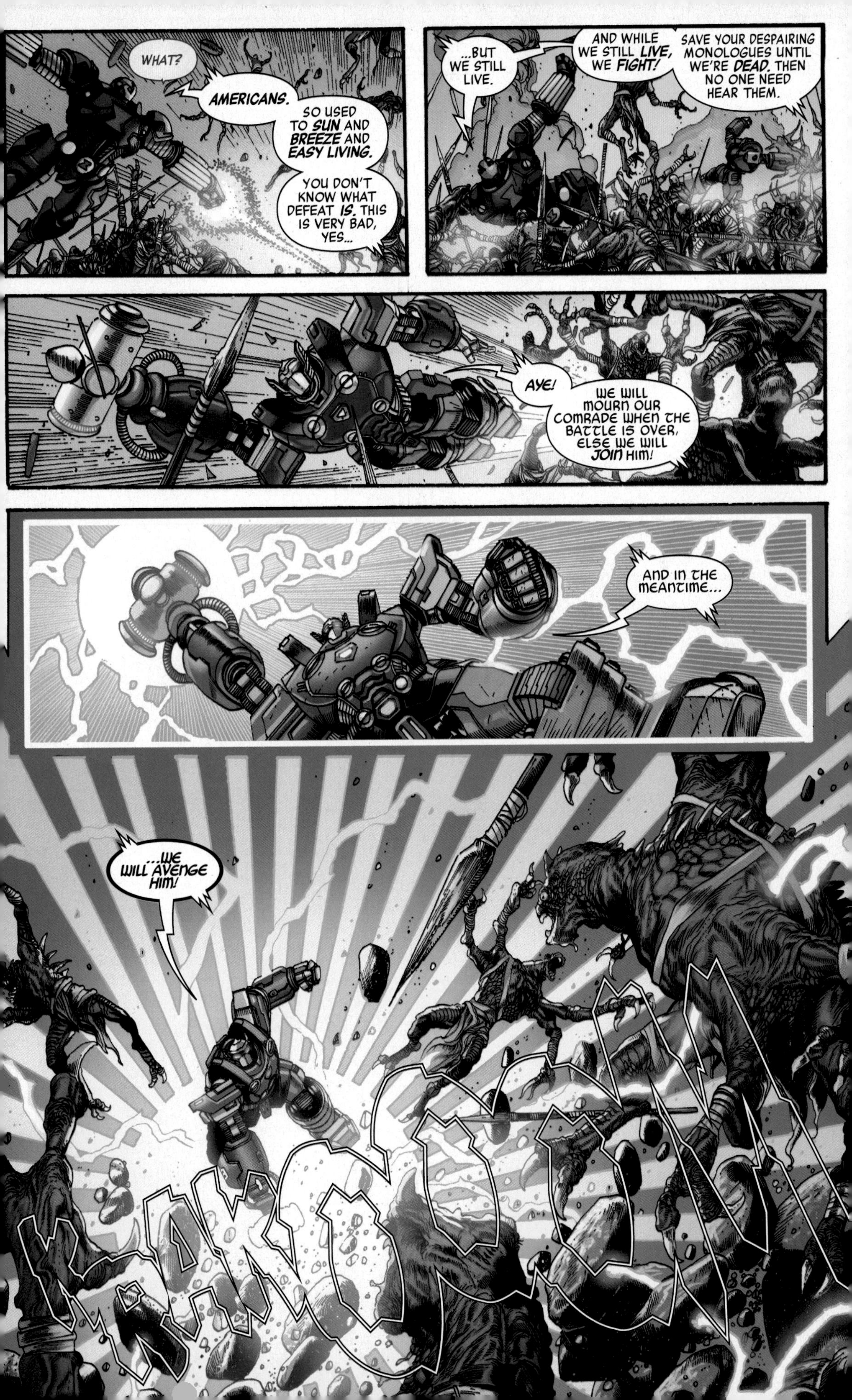
WHAT?
AMERICANS.
SO USED TO SUN AND BREEZE AND EASY LIVING.
YOU DON'T KNOW WHAT DEFEAT IS. THIS IS VERY BAD, YES...
...BUT WE STILL LIVE.
AND WHILE WE STILL LIVE, WE FIGHT!
SAVE YOUR DESPAIRING MONOLOGUES UNTIL WE'RE DEAD. THEN NO ONE NEED HEAR THEM.
AYE!
WE WILL MOURN OUR COMRADE WHEN THE BATTLE IS OVER, ELSE WE WILL JOIN HIM!
AND IN THE MEANTIME...
...WE WILL AVENGE HIM!

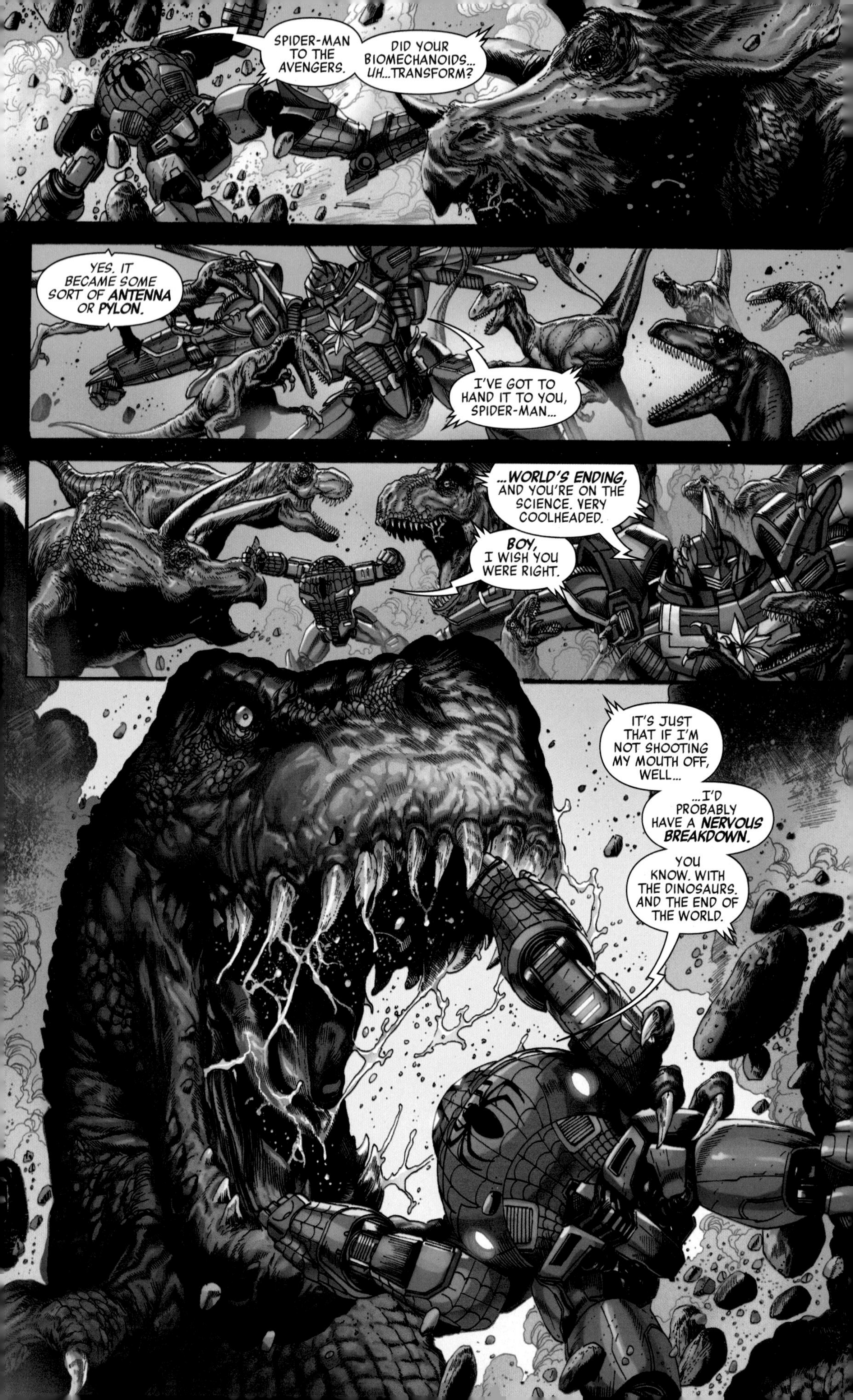
SPIDER-MAN TO THE AVENGERS.
DID YOUR BIOMECHANOIDS... UH...TRANSFORM?
YES. IT BECAME SOME SORT OF ANTENNA OR PYLON.
I'VE GOT TO HAND IT TO YOU, SPIDER-MAN...
...WORLD'S ENDING, AND YOU'RE ON THE SCIENCE. VERY COOLHEADED.
BOY, I WISH YOU WERE RIGHT.
IT'S JUST THAT IF I'M NOT SHOOTING MY MOUTH OFF, WELL...
...I'D PROBABLY HAVE A NERVOUS BREAKDOWN.
YOU KNOW. WITH THE DINOSAURS. AND THE END OF THE WORLD.

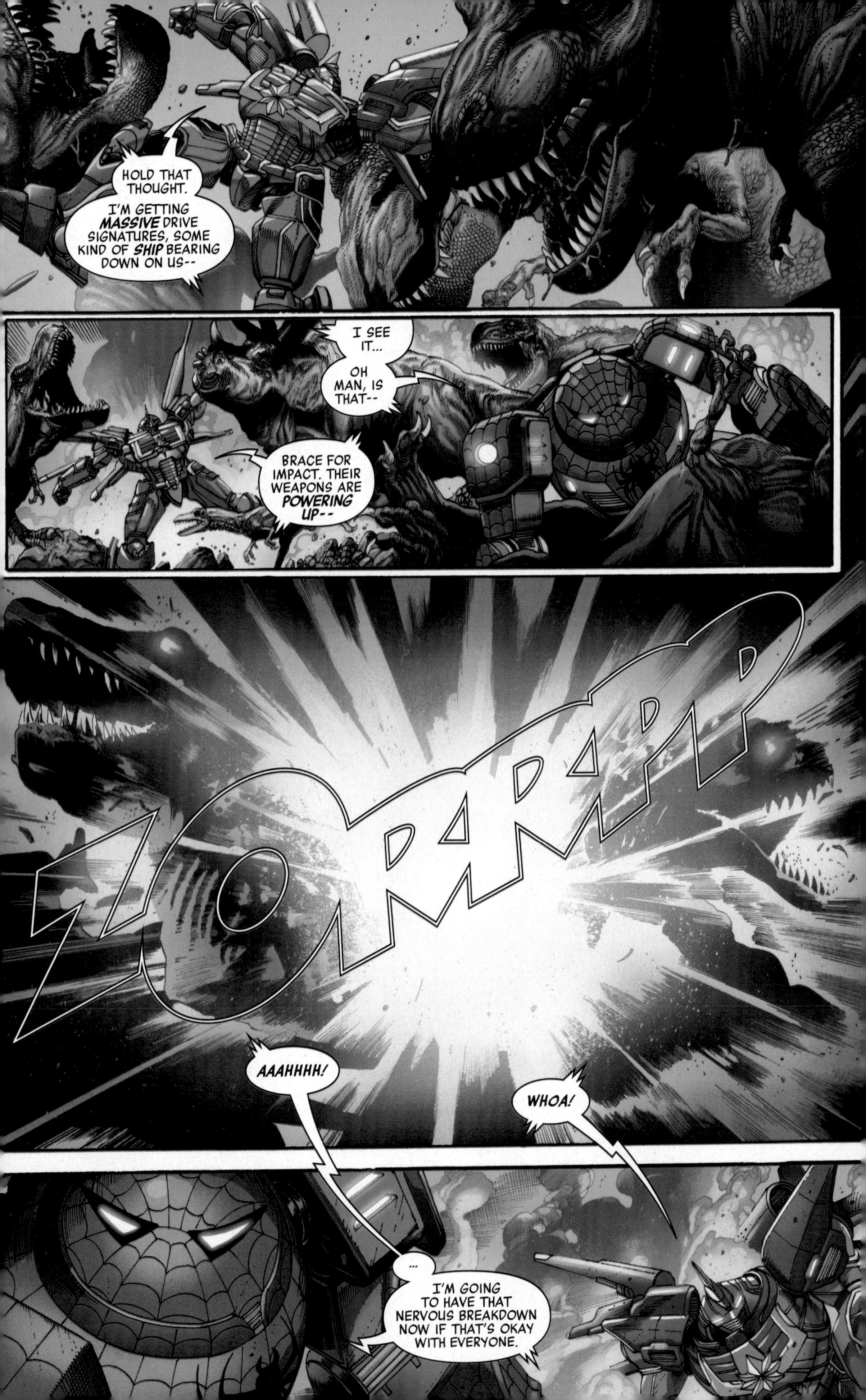
HOLD THAT THOUGHT.
I'M GETTING **MASSIVE** DRIVE SIGNATURES, SOME KIND OF **SHIP** BEARING DOWN ON US--
I SEE IT...
OH MAN, IS THAT--
BRACE FOR IMPACT. THEIR WEAPONS ARE **POWERING UP**--
ZORRRPP
AAAHHHH!
WHOA!
...
I'M GOING TO HAVE THAT NERVOUS BREAKDOWN NOW IF THAT'S OKAY WITH EVERYONE.

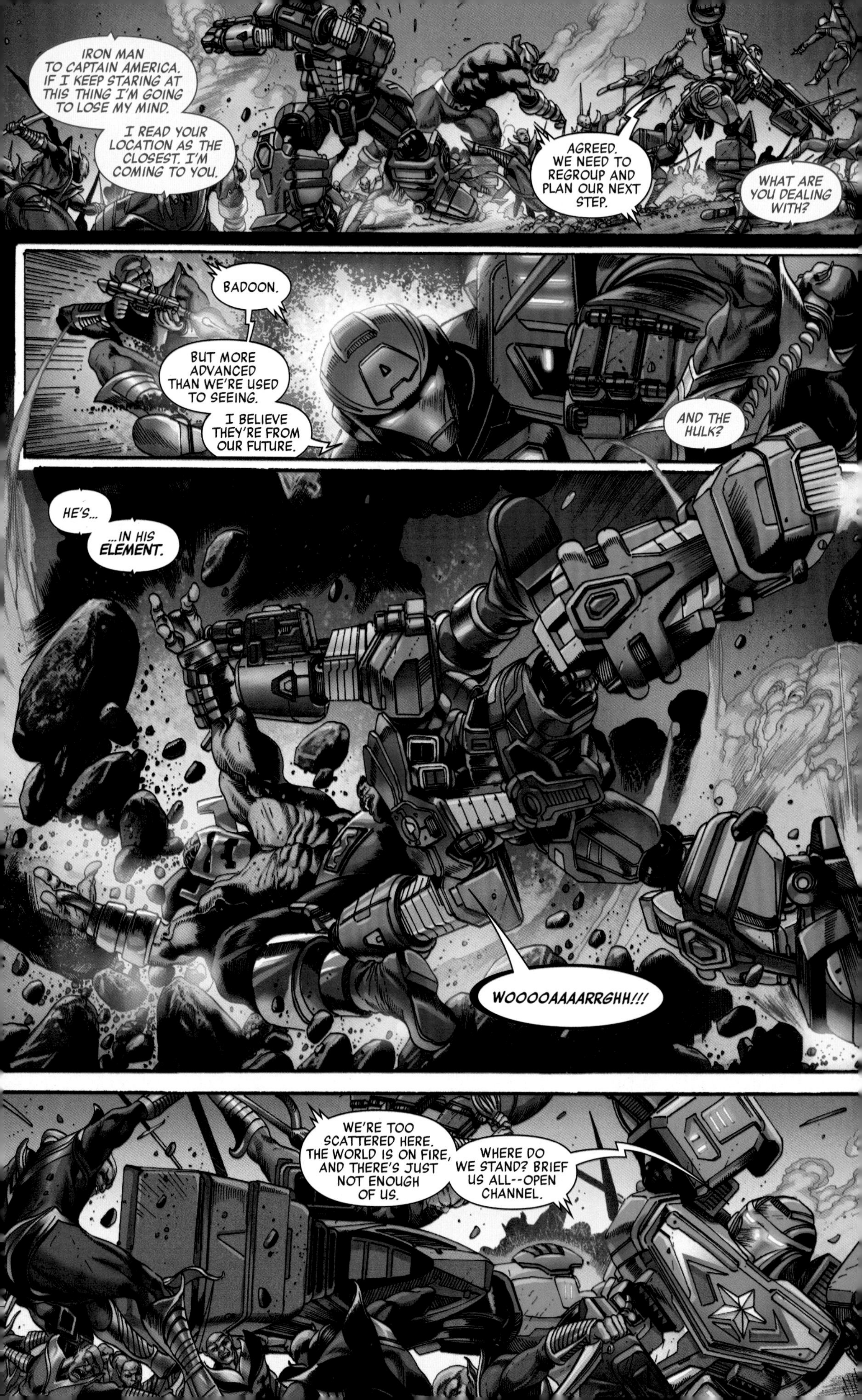
IRON MAN TO CAPTAIN AMERICA. IF I KEEP STARING AT THIS THING I'M GOING TO LOSE MY MIND.
I READ YOUR LOCATION AS THE CLOSEST. I'M COMING TO YOU.
AGREED. WE NEED TO REGROUP AND PLAN OUR NEXT STEP.
WHAT ARE YOU DEALING WITH?
BADOON.
BUT MORE ADVANCED THAN WE'RE USED TO SEEING.
I BELIEVE THEY'RE FROM OUR FUTURE.
AND THE HULK?
HE'S...
...IN HIS ELEMENT.
WOOOOAAAARRGHH!!!
WE'RE TOO SCATTERED HERE. THE WORLD IS ON FIRE, AND THERE'S JUST NOT ENOUGH OF US.
WHERE DO WE STAND? BRIEF US ALL--OPEN CHANNEL.

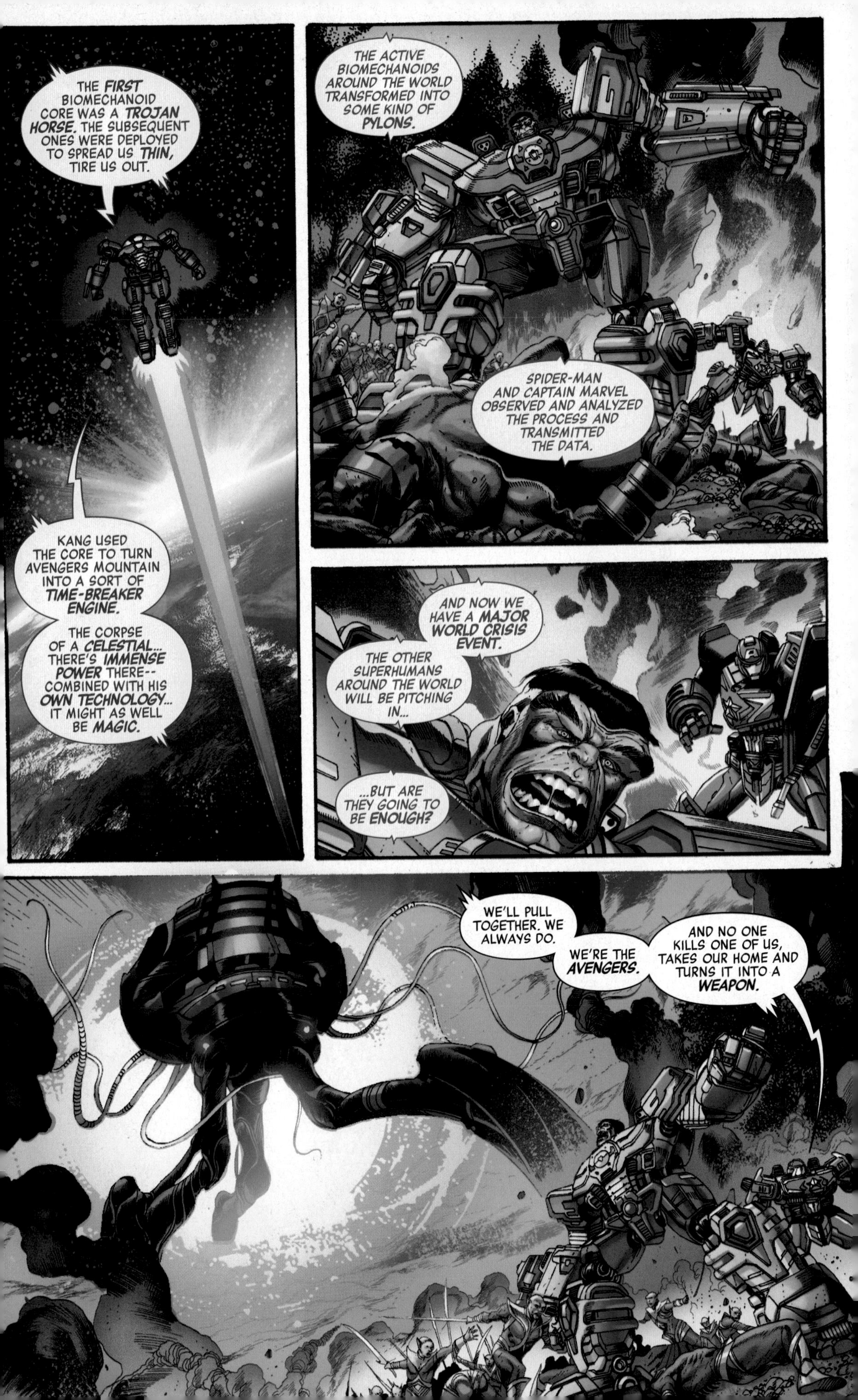
THE FIRST BIOMECHANOID CORE WAS A TROJAN HORSE. THE SUBSEQUENT ONES WERE DEPLOYED TO SPREAD US THIN, TIRE US OUT.
KANG USED THE CORE TO TURN AVENGERS MOUNTAIN INTO A SORT OF TIME-BREAKER ENGINE.
THE CORPSE OF A CELESTIAL... THERE'S IMMENSE POWER THERE--COMBINED WITH HIS OWN TECHNOLOGY... IT MIGHT AS WELL BE MAGIC.
THE ACTIVE BIOMECHANOIDS AROUND THE WORLD TRANSFORMED INTO SOME KIND OF PYLONS.
SPIDER-MAN AND CAPTAIN MARVEL OBSERVED AND ANALYZED THE PROCESS AND TRANSMITTED THE DATA.
AND NOW WE HAVE A MAJOR WORLD CRISIS EVENT.
THE OTHER SUPERHUMANS AROUND THE WORLD WILL BE PITCHING IN...
...BUT ARE THEY GOING TO BE ENOUGH?
WE'LL PULL TOGETHER. WE ALWAYS DO.
WE'RE THE AVENGERS.
AND NO ONE KILLS ONE OF US, TAKES OUR HOME AND TURNS IT INTO A WEAPON.

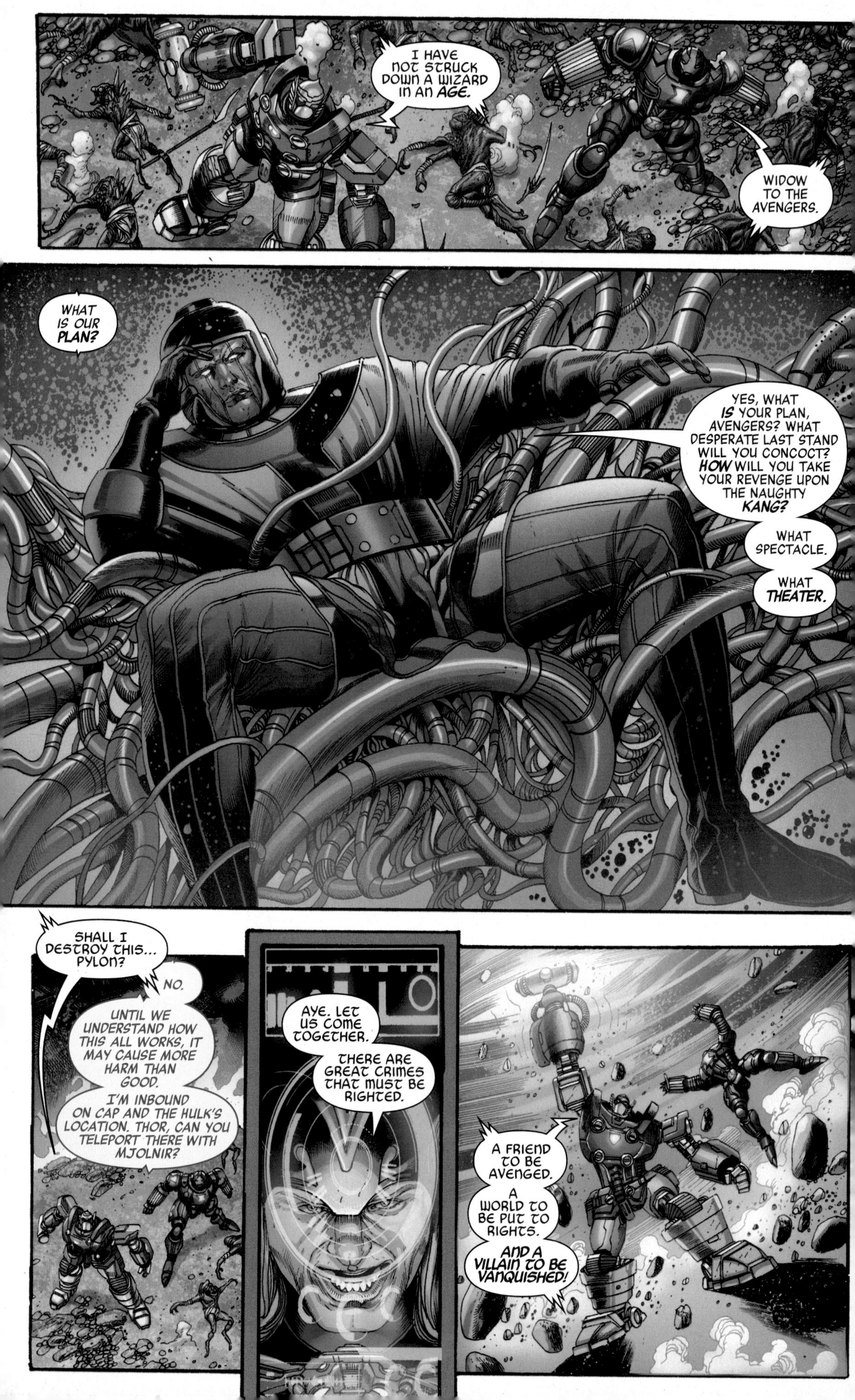
I HAVE NOT STRUCK DOWN A WIZARD IN AN AGE.
WIDOW TO THE AVENGERS.
WHAT IS OUR PLAN?
YES, WHAT IS YOUR PLAN, AVENGERS? WHAT DESPERATE LAST STAND WILL YOU CONCOCT? HOW WILL YOU TAKE YOUR REVENGE UPON THE NAUGHTY KANG?
WHAT SPECTACLE.
WHAT THEATER.
SHALL I DESTROY THIS... PYLON?
NO.
UNTIL WE UNDERSTAND HOW THIS ALL WORKS, IT MAY CAUSE MORE HARM THAN GOOD.
I'M INBOUND ON CAP AND THE HULK'S LOCATION. THOR, CAN YOU TELEPORT THERE WITH MJOLNIR?
AYE. LET US COME TOGETHER.
THERE ARE GREAT CRIMES THAT MUST BE RIGHTED.
A FRIEND TO BE AVENGED.
A WORLD TO BE PUT TO RIGHTS.
AND A VILLAIN TO BE VANQUISHED!

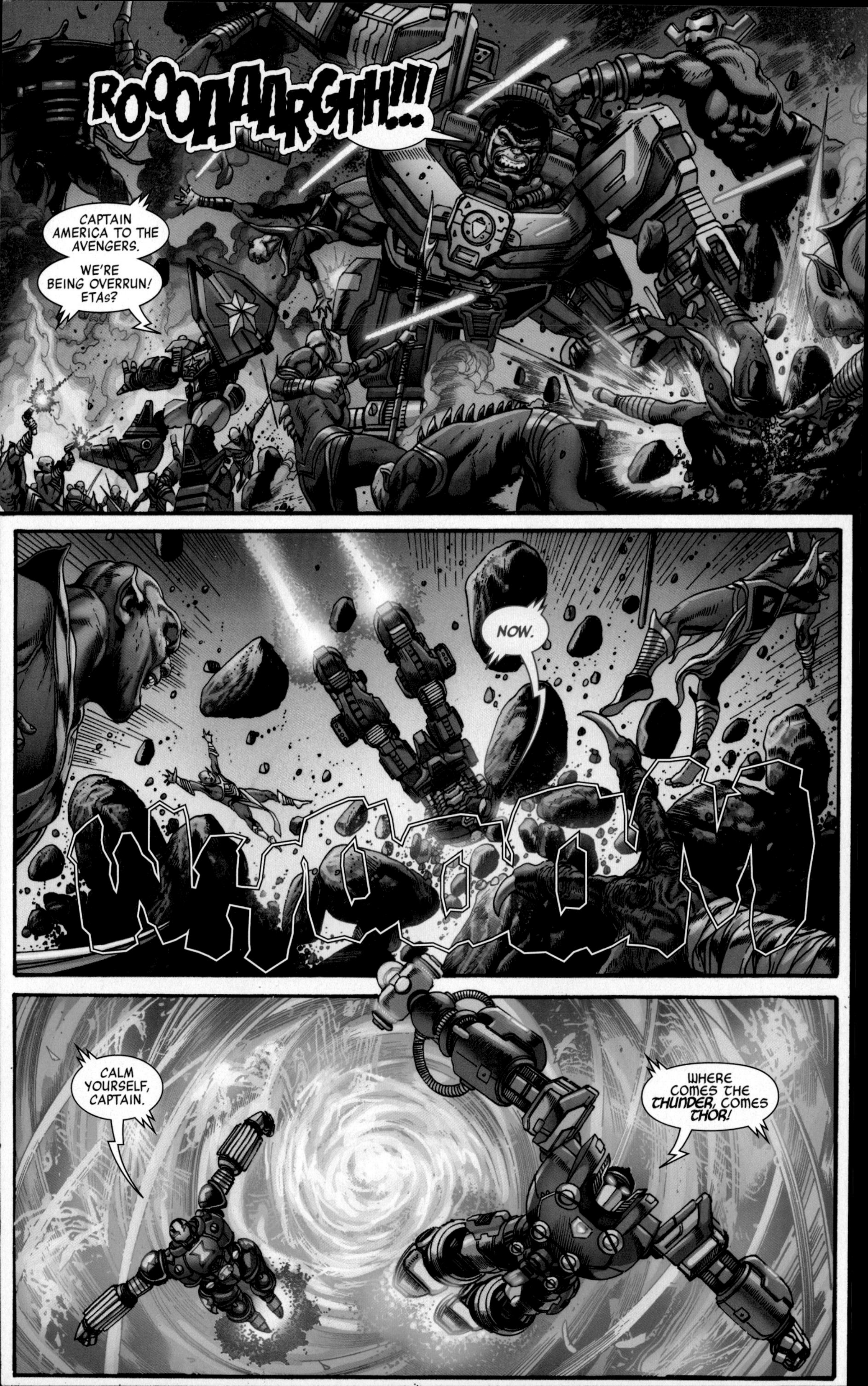
ROOOAAARGHH!!!
CAPTAIN AMERICA TO THE AVENGERS.
WE'RE BEING OVERRUN! ETAs?
NOW.
WHOOOOM
CALM YOURSELF, CAPTAIN.
WHERE COMES THE THUNDER, COMES THOR!

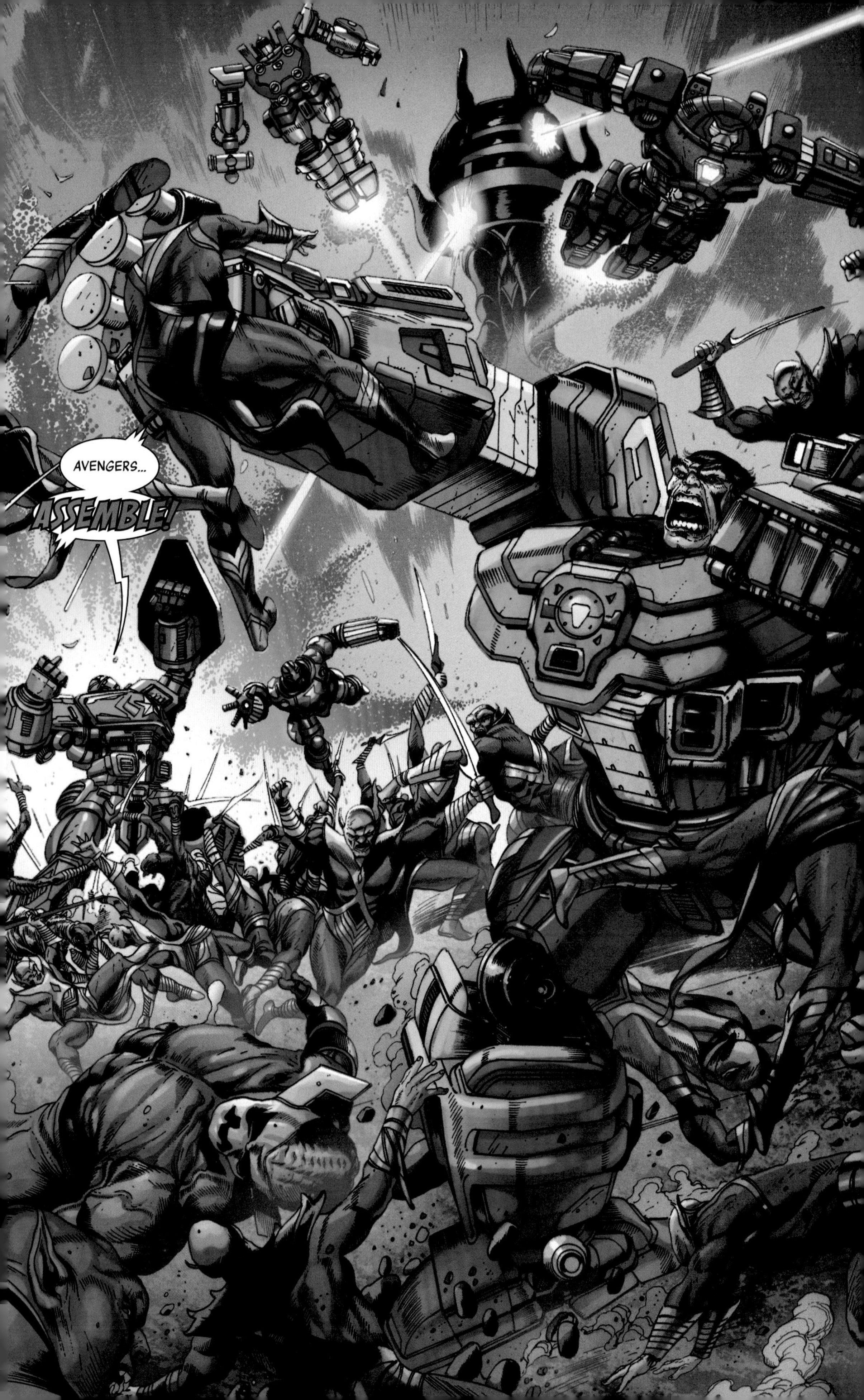

AVENGERS...
ASSEMBLE!

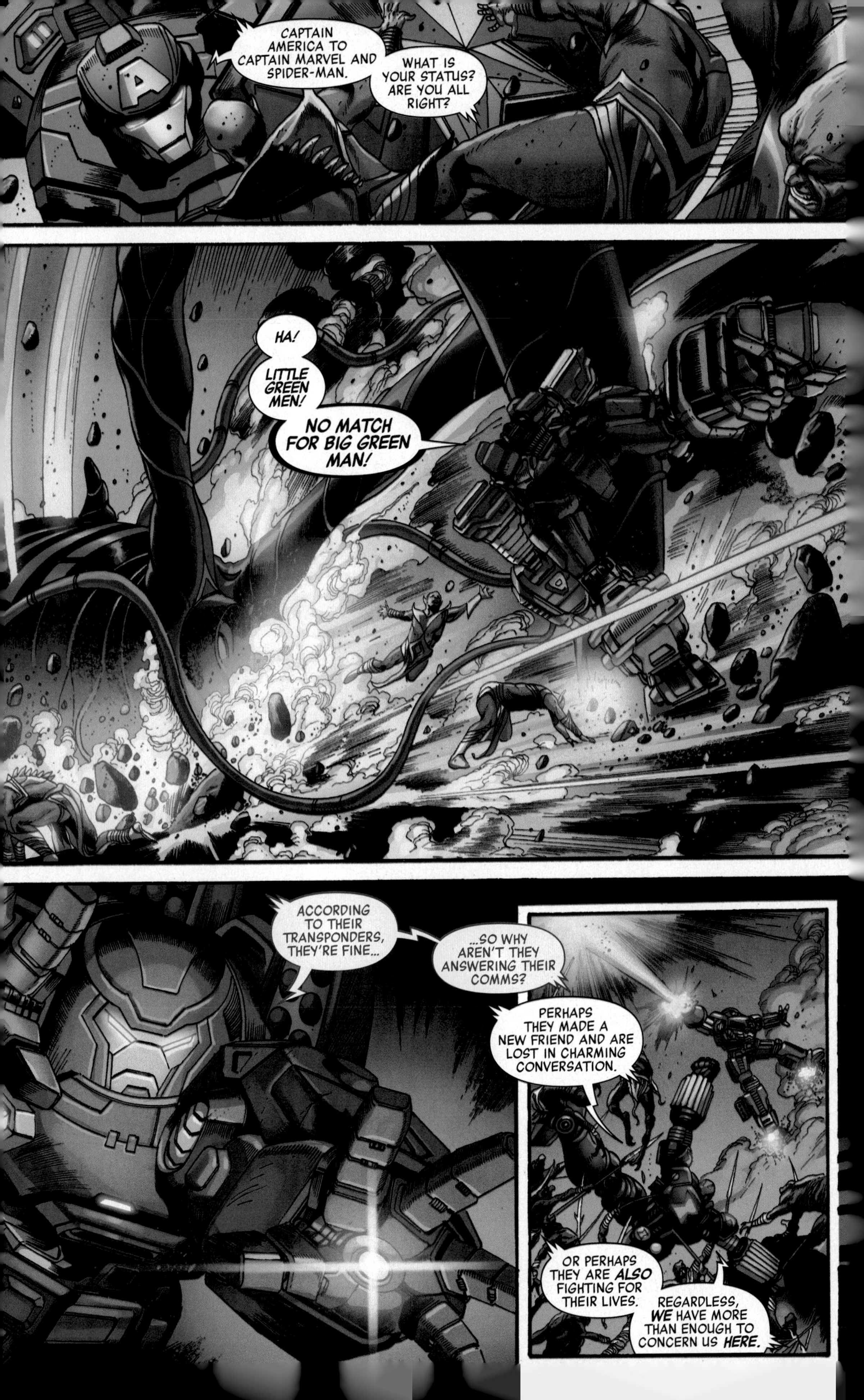
CAPTAIN AMERICA TO CAPTAIN MARVEL AND SPIDER-MAN.
WHAT IS YOUR STATUS? ARE YOU ALL RIGHT?
HA!
LITTLE GREEN MEN!
NO MATCH FOR BIG GREEN MAN!
ACCORDING TO THEIR TRANSPONDERS, THEY'RE FINE...
...SO WHY AREN'T THEY ANSWERING THEIR COMMS?
PERHAPS THEY MADE A NEW FRIEND AND ARE LOST IN CHARMING CONVERSATION.
OR PERHAPS THEY ARE ALSO FIGHTING FOR THEIR LIVES.
REGARDLESS, WE HAVE MORE THAN ENOUGH TO CONCERN US HERE.

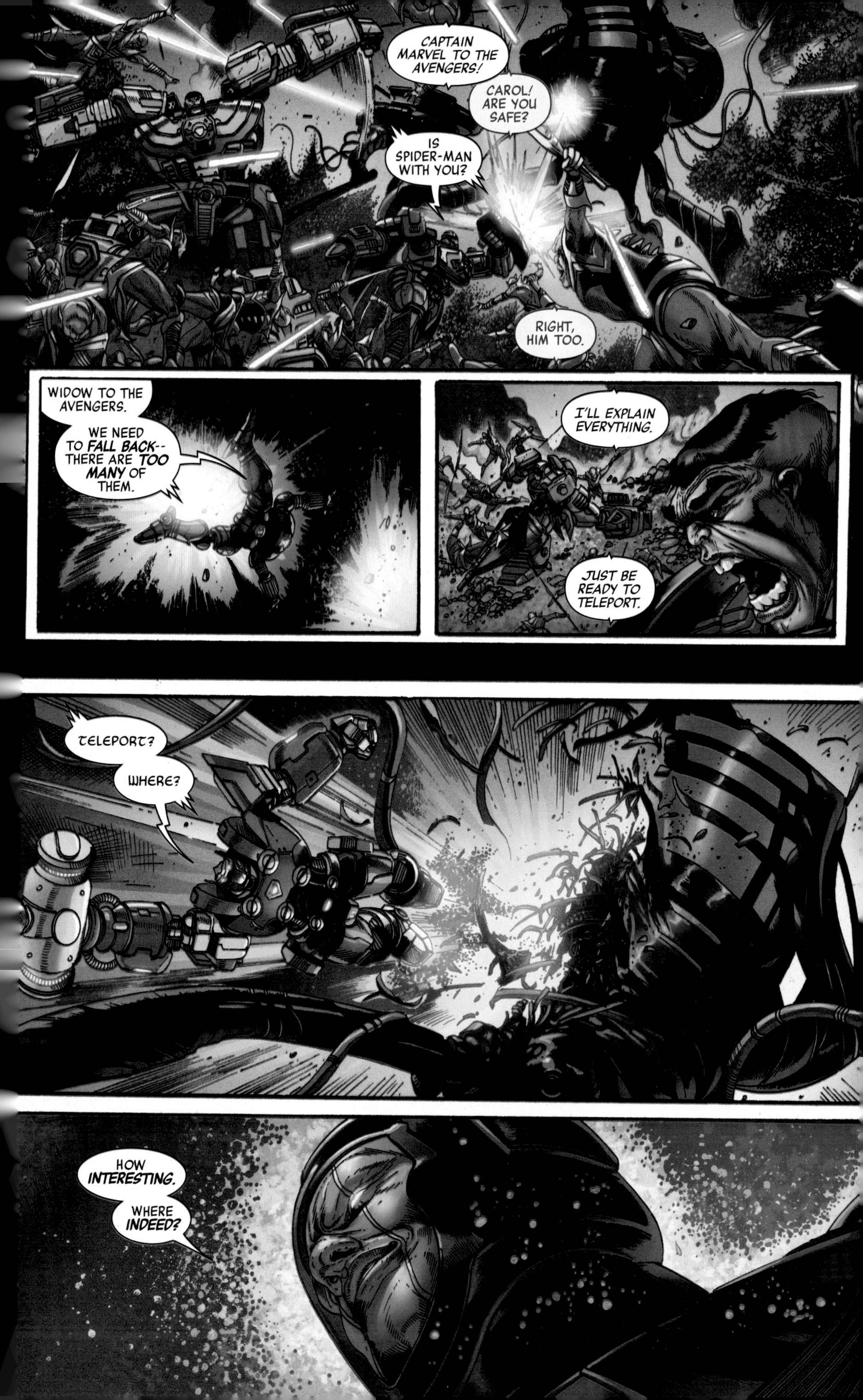
CAPTAIN MARVEL TO THE AVENGERS!
CAROL! ARE YOU SAFE?
IS SPIDER-MAN WITH YOU?
RIGHT, HIM TOO.
WIDOW TO THE AVENGERS.
WE NEED TO FALL BACK-- THERE ARE TOO MANY OF THEM.
I'LL EXPLAIN EVERYTHING.
JUST BE READY TO TELEPORT.
TELEPORT?
WHERE?
HOW INTERESTING.
WHERE INDEED?

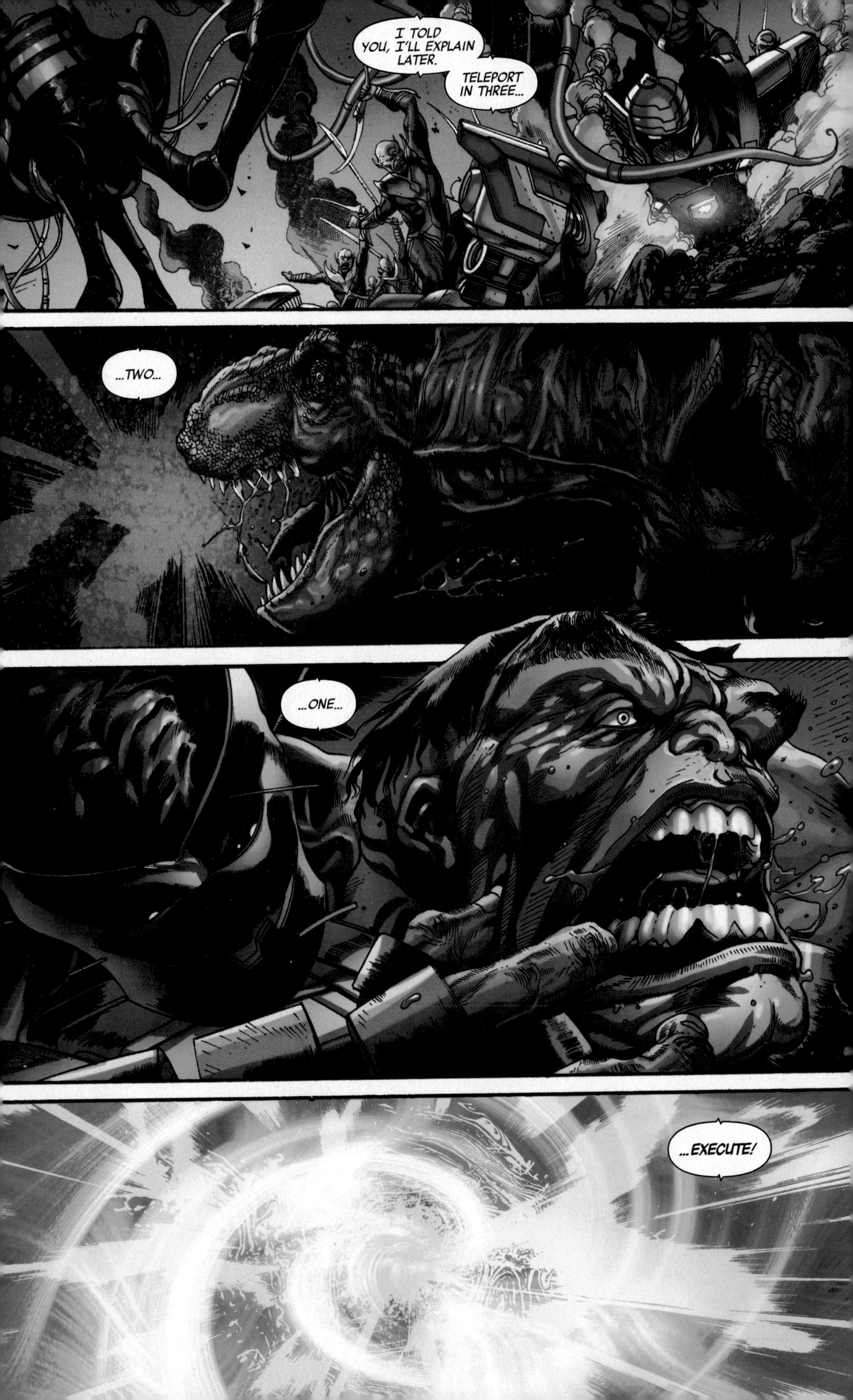
I TOLD YOU, I'LL EXPLAIN LATER.
TELEPORT IN THREE...
...TWO...
...ONE...
...EXECUTE!

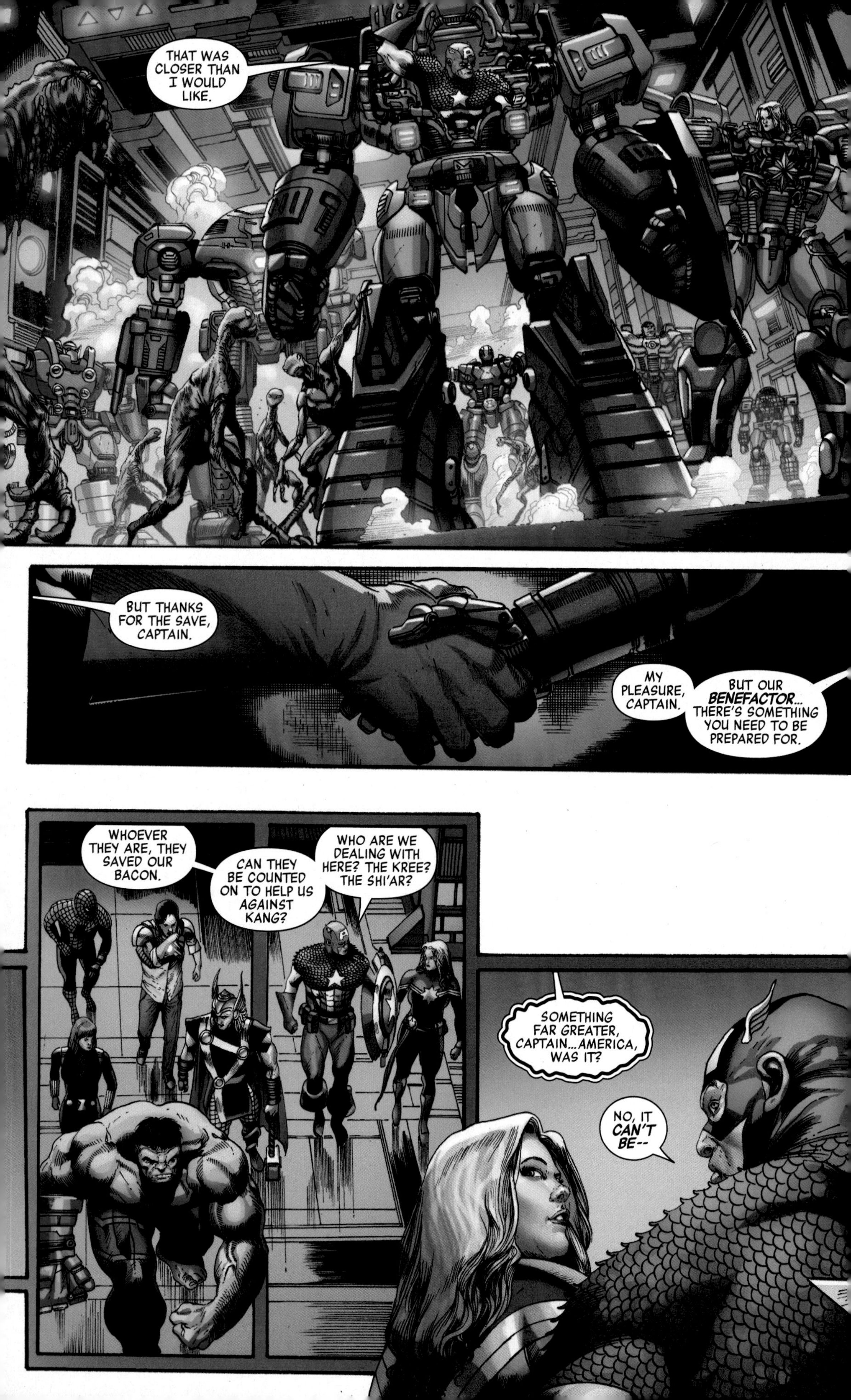
THAT WAS CLOSER THAN I WOULD LIKE.
BUT THANKS FOR THE SAVE, CAPTAIN.
MY PLEASURE, CAPTAIN.
BUT OUR BENEFACTOR... THERE'S SOMETHING YOU NEED TO BE PREPARED FOR.
WHOEVER THEY ARE, THEY SAVED OUR BACON.
CAN THEY BE COUNTED ON TO HELP US AGAINST KANG?
WHO ARE WE DEALING WITH HERE? THE KREE? THE SHI'AR?
SOMETHING FAR GREATER, CAPTAIN...AMERICA, WAS IT?
NO, IT CAN'T BE--

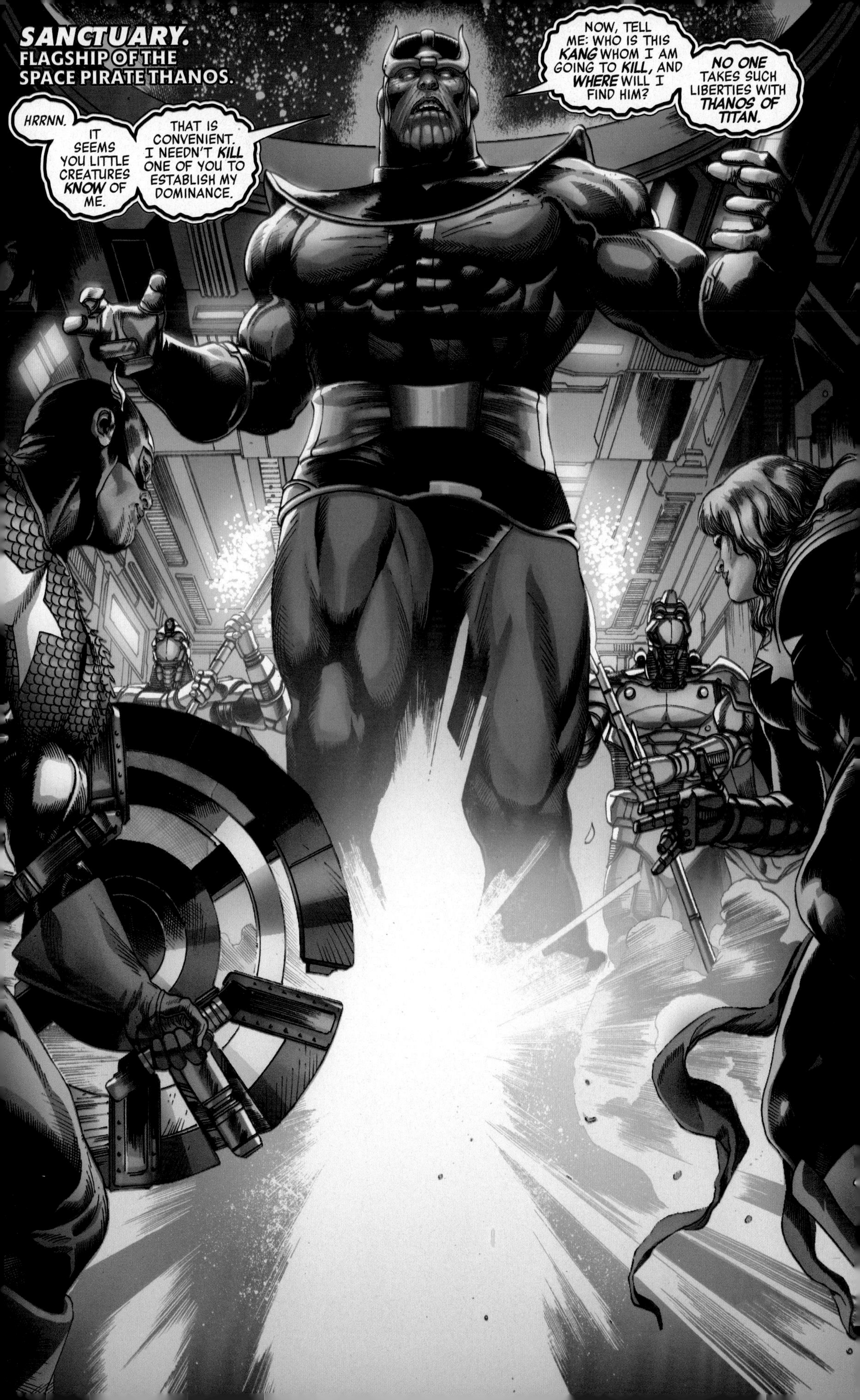
SANCTUARY.
FLAGSHIP OF THE SPACE PIRATE THANOS.
HRRNN.
IT SEEMS YOU LITTLE CREATURES KNOW OF ME.
THAT IS CONVENIENT. I NEEDN'T KILL ONE OF YOU TO ESTABLISH MY DOMINANCE.
NOW, TELL ME: WHO IS THIS KANG WHOM I AM GOING TO KILL, AND WHERE WILL I FIND HIM?
NO ONE TAKES SUCH LIBERTIES WITH THANOS OF TITAN.

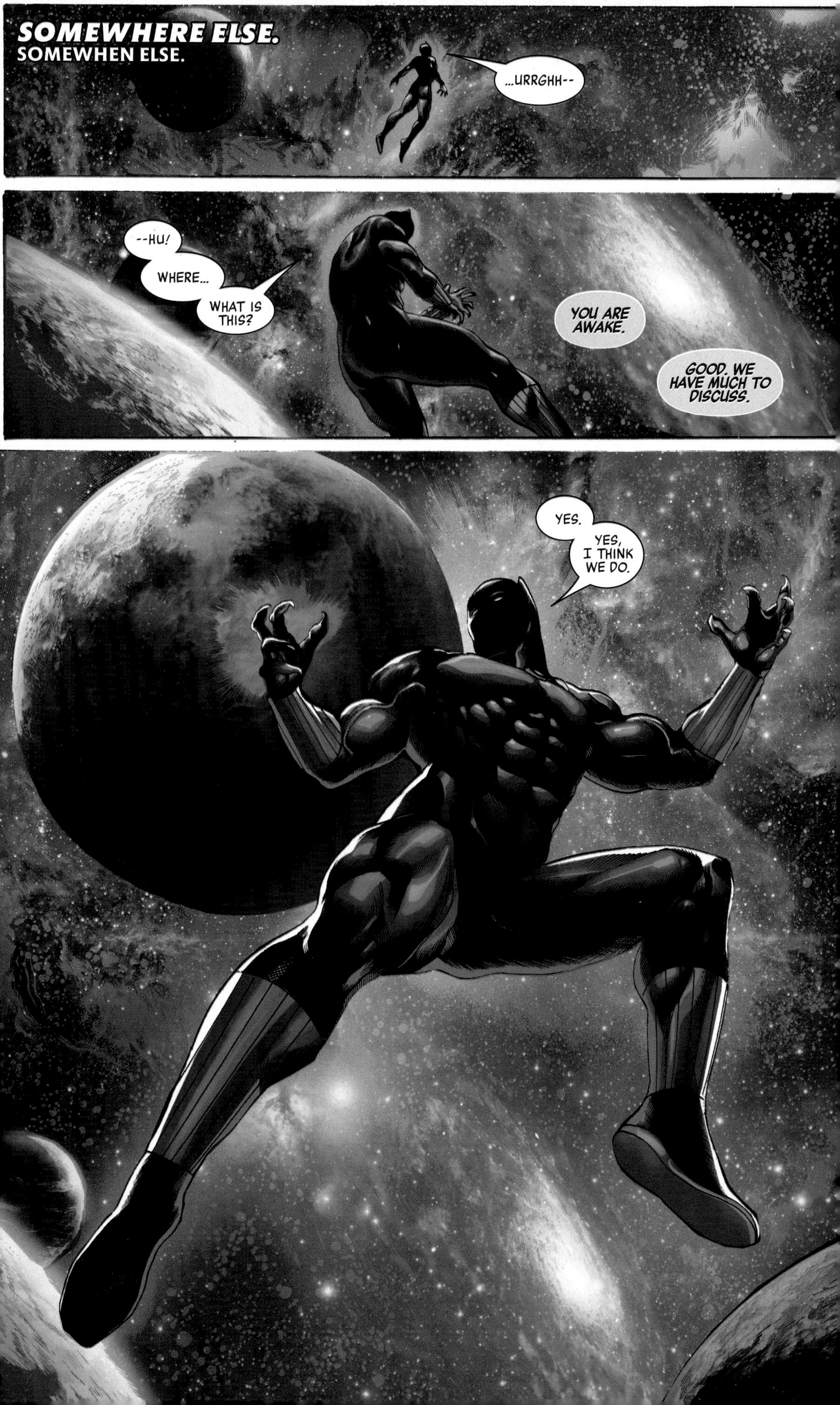
SOMEWHERE ELSE.
SOMEWHEN ELSE.
...URRGHH--
--HU!
WHERE...
WHAT IS THIS?
YOU ARE AWAKE.
GOOD. WE HAVE MUCH TO DISCUSS.
YES.
YES, I THINK WE DO.

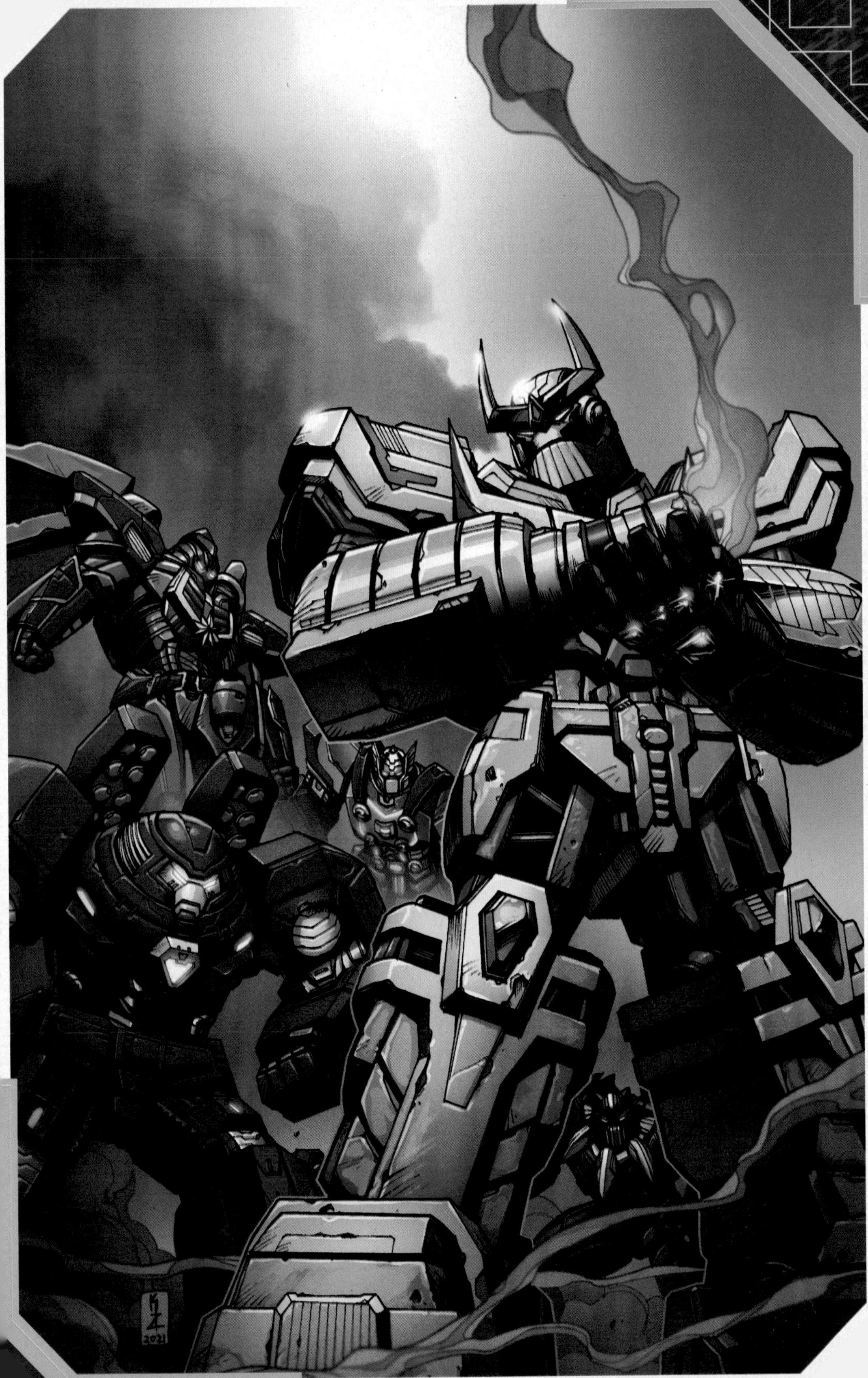

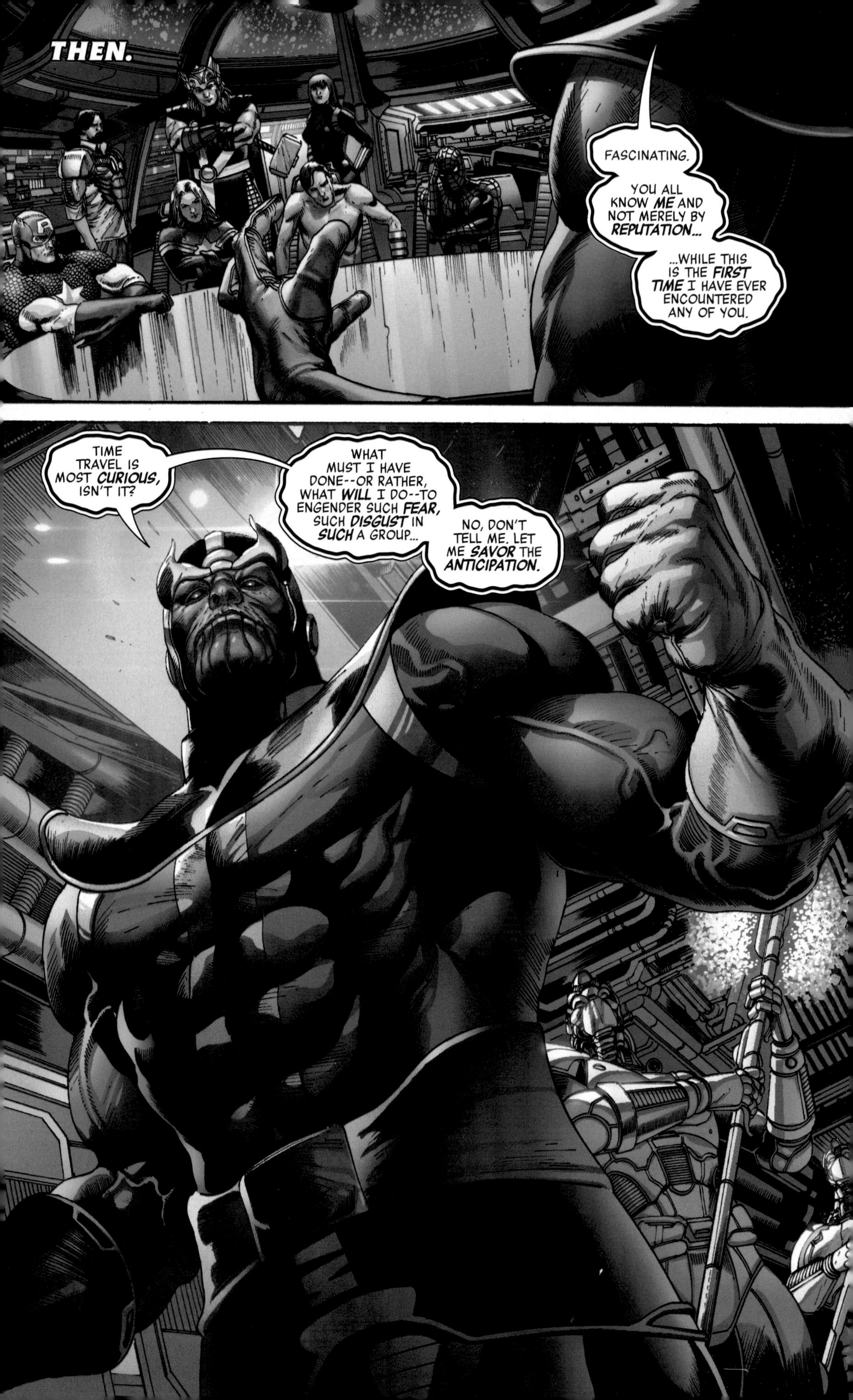
THEN.
FASCINATING.
YOU ALL KNOW ME AND NOT MERELY BY REPUTATION...
...WHILE THIS IS THE FIRST TIME I HAVE EVER ENCOUNTERED ANY OF YOU.
TIME TRAVEL IS MOST CURIOUS, ISN'T IT?
WHAT MUST I HAVE DONE--OR RATHER, WHAT WILL I DO--TO ENGENDER SUCH FEAR, SUCH DISGUST IN SUCH A GROUP...
NO, DON'T TELL ME. LET ME SAVOR THE ANTICIPATION.

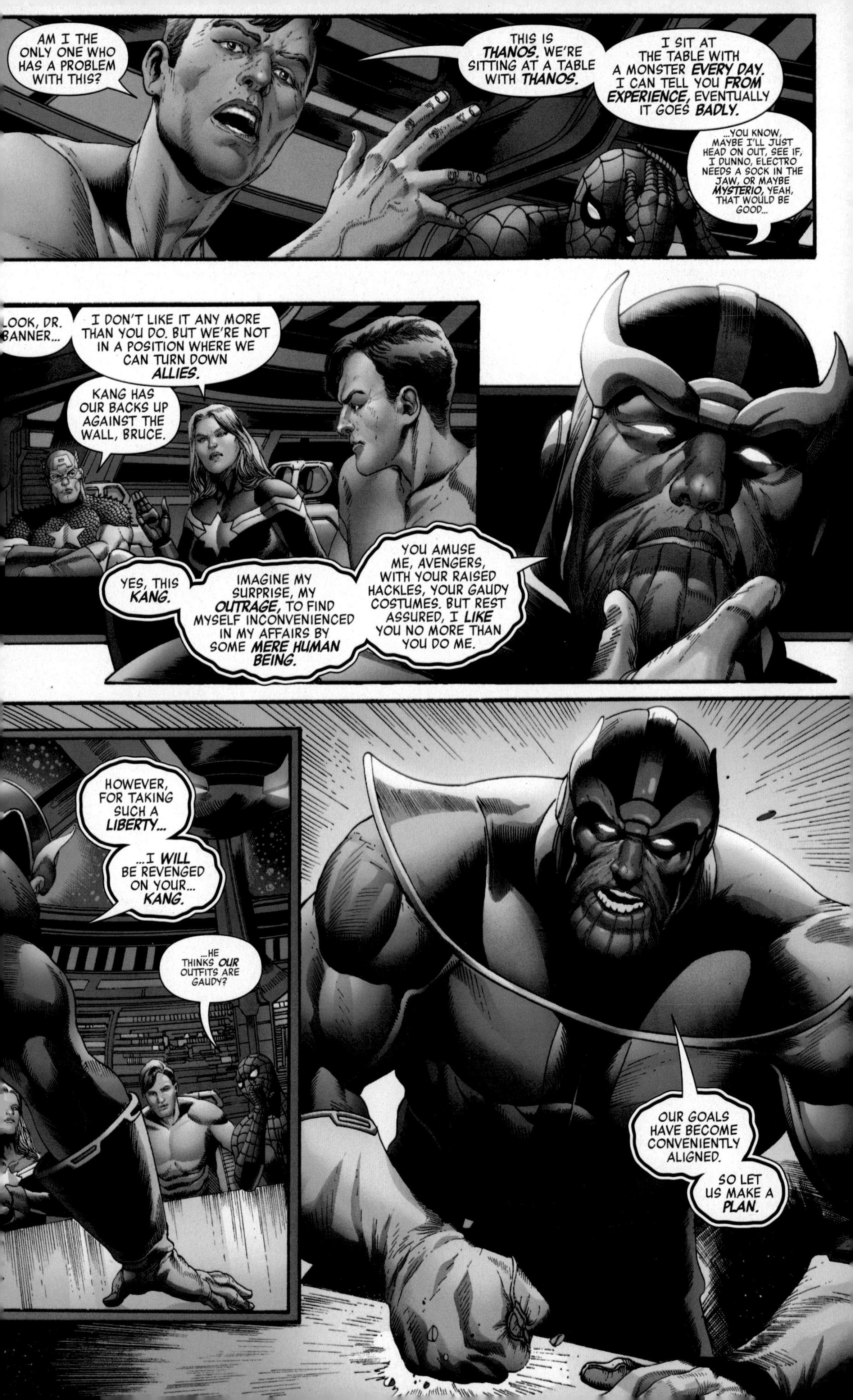
AM I THE ONLY ONE WHO HAS A PROBLEM WITH THIS?
THIS IS THANOS. WE'RE SITTING AT A TABLE WITH THANOS.
I SIT AT THE TABLE WITH A MONSTER EVERY DAY. I CAN TELL YOU FROM EXPERIENCE, EVENTUALLY IT GOES BADLY.
...YOU KNOW, MAYBE I'LL JUST HEAD ON OUT, SEE IF, I DUNNO, ELECTRO NEEDS A SOCK IN THE JAW, OR MAYBE MYSTERIO, YEAH, THAT WOULD BE GOOD...
LOOK, DR. BANNER...
I DON'T LIKE IT ANY MORE THAN YOU DO. BUT WE'RE NOT IN A POSITION WHERE WE CAN TURN DOWN ALLIES.
KANG HAS OUR BACKS UP AGAINST THE WALL, BRUCE.
YOU AMUSE ME, AVENGERS, WITH YOUR RAISED HACKLES, YOUR GAUDY COSTUMES. BUT REST ASSURED, I LIKE YOU NO MORE THAN YOU DO ME.
IMAGINE MY SURPRISE, MY OUTRAGE, TO FIND MYSELF INCONVENIENCED IN MY AFFAIRS BY SOME MERE HUMAN BEING.
YES, THIS KANG.
HOWEVER, FOR TAKING SUCH A LIBERTY...
...I WILL BE REVENGED ON YOUR... KANG.
...HE THINKS OUR OUTFITS ARE GAUDY?
OUR GOALS HAVE BECOME CONVENIENTLY ALIGNED.
SO LET US MAKE A PLAN.

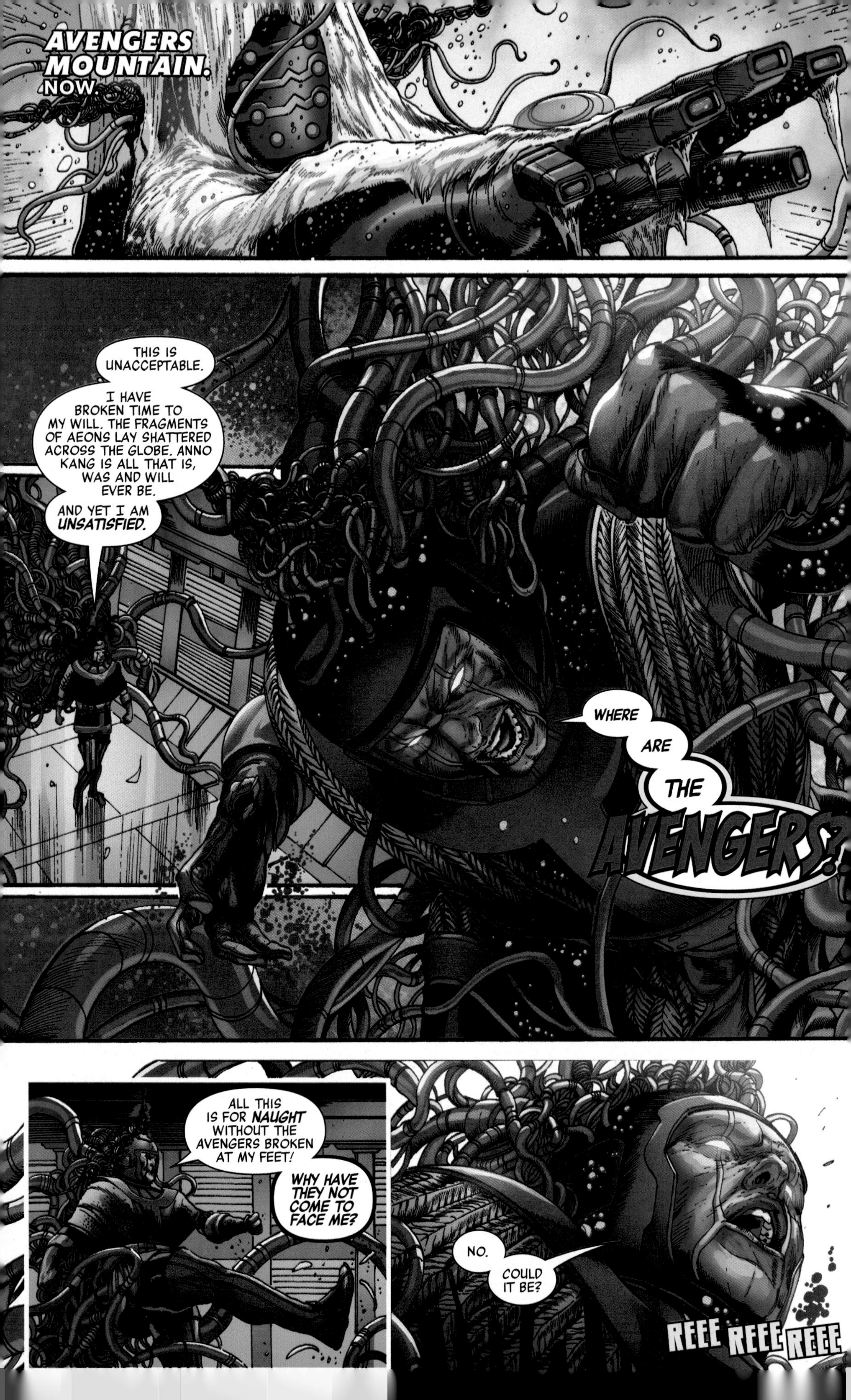
AVENGERS MOUNTAIN. NOW.
THIS IS UNACCEPTABLE.
I HAVE BROKEN TIME TO MY WILL. THE FRAGMENTS OF AEONS LAY SHATTERED ACROSS THE GLOBE. ANNO KANG IS ALL THAT IS, WAS AND WILL EVER BE.
AND YET I AM UNSATISFIED.
WHERE ARE THE AVENGERS?!
ALL THIS IS FOR NAUGHT WITHOUT THE AVENGERS BROKEN AT MY FEET!
WHY HAVE THEY NOT COME TO FACE ME?
NO.
COULD IT BE?
REEE REEE REEE

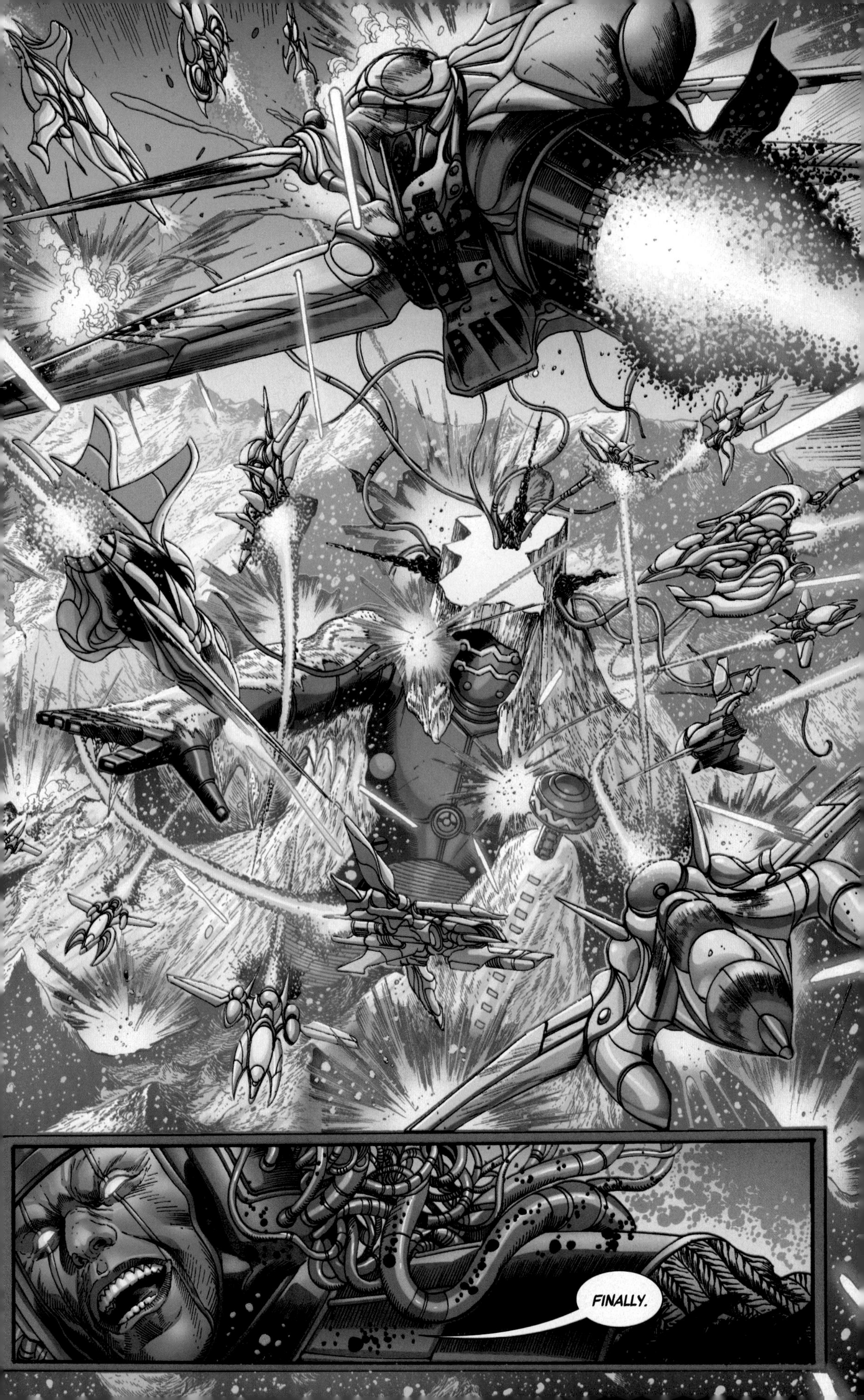
FINALLY.

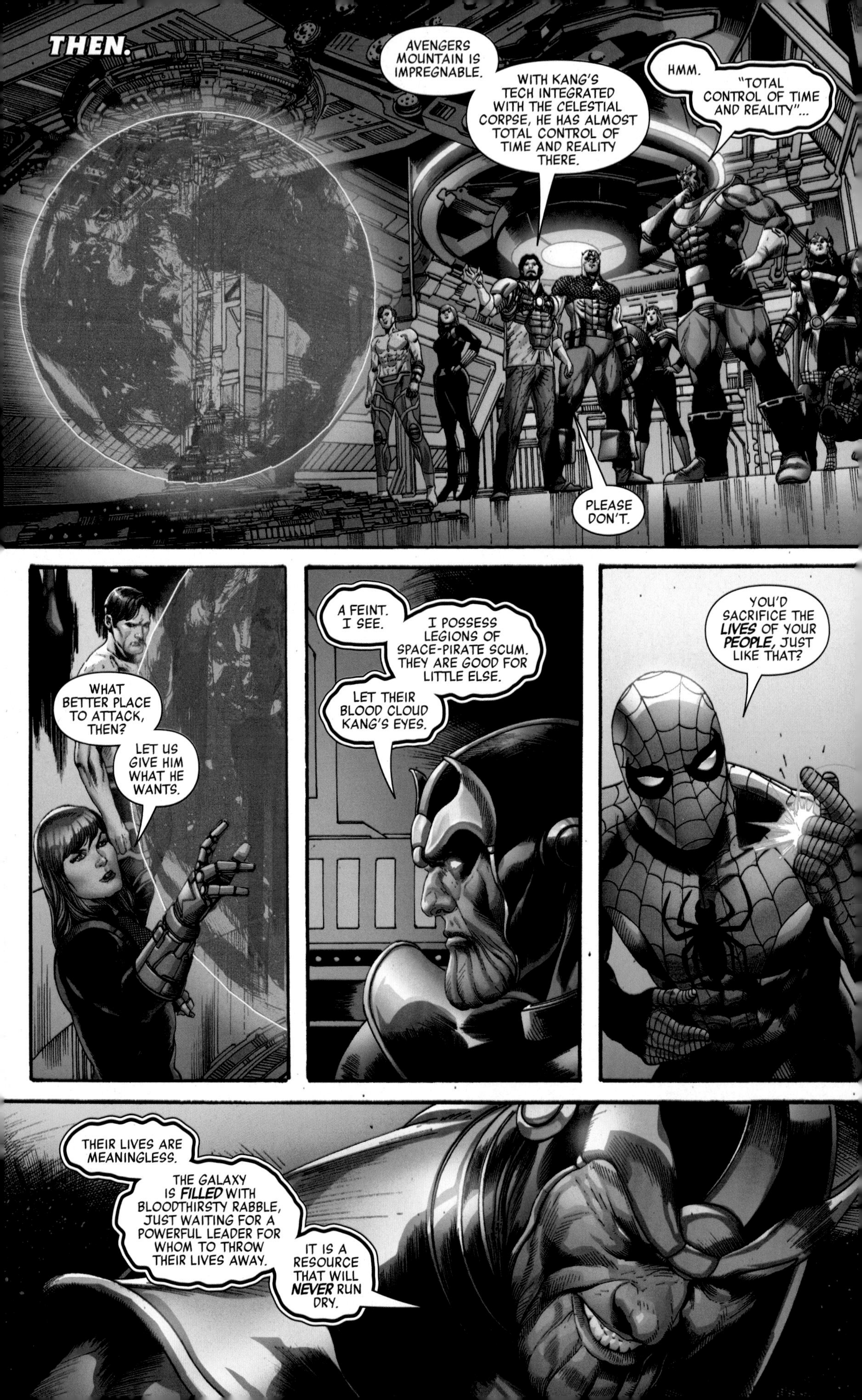
THEN.
AVENGERS MOUNTAIN IS IMPREGNABLE.
WITH KANG'S TECH INTEGRATED WITH THE CELESTIAL CORPSE, HE HAS ALMOST TOTAL CONTROL OF TIME AND REALITY THERE.
HMM.
"TOTAL CONTROL OF TIME AND REALITY"...
PLEASE DON'T.
WHAT BETTER PLACE TO ATTACK, THEN?
LET US GIVE HIM WHAT HE WANTS.
A FEINT. I SEE.
I POSSESS LEGIONS OF SPACE-PIRATE SCUM. THEY ARE GOOD FOR LITTLE ELSE.
LET THEIR BLOOD CLOUD KANG'S EYES.
YOU'D SACRIFICE THE *LIVES* OF YOUR *PEOPLE,* JUST LIKE THAT?
THEIR LIVES ARE MEANINGLESS.
THE GALAXY IS ***FILLED*** WITH BLOODTHIRSTY RABBLE, JUST WAITING FOR A POWERFUL LEADER FOR WHOM TO THROW THEIR LIVES AWAY.
IT IS A RESOURCE THAT WILL ***NEVER*** RUN DRY.

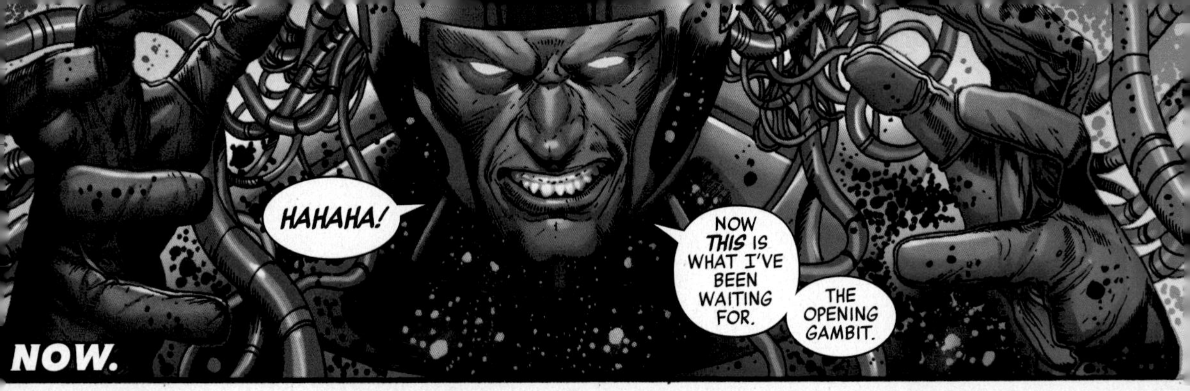
HAHAHA!
NOW THIS IS WHAT I'VE BEEN WAITING FOR.
THE OPENING GAMBIT.
NOW.

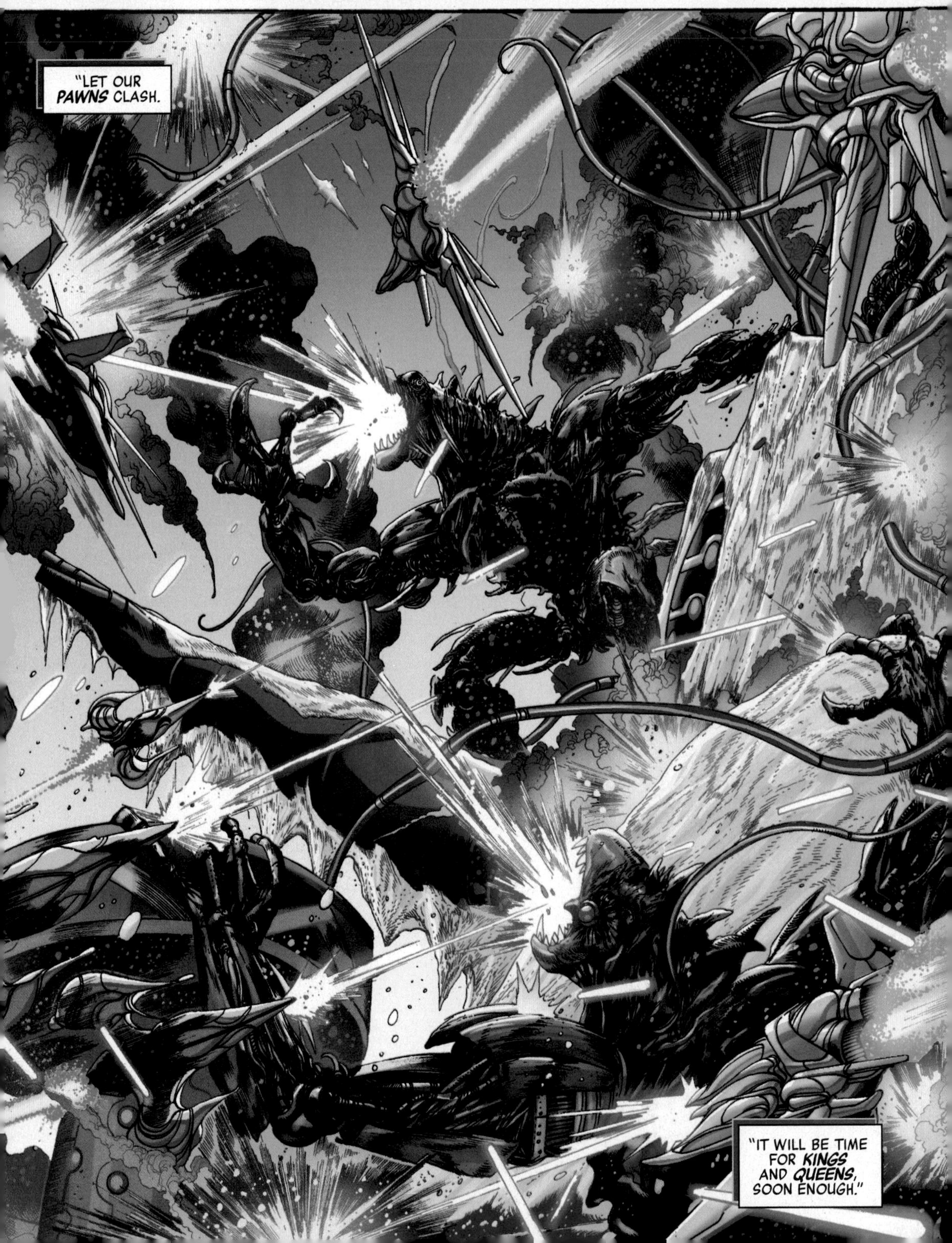
"LET OUR PAWNS CLASH.
"IT WILL BE TIME FOR KINGS AND QUEENS, SOON ENOUGH."

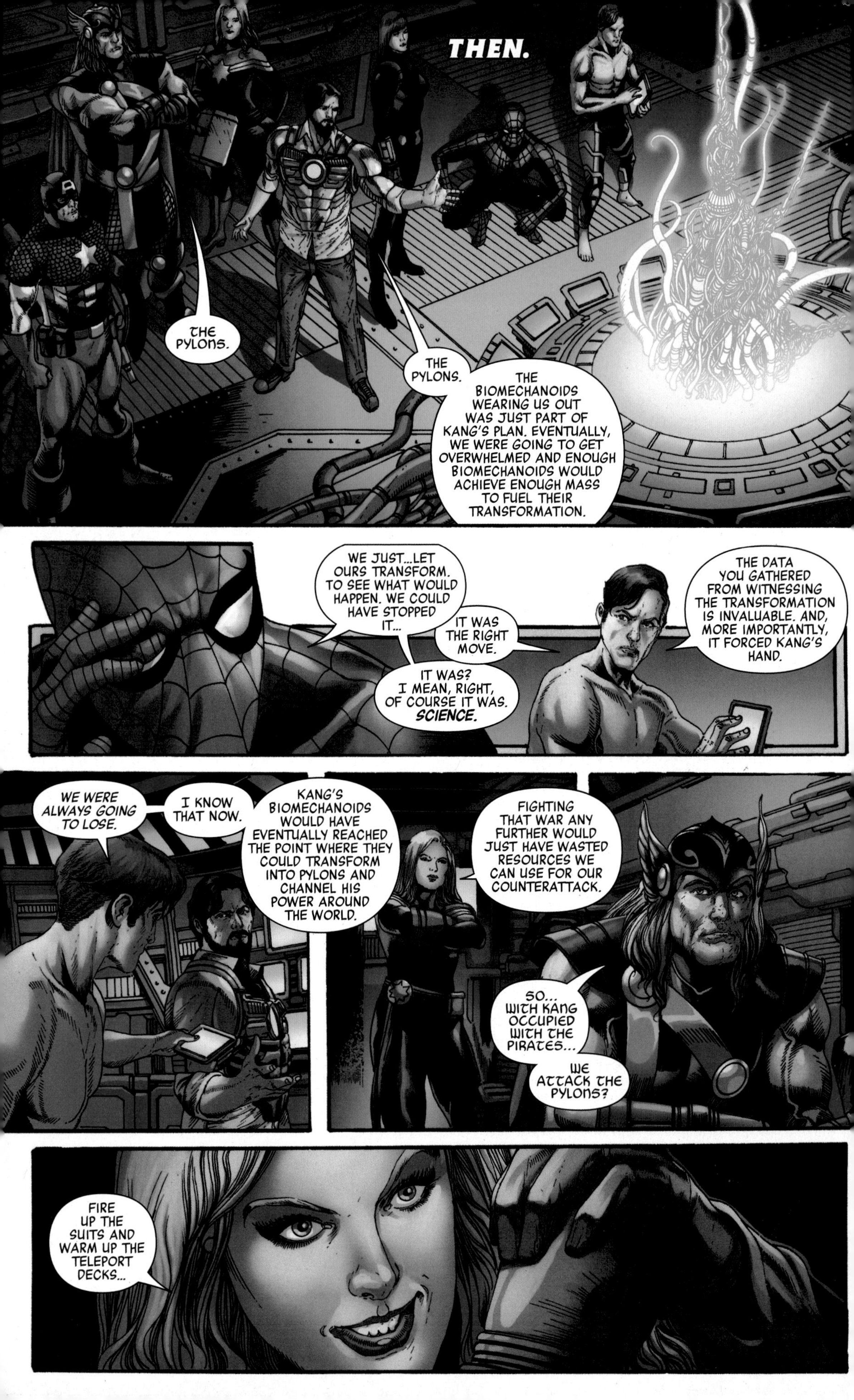
THEN.
THE PYLONS.
THE PYLONS.
THE BIOMECHANOIDS WEARING US OUT WAS JUST PART OF KANG'S PLAN. EVENTUALLY, WE WERE GOING TO GET OVERWHELMED AND ENOUGH BIOMECHANOIDS WOULD ACHIEVE ENOUGH MASS TO FUEL THEIR TRANSFORMATION.
WE JUST...LET OURS TRANSFORM. TO SEE WHAT WOULD HAPPEN. WE COULD HAVE STOPPED IT...
IT WAS THE RIGHT MOVE.
THE DATA YOU GATHERED FROM WITNESSING THE TRANSFORMATION IS INVALUABLE. AND, MORE IMPORTANTLY, IT FORCED KANG'S HAND.
IT WAS? I MEAN, RIGHT, OF COURSE IT WAS. SCIENCE.
WE WERE ALWAYS GOING TO LOSE.
I KNOW THAT NOW.
KANG'S BIOMECHANOIDS WOULD HAVE EVENTUALLY REACHED THE POINT WHERE THEY COULD TRANSFORM INTO PYLONS AND CHANNEL HIS POWER AROUND THE WORLD.
FIGHTING THAT WAR ANY FURTHER WOULD JUST HAVE WASTED RESOURCES WE CAN USE FOR OUR COUNTERATTACK.
SO... WITH KANG OCCUPIED WITH THE PIRATES...
WE ATTACK THE PYLONS?
FIRE UP THE SUITS AND WARM UP THE TELEPORT DECKS...

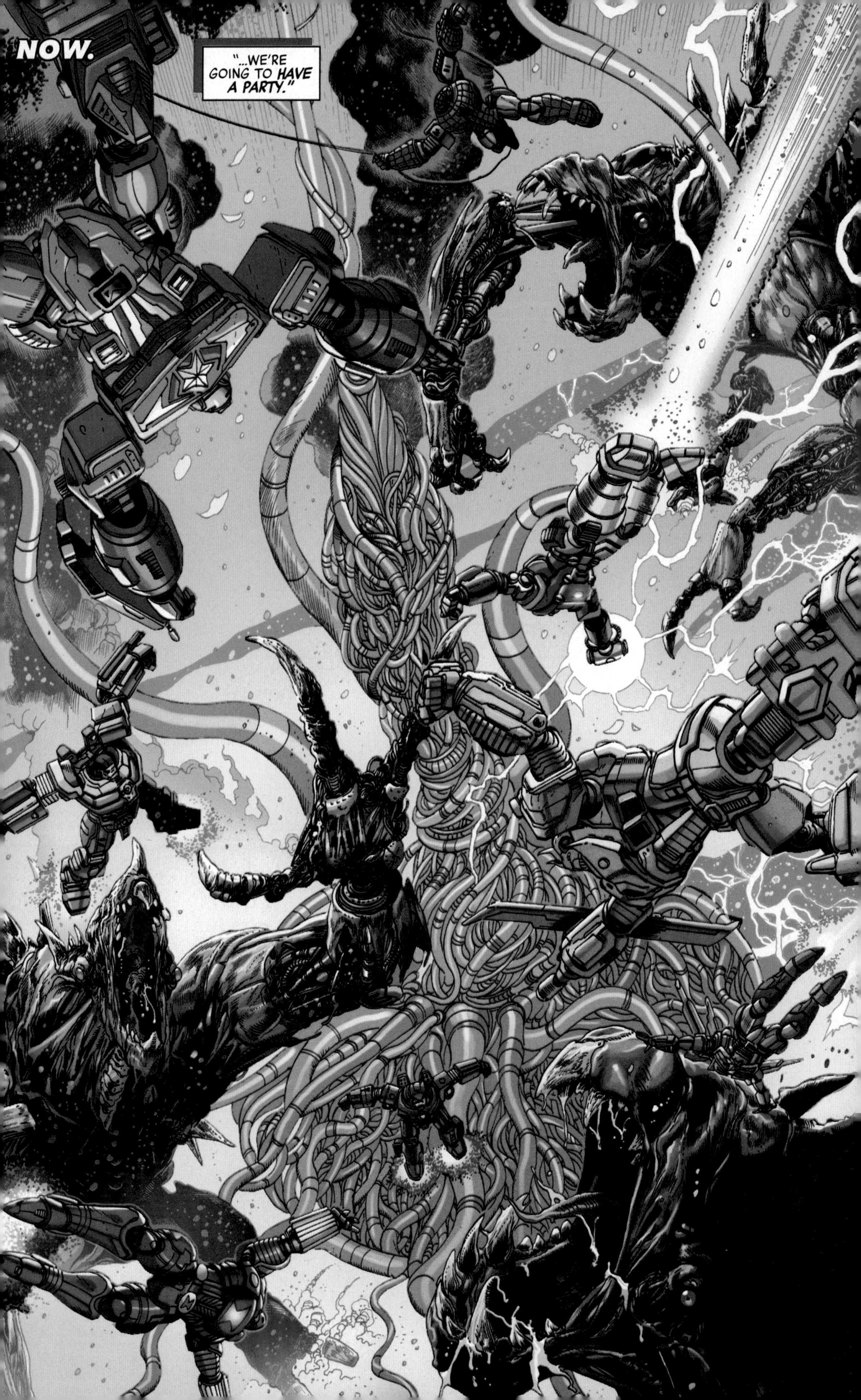
NOW.
"...WE'RE GOING TO HAVE A PARTY."

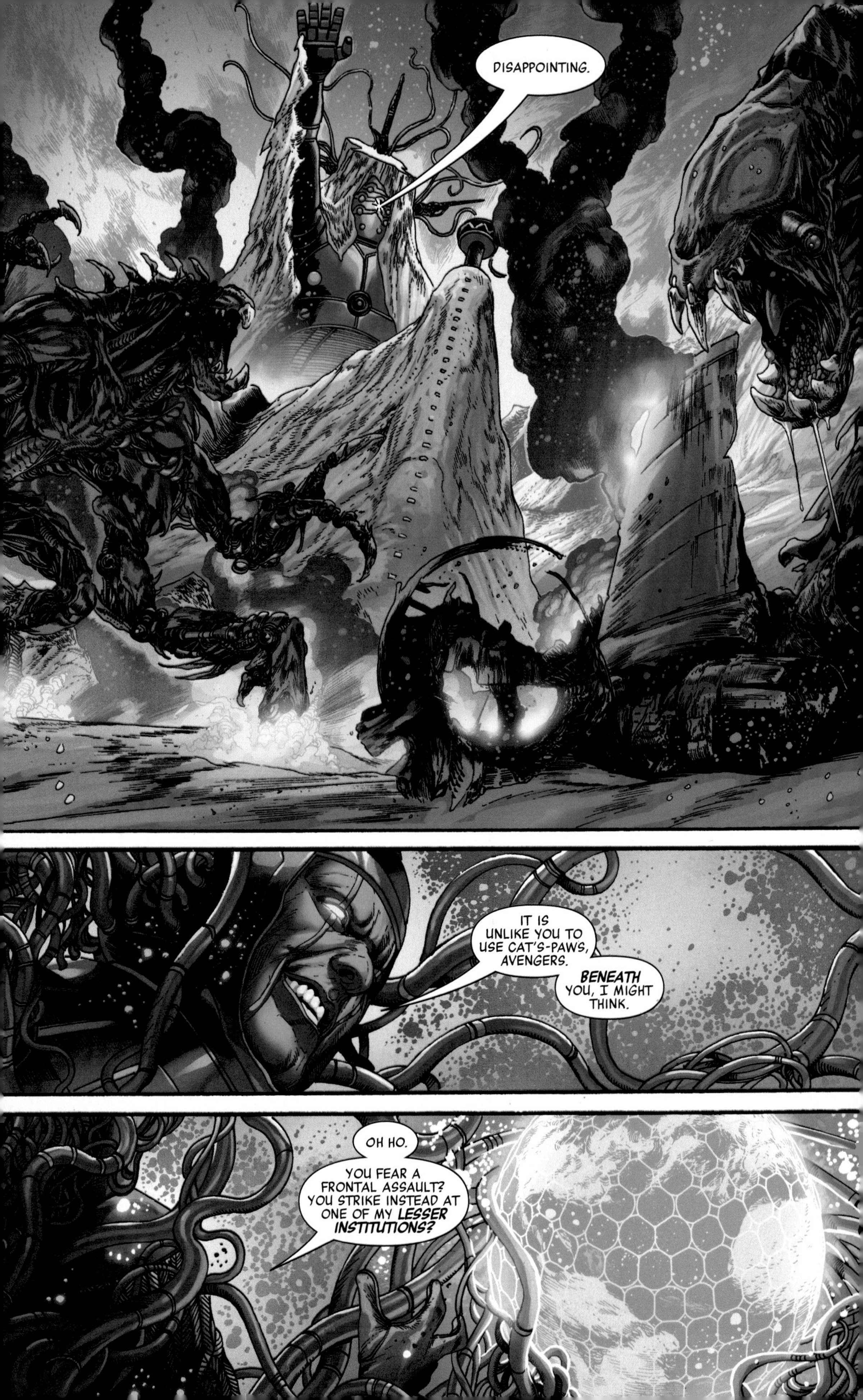
DISAPPOINTING.
IT IS UNLIKE YOU TO USE CAT'S-PAWS, AVENGERS.
BENEATH YOU, I MIGHT THINK.
OH HO.
YOU FEAR A FRONTAL ASSAULT? YOU STRIKE INSTEAD AT ONE OF MY LESSER INSTITUTIONS?

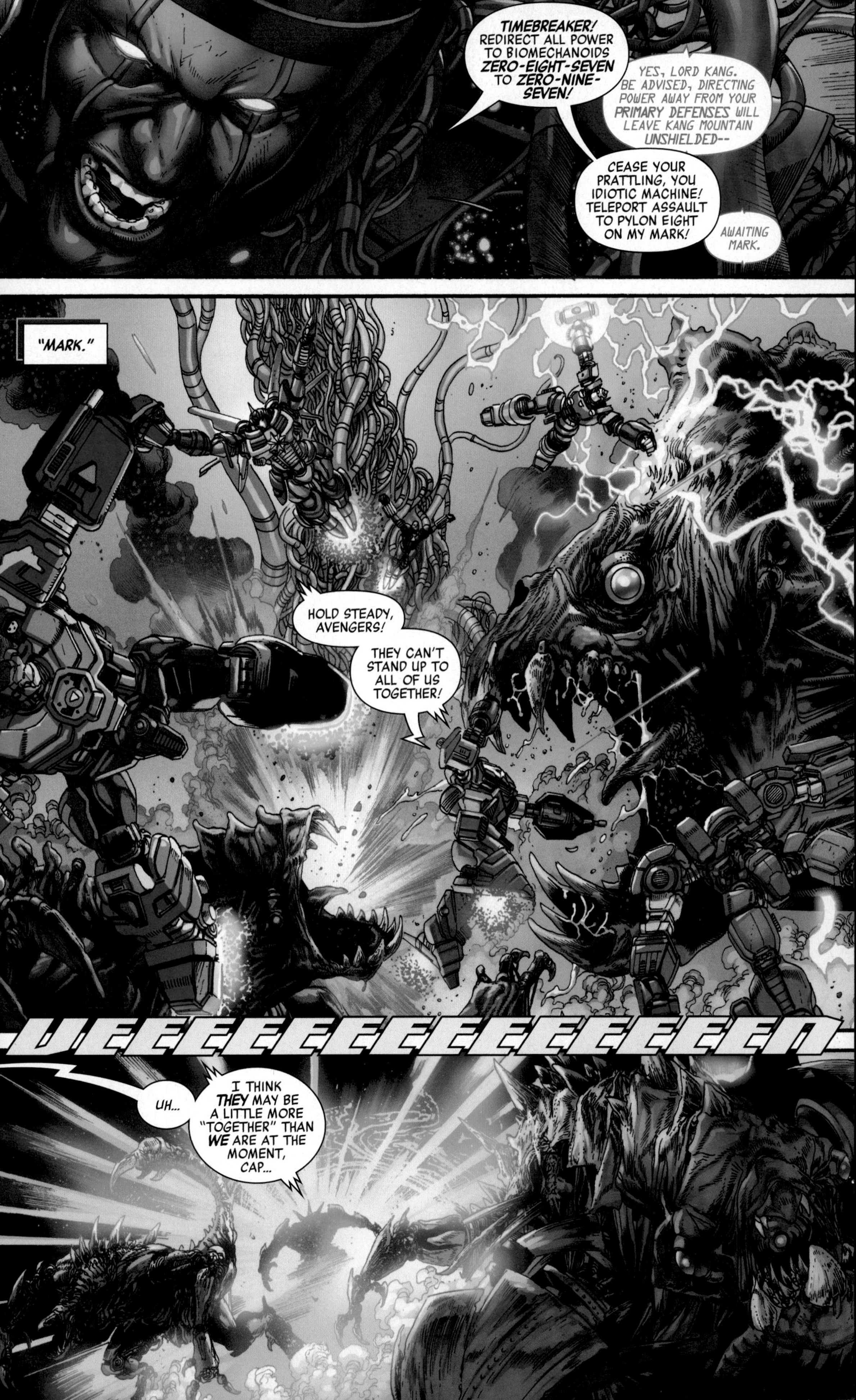
TIMEBREAKER! REDIRECT ALL POWER TO BIOMECHANOIDS ZERO-EIGHT-SEVEN TO ZERO-NINE-SEVEN!
YES, LORD KANG. BE ADVISED, DIRECTING POWER AWAY FROM YOUR PRIMARY DEFENSES WILL LEAVE KANG MOUNTAIN UNSHIELDED--
CEASE YOUR PRATTLING, YOU IDIOTIC MACHINE! TELEPORT ASSAULT TO PYLON EIGHT ON MY MARK!
AWAITING MARK.
"MARK."
HOLD STEADY, AVENGERS!
THEY CAN'T STAND UP TO ALL OF US TOGETHER!
VEEEEEEEEEEEEEEN
UH...
I THINK THEY MAY BE A LITTLE MORE "TOGETHER" THAN WE ARE AT THE MOMENT, CAP...

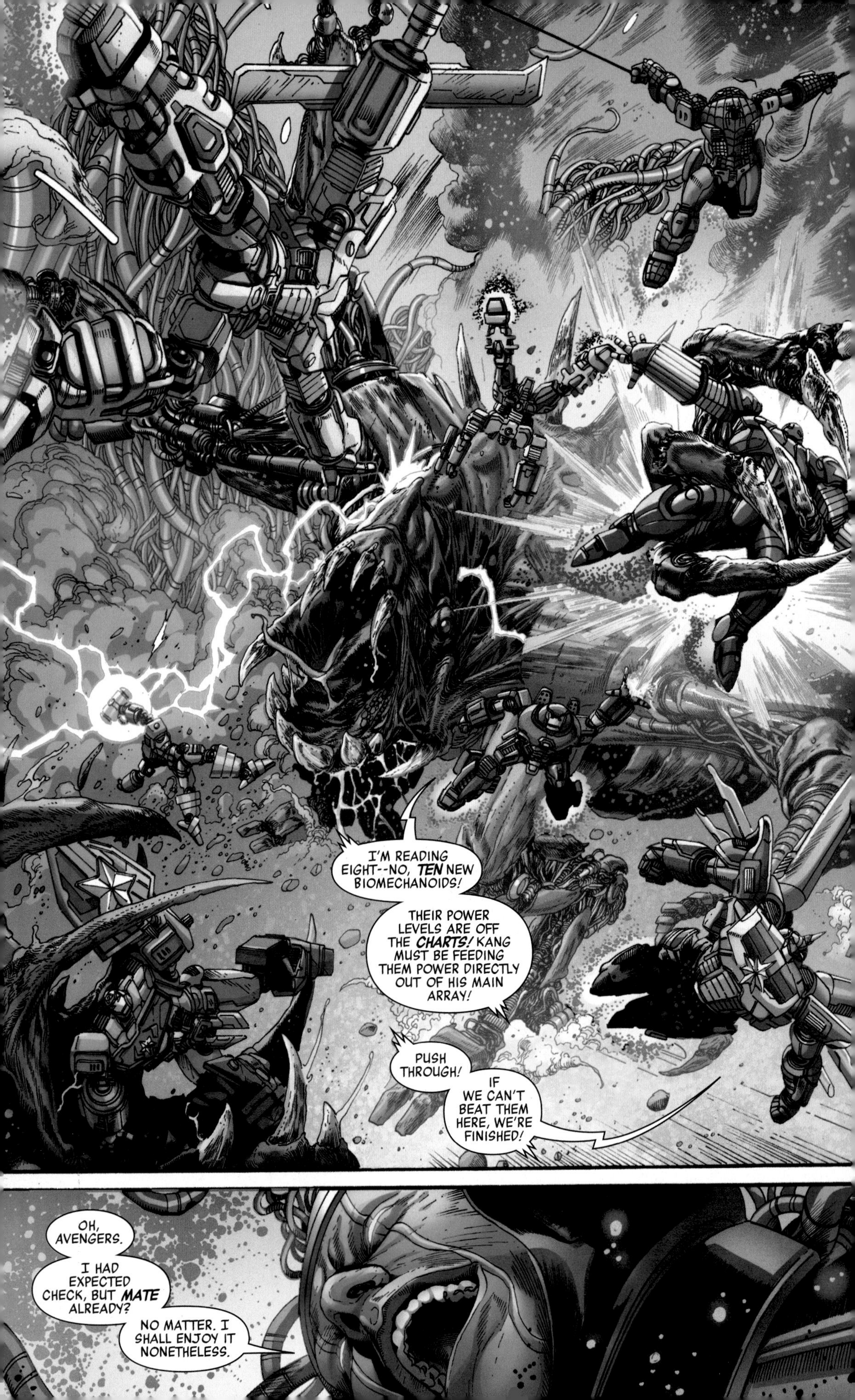
I'M READING EIGHT--NO, TEN NEW BIOMECHANOIDS!
THEIR POWER LEVELS ARE OFF THE CHARTS! KANG MUST BE FEEDING THEM POWER DIRECTLY OUT OF HIS MAIN ARRAY!
PUSH THROUGH!
IF WE CAN'T BEAT THEM HERE, WE'RE FINISHED!
OH, AVENGERS.
I HAD EXPECTED CHECK, BUT MATE ALREADY?
NO MATTER. I SHALL ENJOY IT NONETHELESS.

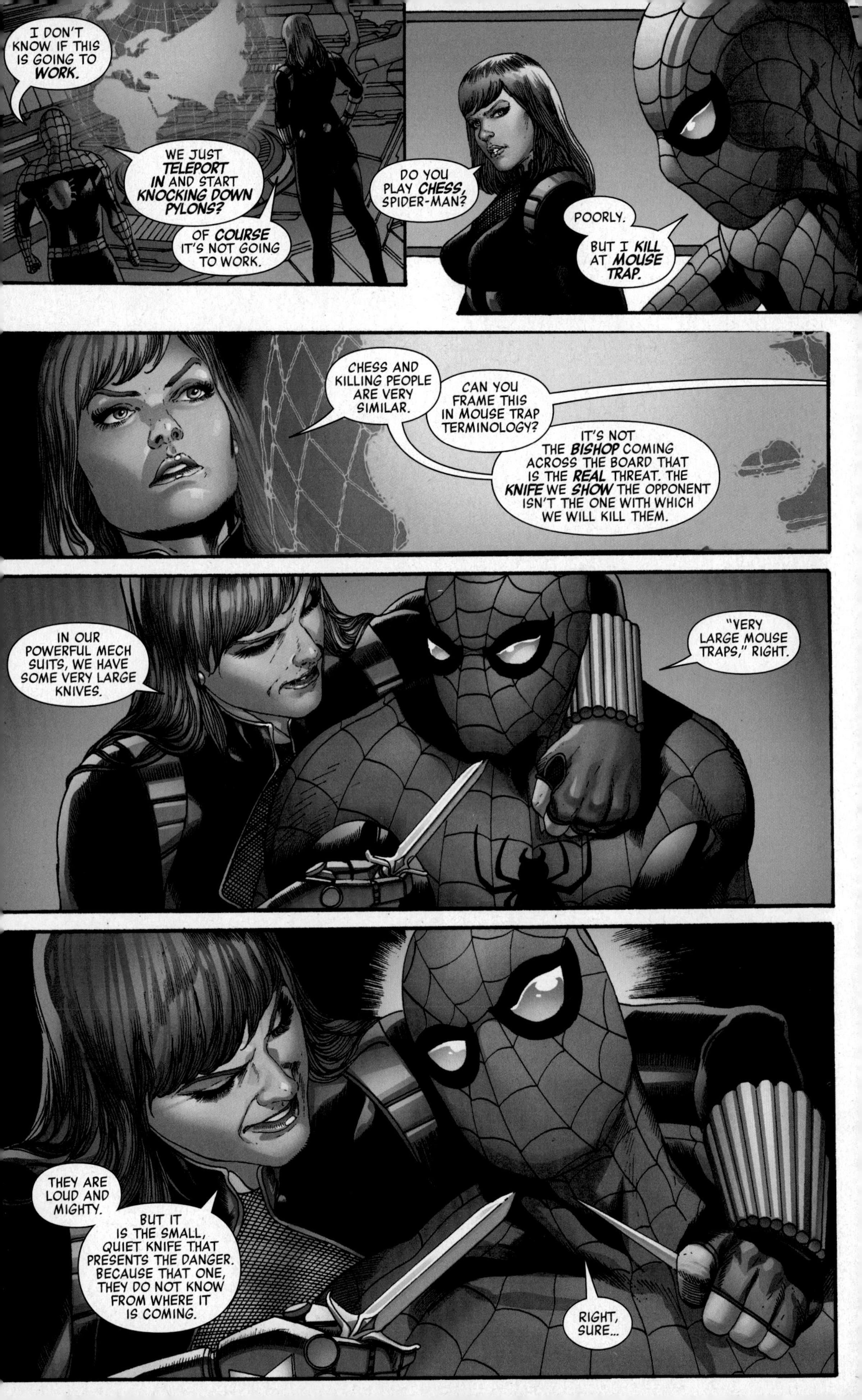
I DON'T KNOW IF THIS IS GOING TO WORK.
WE JUST TELEPORT IN AND START KNOCKING DOWN PYLONS?
OF COURSE IT'S NOT GOING TO WORK.
DO YOU PLAY CHESS, SPIDER-MAN?
POORLY.
BUT I KILL AT MOUSE TRAP.
CHESS AND KILLING PEOPLE ARE VERY SIMILAR.
CAN YOU FRAME THIS IN MOUSE TRAP TERMINOLOGY?
IT'S NOT THE BISHOP COMING ACROSS THE BOARD THAT IS THE REAL THREAT. THE KNIFE WE SHOW THE OPPONENT ISN'T THE ONE WITH WHICH WE WILL KILL THEM.
IN OUR POWERFUL MECH SUITS, WE HAVE SOME VERY LARGE KNIVES.
"VERY LARGE MOUSE TRAPS," RIGHT.
THEY ARE LOUD AND MIGHTY.
BUT IT IS THE SMALL, QUIET KNIFE THAT PRESENTS THE DANGER. BECAUSE THAT ONE, THEY DO NOT KNOW FROM WHERE IT IS COMING.
RIGHT, SURE...

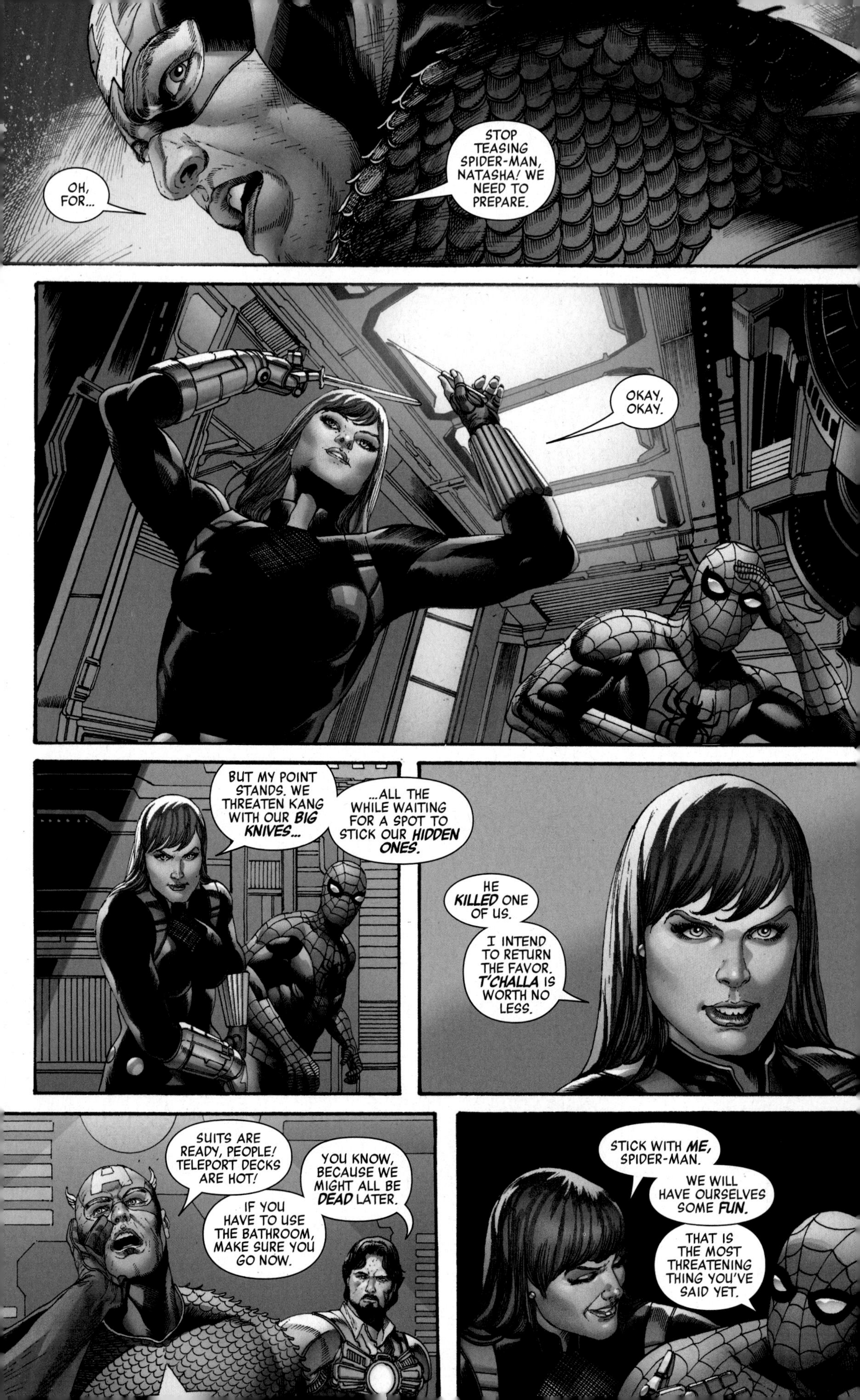
OH, FOR...
STOP TEASING SPIDER-MAN, NATASHA! WE NEED TO PREPARE.
OKAY, OKAY.
BUT MY POINT STANDS. WE THREATEN KANG WITH OUR BIG KNIVES...
...ALL THE WHILE WAITING FOR A SPOT TO STICK OUR HIDDEN ONES.
HE KILLED ONE OF US.
I INTEND TO RETURN THE FAVOR. T'CHALLA IS WORTH NO LESS.
SUITS ARE READY, PEOPLE! TELEPORT DECKS ARE HOT!
IF YOU HAVE TO USE THE BATHROOM, MAKE SURE YOU GO NOW.
YOU KNOW, BECAUSE WE MIGHT ALL BE DEAD LATER.
STICK WITH ME, SPIDER-MAN.
WE WILL HAVE OURSELVES SOME FUN.
THAT IS THE MOST THREATENING THING YOU'VE SAID YET.

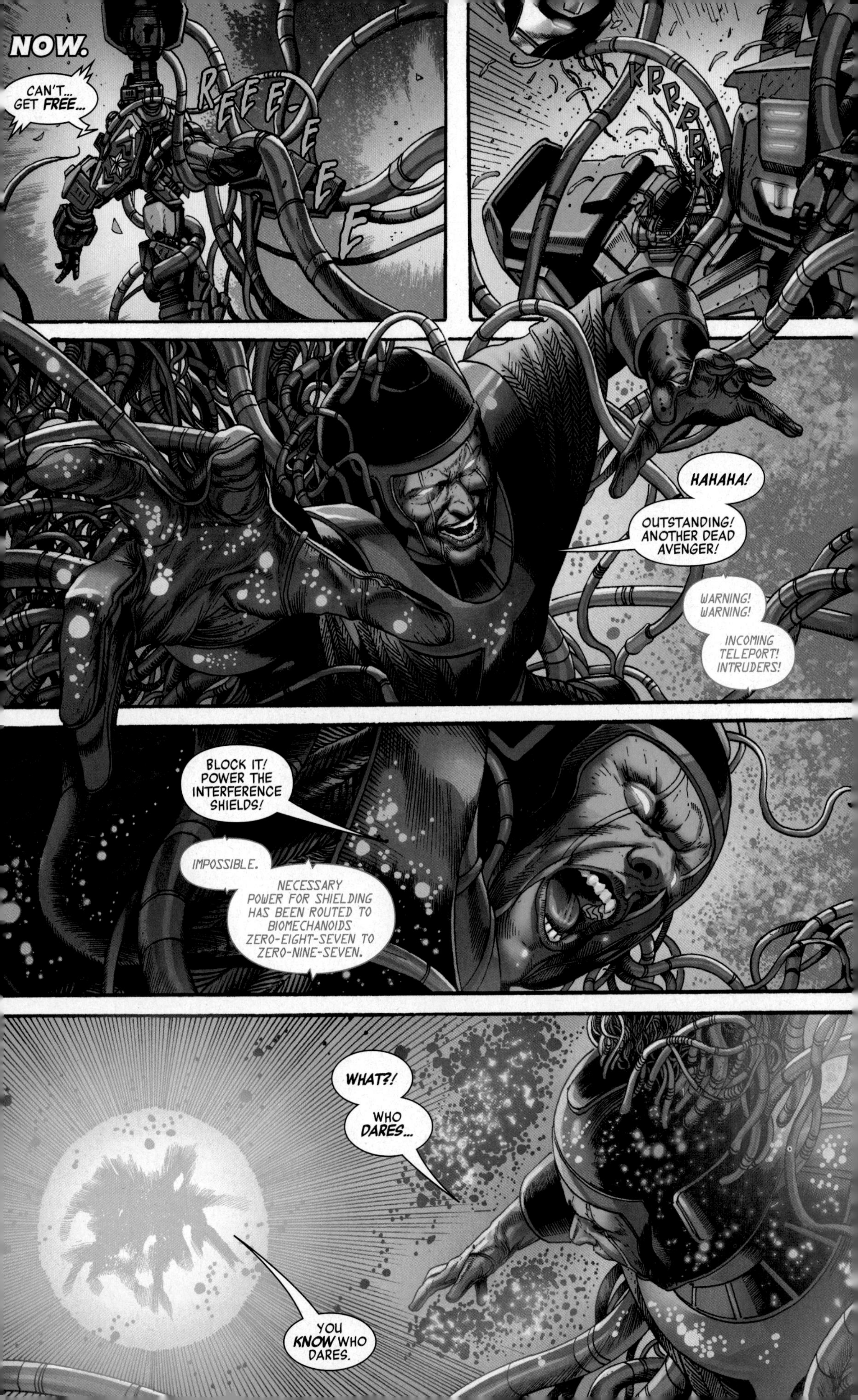
NOW.
CAN'T... GET FREE...
REEEEEEEE
KRRRRRK
HAHAHA!
OUTSTANDING! ANOTHER DEAD AVENGER!
WARNING! WARNING!
INCOMING TELEPORT! INTRUDERS!
BLOCK IT! POWER THE INTERFERENCE SHIELDS!
IMPOSSIBLE.
NECESSARY POWER FOR SHIELDING HAS BEEN ROUTED TO BIOMECHANOIDS ZERO-EIGHT-SEVEN TO ZERO-NINE-SEVEN.
WHAT?!
WHO DARES...
YOU KNOW WHO DARES.

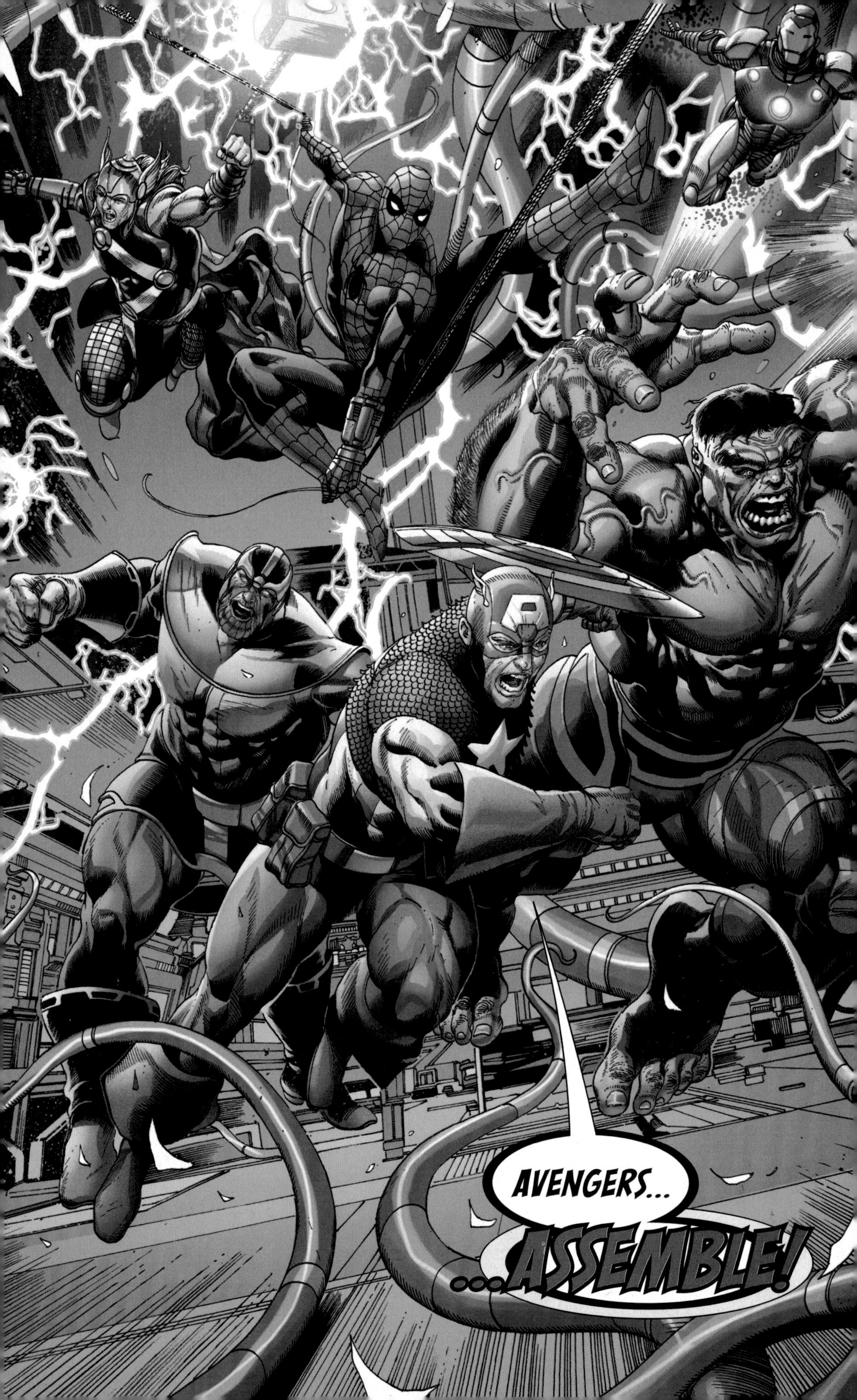
AVENGERS...
...ASSEMBLE!

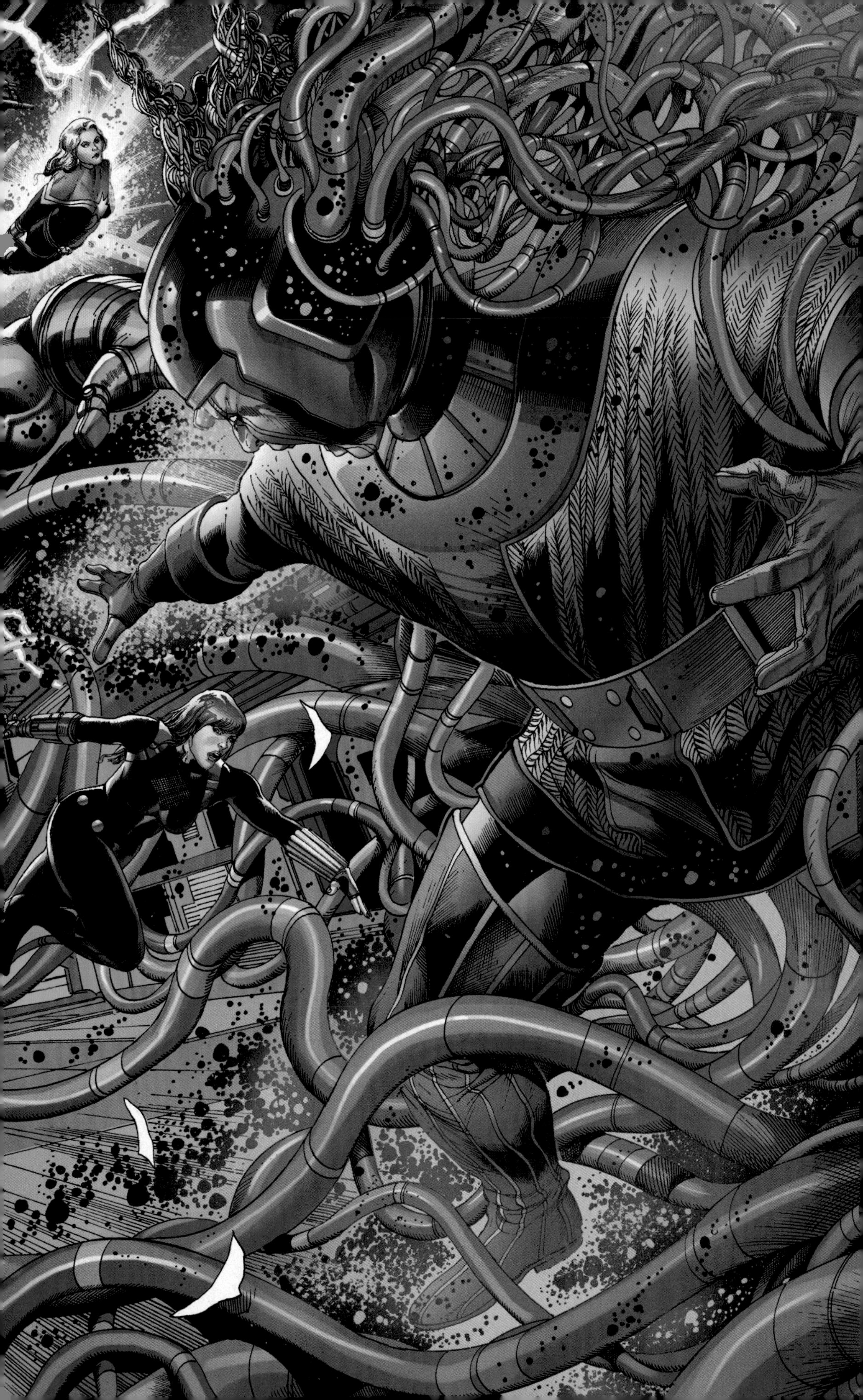

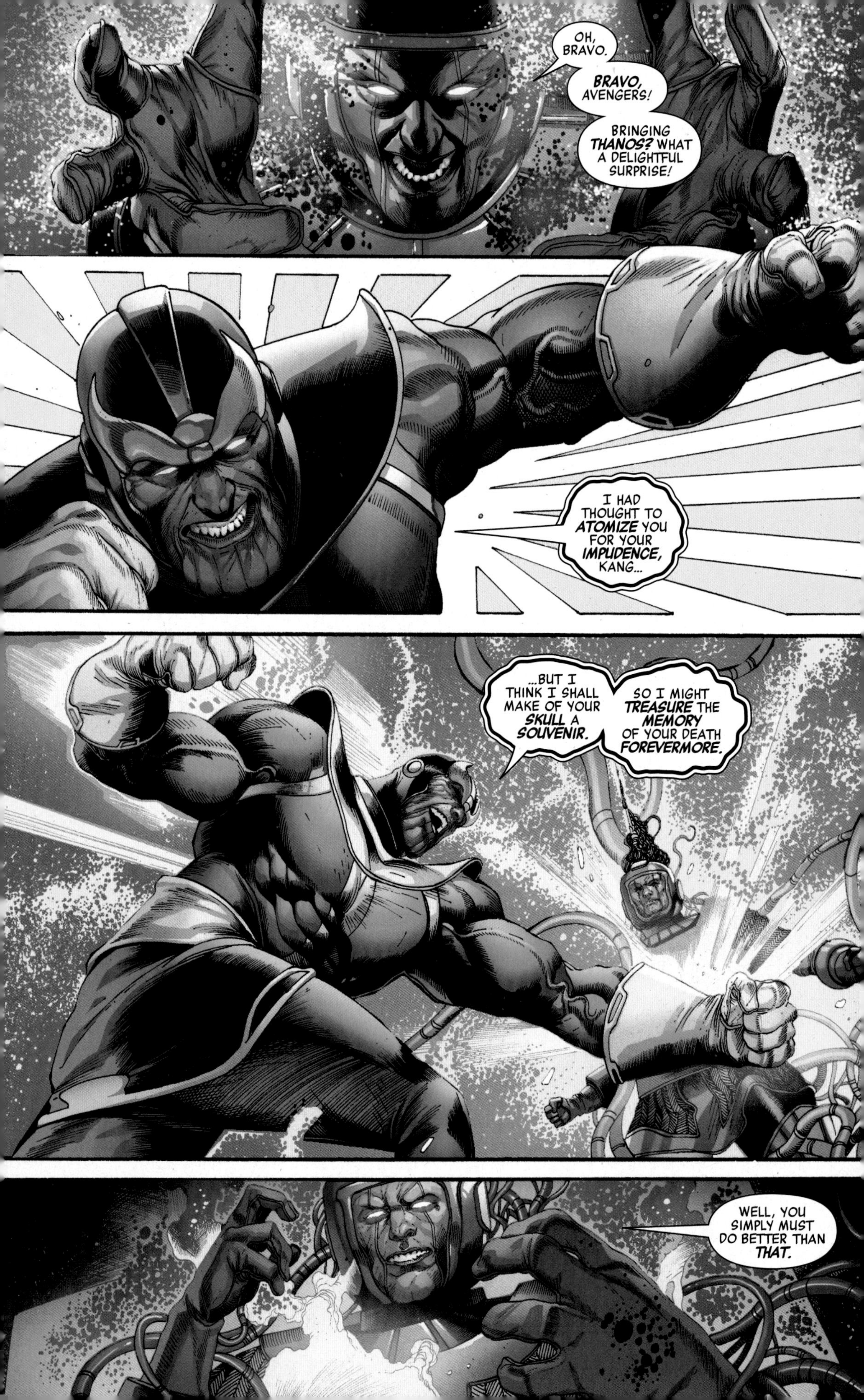
OH, BRAVO.
BRAVO, AVENGERS!
BRINGING THANOS? WHAT A DELIGHTFUL SURPRISE!
I HAD THOUGHT TO ATOMIZE YOU FOR YOUR IMPUDENCE, KANG...
...BUT I THINK I SHALL MAKE OF YOUR SKULL A SOUVENIR.
SO I MIGHT TREASURE THE MEMORY OF YOUR DEATH FOREVERMORE.
WELL, YOU SIMPLY MUST DO BETTER THAN THAT.

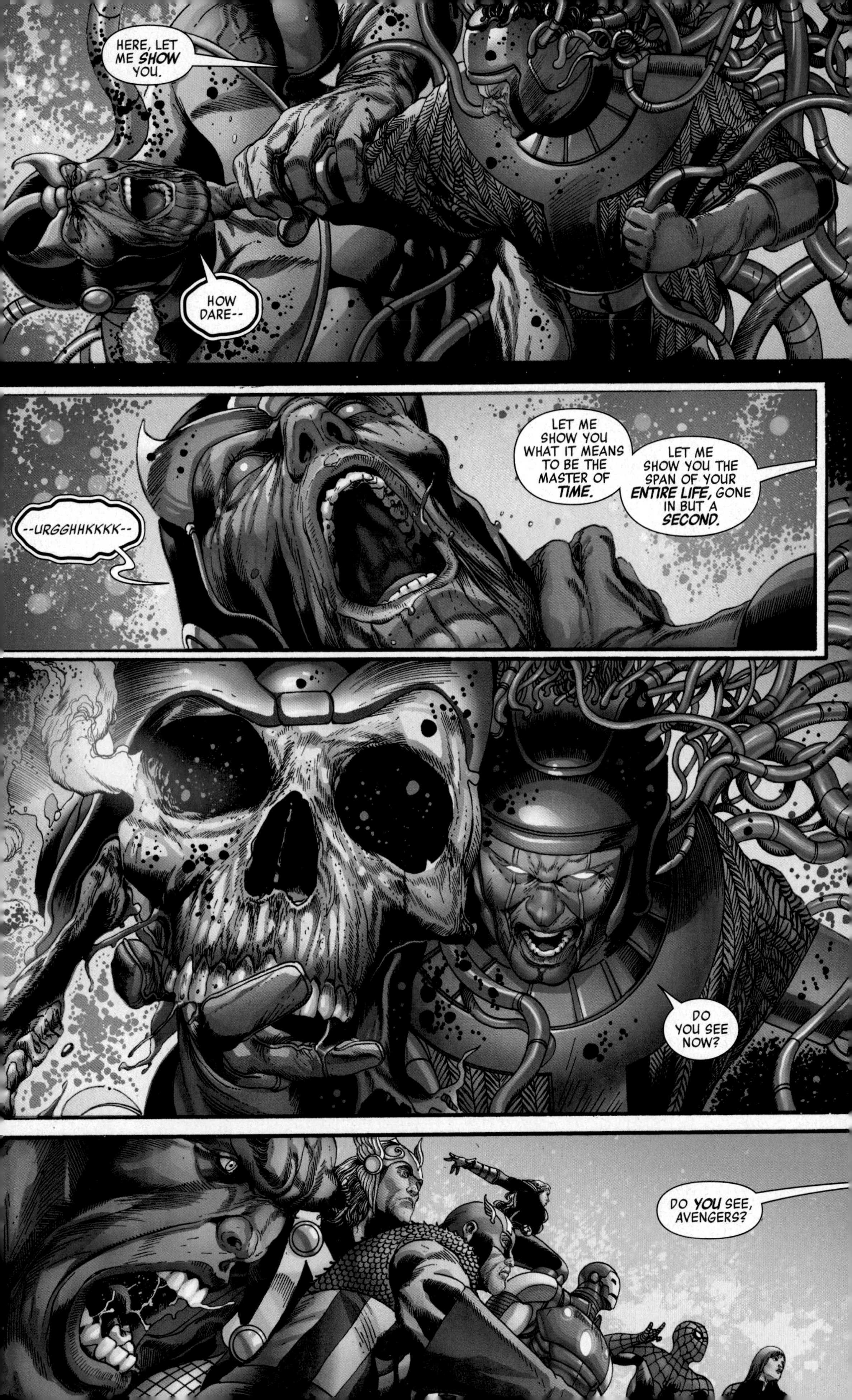
HERE, LET ME SHOW YOU.
HOW DARE--
LET ME SHOW YOU WHAT IT MEANS TO BE THE MASTER OF TIME.
LET ME SHOW YOU THE SPAN OF YOUR ENTIRE LIFE, GONE IN BUT A SECOND.
--URGGHHKKKK--
DO YOU SEE NOW?
DO YOU SEE, AVENGERS?

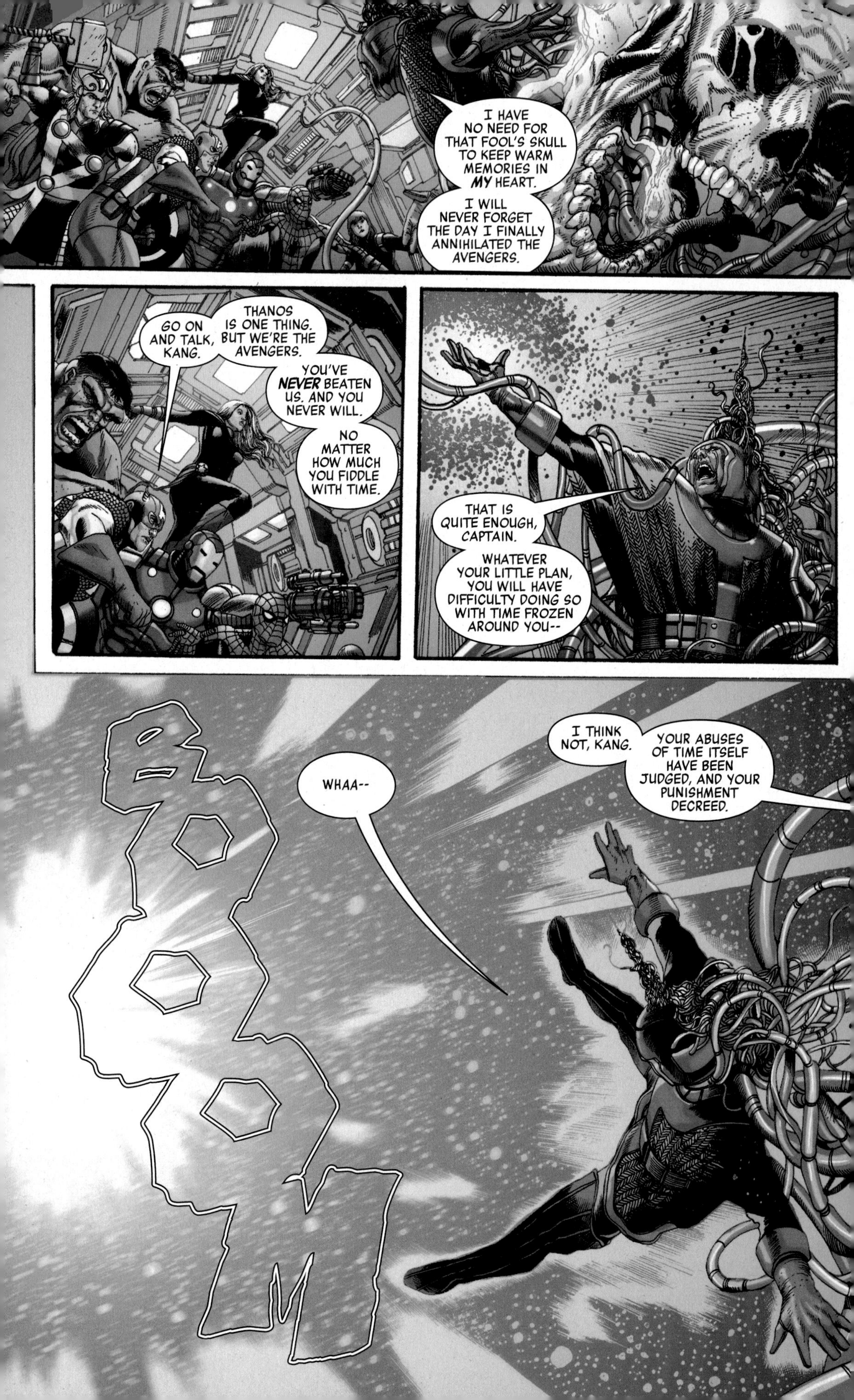
I HAVE NO NEED FOR THAT FOOL'S SKULL TO KEEP WARM MEMORIES IN *MY* HEART.
I WILL NEVER FORGET THE DAY I FINALLY ANNIHILATED THE AVENGERS.
GO ON AND TALK, KANG.
THANOS IS ONE THING. BUT WE'RE THE AVENGERS.
YOU'VE *NEVER* BEATEN US. AND YOU NEVER WILL.
NO MATTER HOW MUCH YOU FIDDLE WITH TIME.
THAT IS QUITE ENOUGH, CAPTAIN.
WHATEVER YOUR LITTLE PLAN, YOU WILL HAVE DIFFICULTY DOING SO WITH TIME FROZEN AROUND YOU--
BOOOM
WHAA--
I THINK NOT, KANG.
YOUR ABUSES OF TIME ITSELF HAVE BEEN JUDGED, AND YOUR PUNISHMENT DECREED.

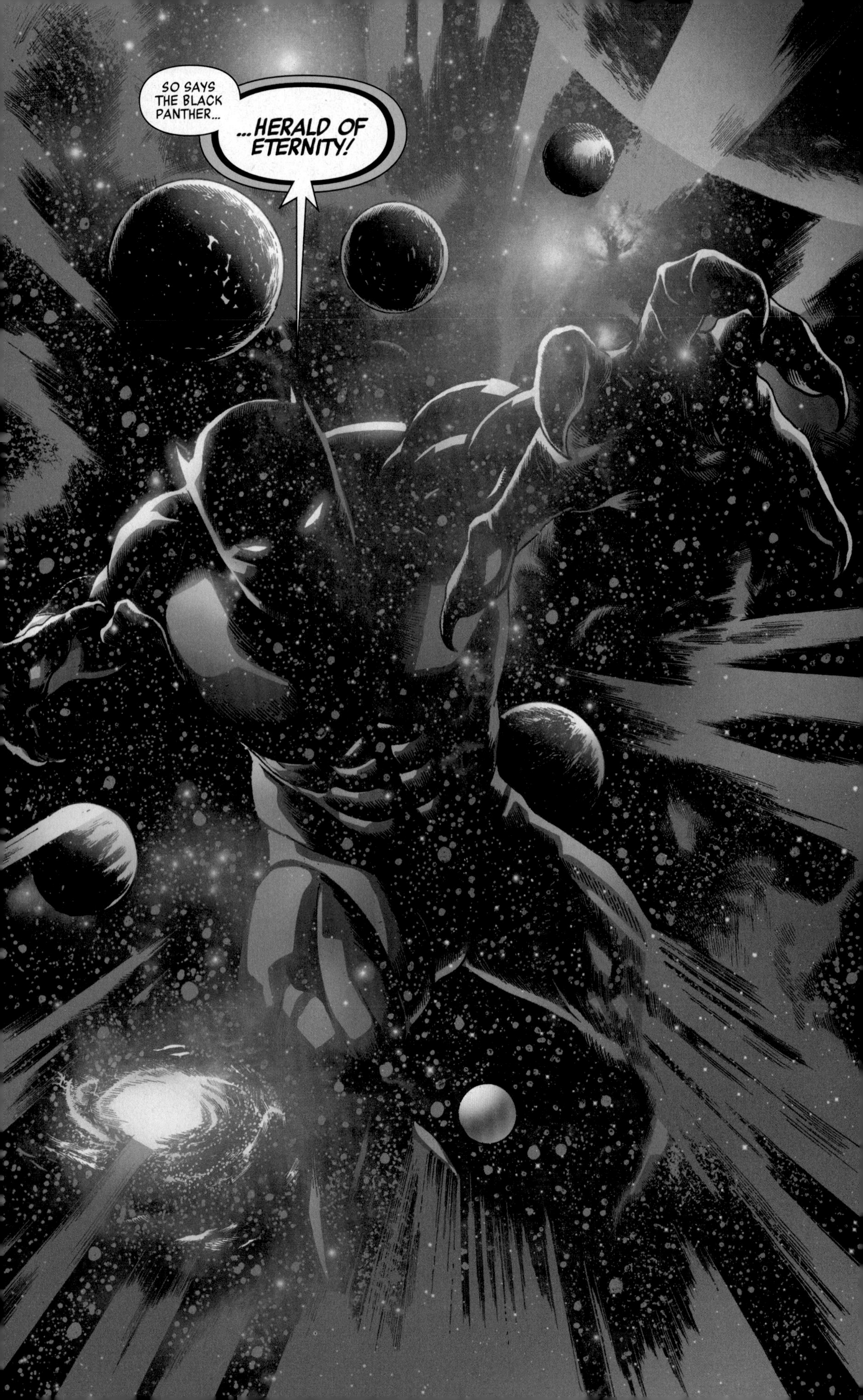
SO SAYS THE BLACK PANTHER...
...HERALD OF ETERNITY!

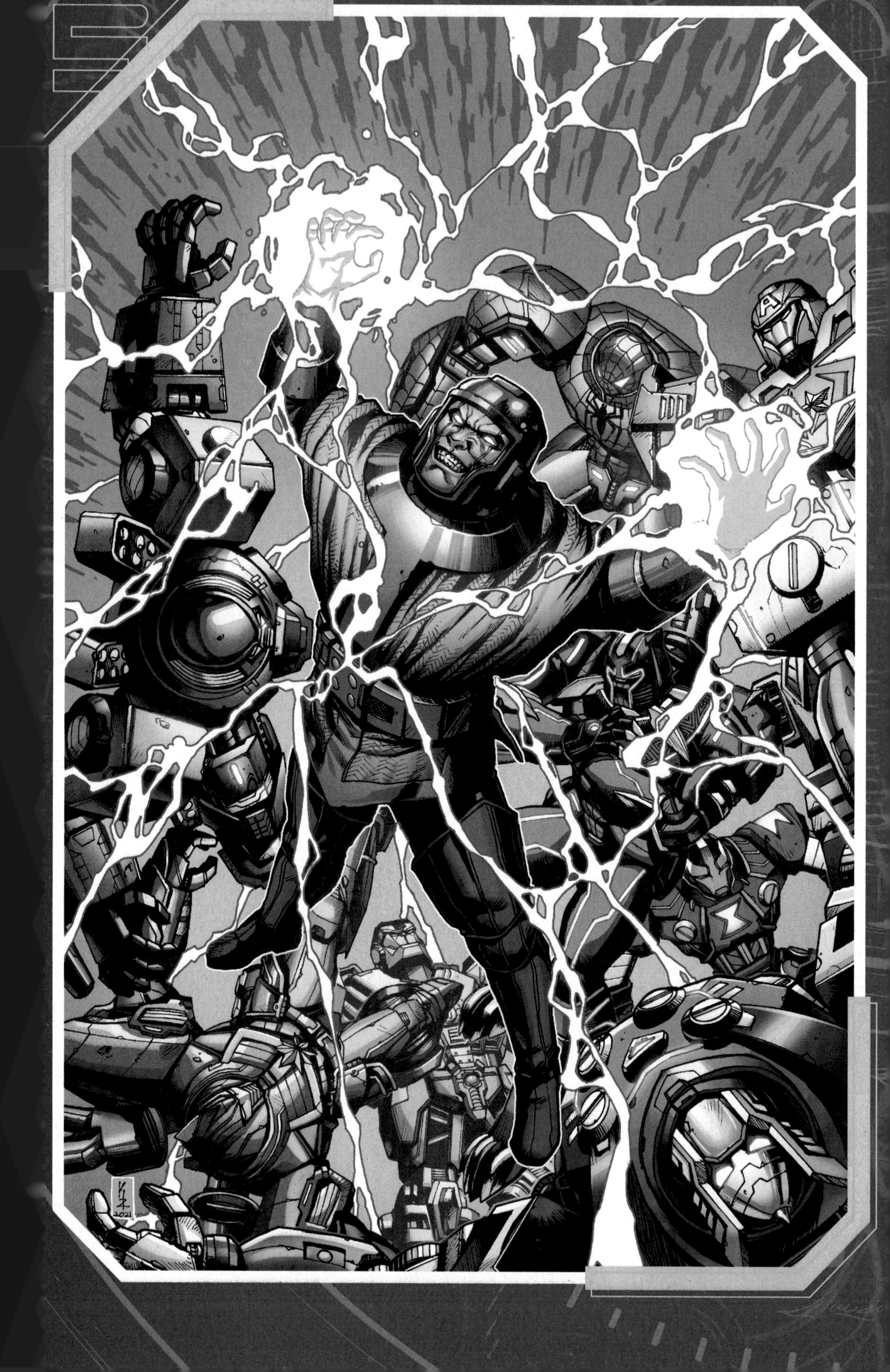

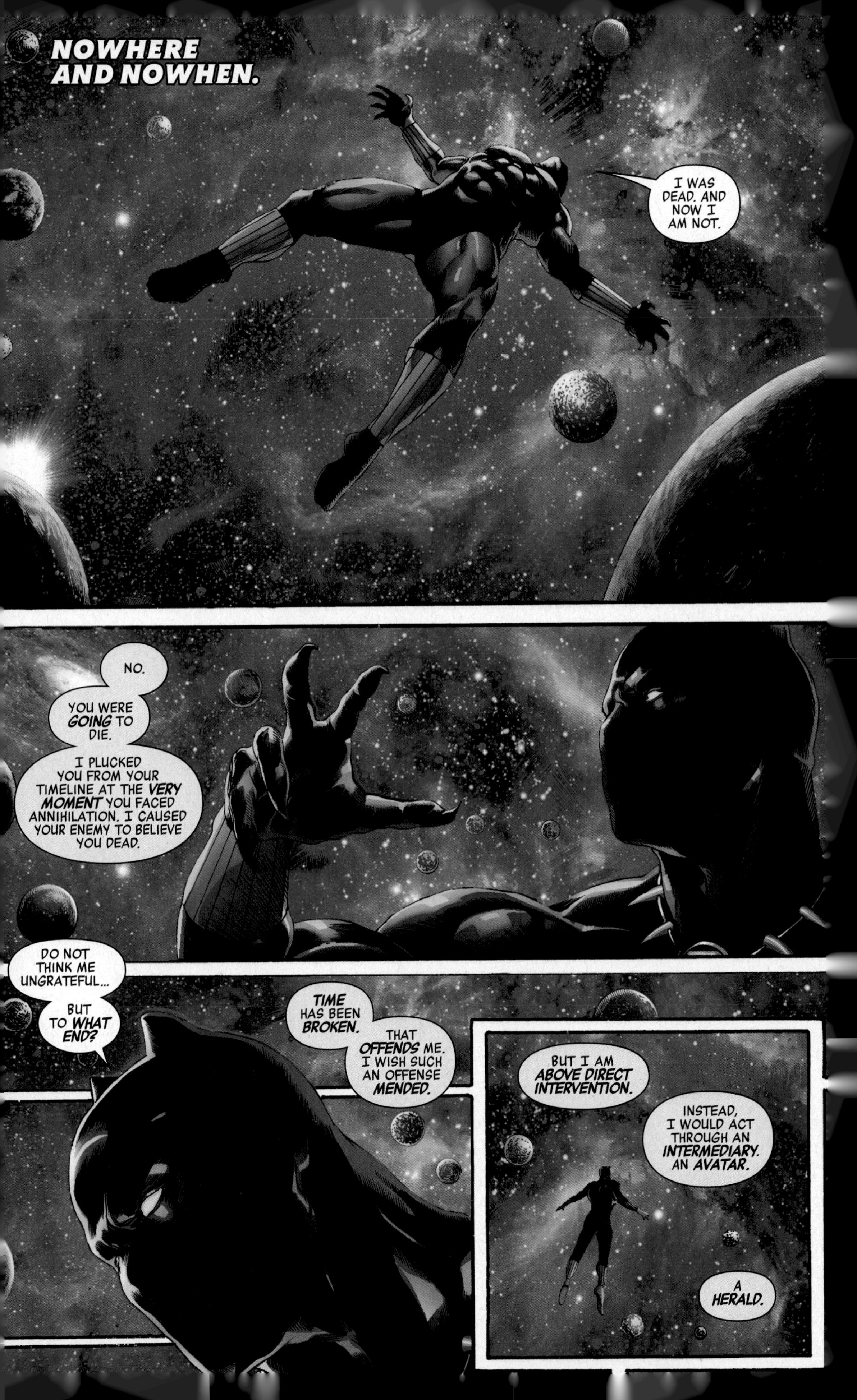
NOWHERE AND NOWHEN.
I WAS DEAD. AND NOW I AM NOT.
NO.
YOU WERE GOING TO DIE.
I PLUCKED YOU FROM YOUR TIMELINE AT THE VERY MOMENT YOU FACED ANNIHILATION. I CAUSED YOUR ENEMY TO BELIEVE YOU DEAD.
DO NOT THINK ME UNGRATEFUL...
BUT TO WHAT END?
TIME HAS BEEN BROKEN.
THAT OFFENDS ME. I WISH SUCH AN OFFENSE MENDED.
BUT I AM ABOVE DIRECT INTERVENTION.
INSTEAD, I WOULD ACT THROUGH AN INTERMEDIARY. AN AVATAR.
A HERALD.

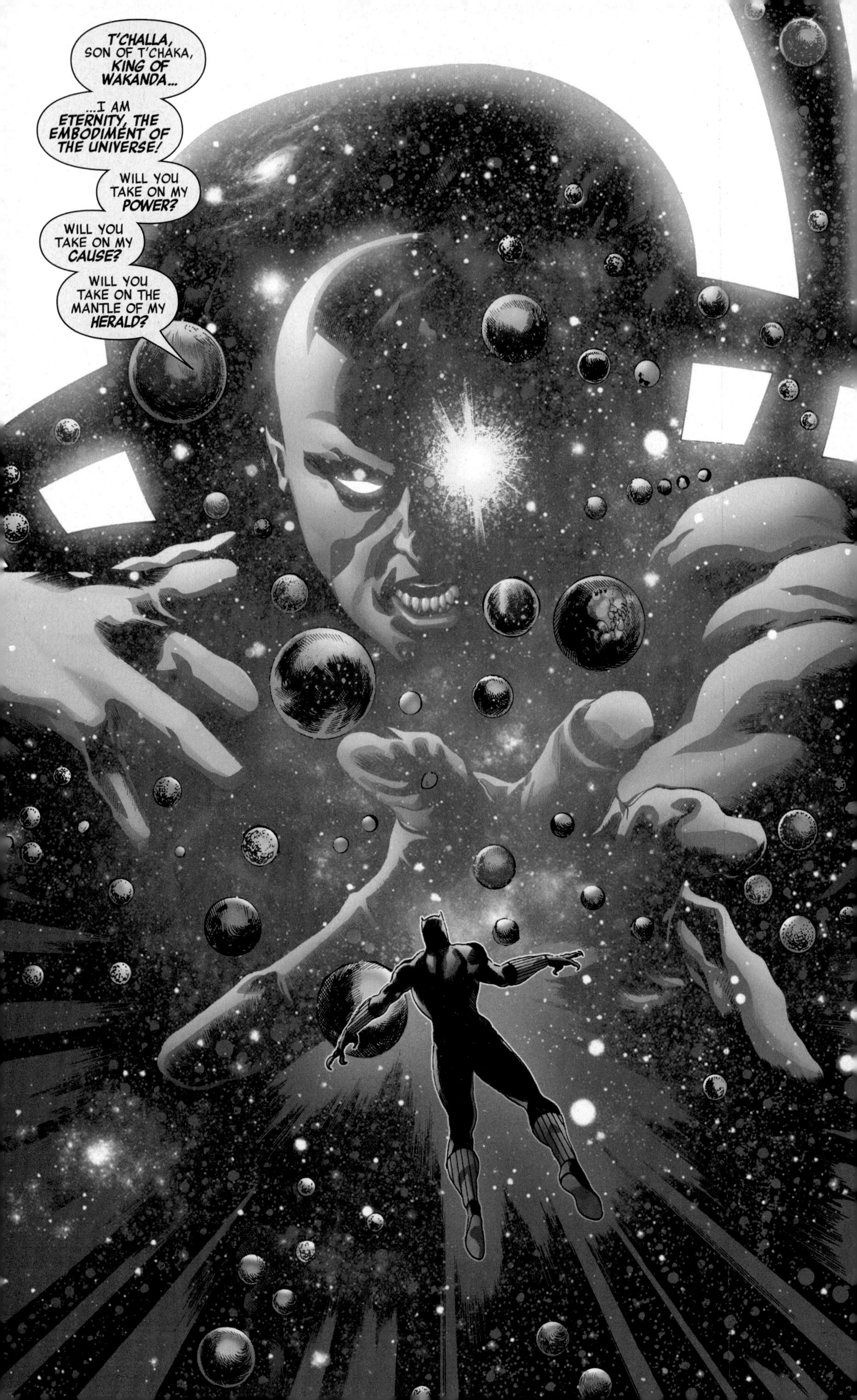
T'CHALLA, SON OF T'CHAKA, KING OF WAKANDA...
...I AM ETERNITY, THE EMBODIMENT OF THE UNIVERSE!
WILL YOU TAKE ON MY POWER?
WILL YOU TAKE ON MY CAUSE?
WILL YOU TAKE ON THE MANTLE OF MY HERALD?

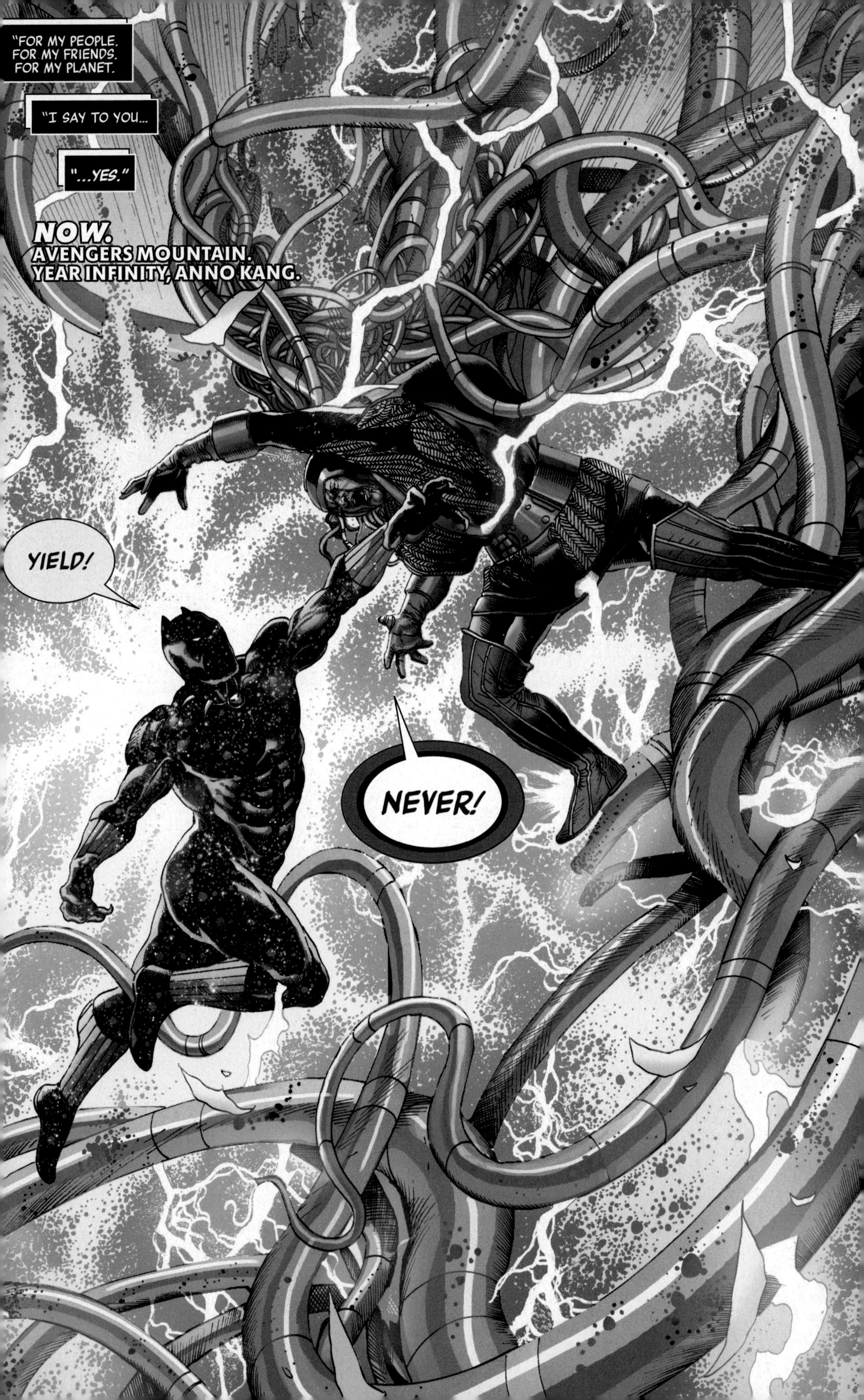
"FOR MY PEOPLE. FOR MY FRIENDS. FOR MY PLANET.
"I SAY TO YOU...
"...YES."
NOW.
AVENGERS MOUNTAIN.
YEAR INFINITY, ANNO KANG.
YIELD!
NEVER!

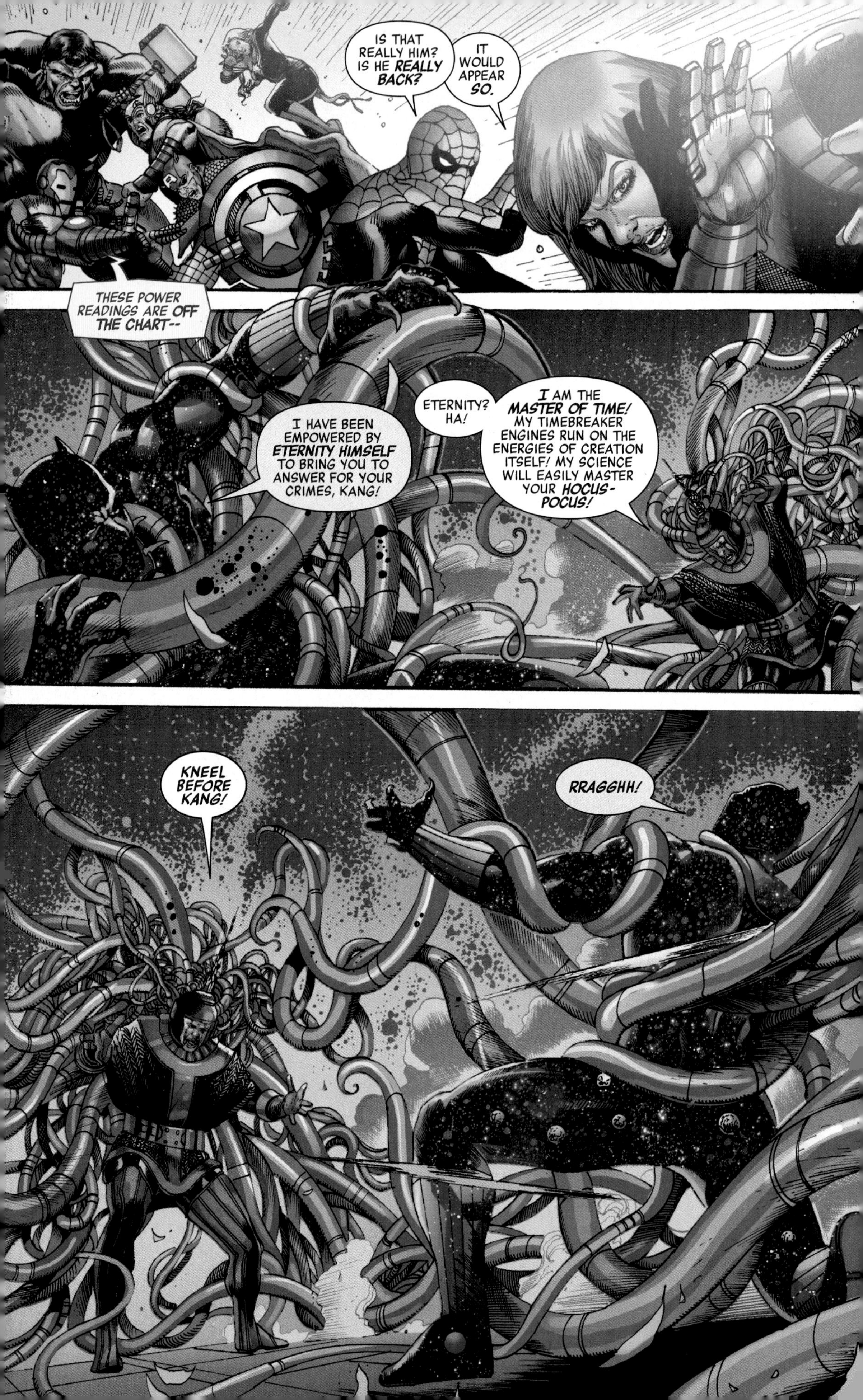
IS THAT REALLY HIM? IS HE REALLY BACK?
IT WOULD APPEAR SO.
THESE POWER READINGS ARE OFF THE CHART--
I HAVE BEEN EMPOWERED BY ETERNITY HIMSELF TO BRING YOU TO ANSWER FOR YOUR CRIMES, KANG!
ETERNITY? HA!
I AM THE MASTER OF TIME! MY TIMEBREAKER ENGINES RUN ON THE ENERGIES OF CREATION ITSELF! MY SCIENCE WILL EASILY MASTER YOUR HOCUS-POCUS!
KNEEL BEFORE KANG!
RRAGGHH!

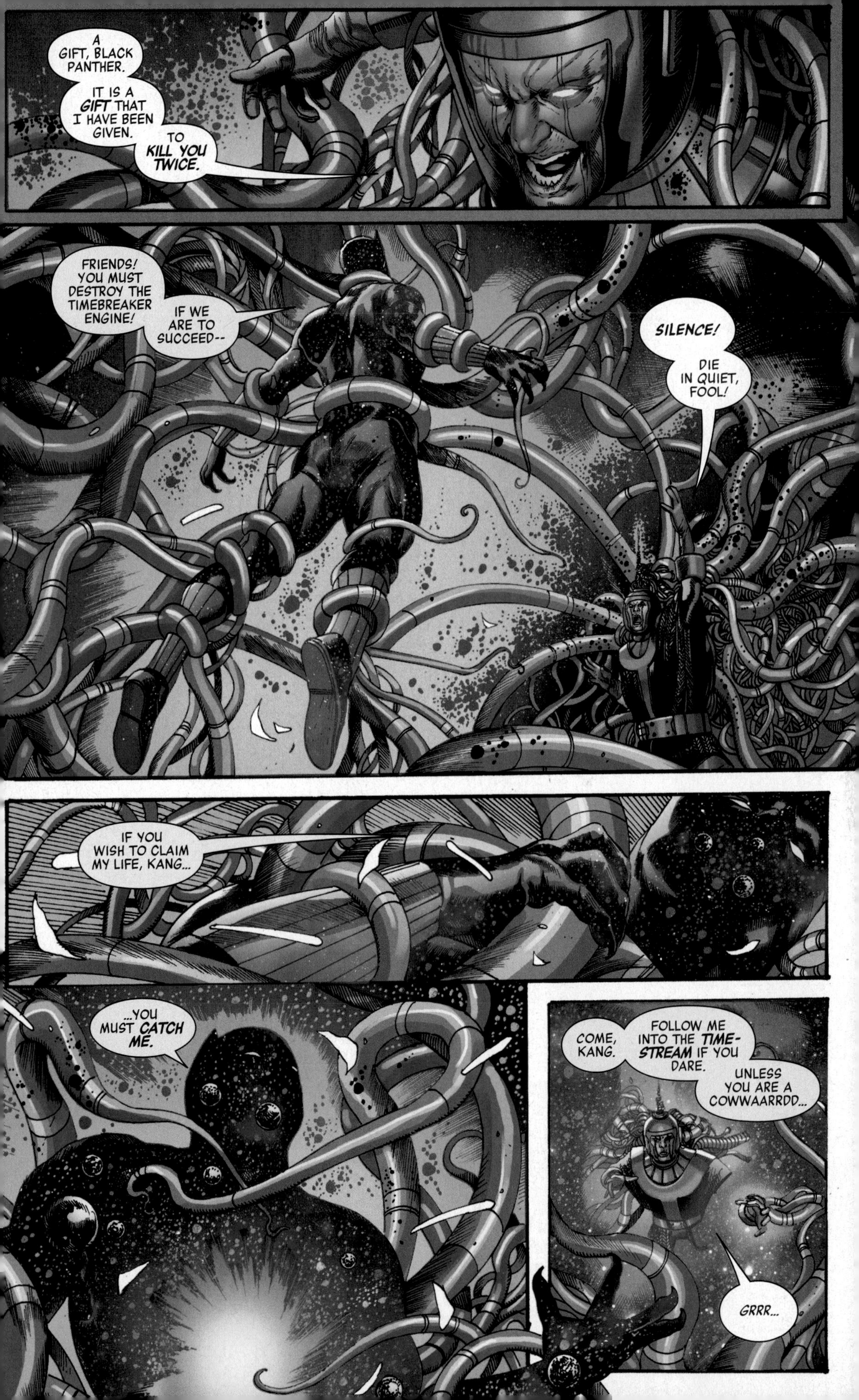
A GIFT, BLACK PANTHER.
IT IS A GIFT THAT I HAVE BEEN GIVEN.
TO KILL YOU TWICE.
FRIENDS! YOU MUST DESTROY THE TIMEBREAKER ENGINE!
IF WE ARE TO SUCCEED--
SILENCE!
DIE IN QUIET, FOOL!
IF YOU WISH TO CLAIM MY LIFE, KANG...
...YOU MUST CATCH ME.
COME, KANG.
FOLLOW ME INTO THE TIME-STREAM IF YOU DARE.
UNLESS YOU ARE A COWWAARRDD...
GRRR...

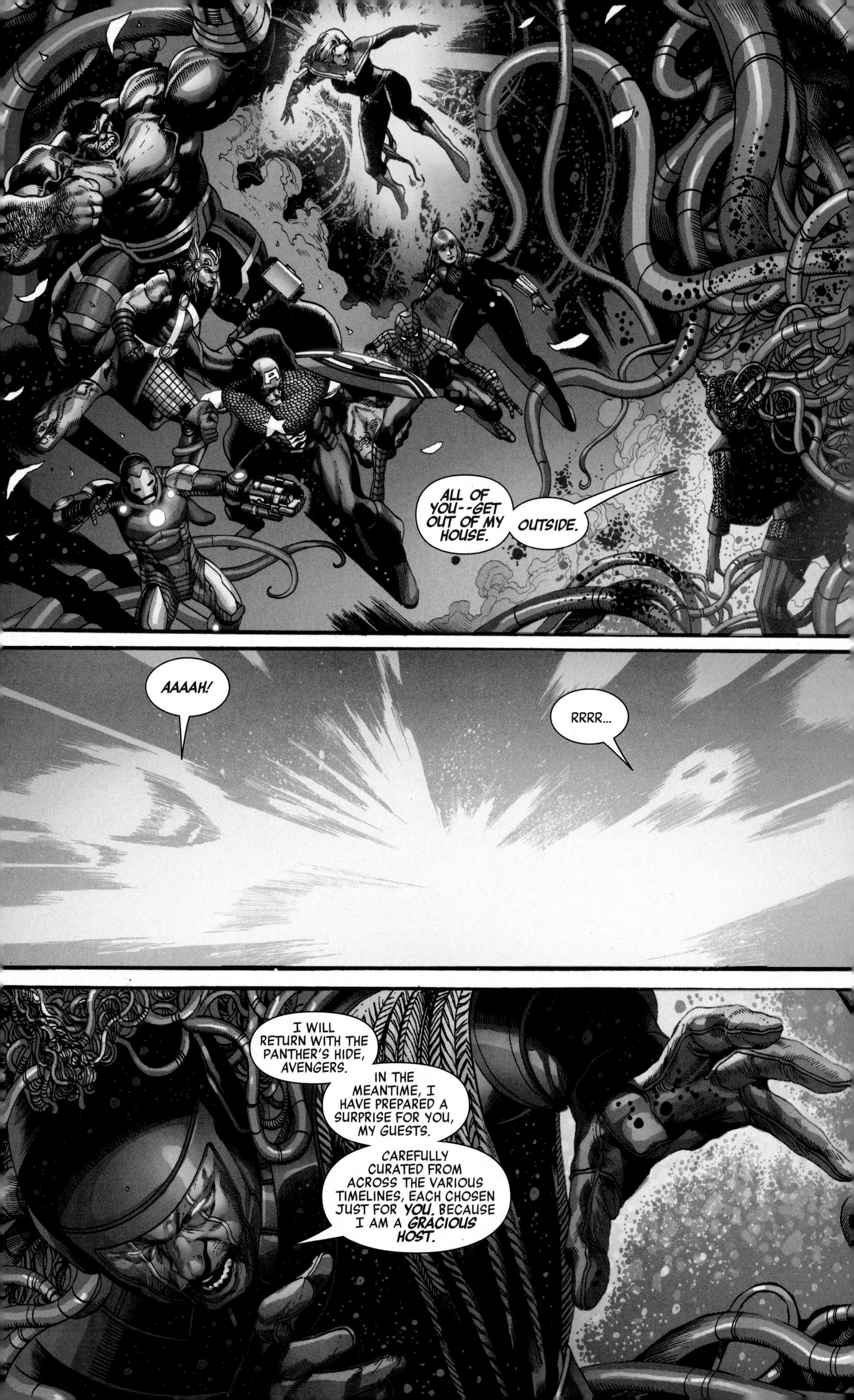
ALL OF YOU--GET OUT OF MY HOUSE.
OUTSIDE.
AAAAH!
RRRR...
I WILL RETURN WITH THE PANTHER'S HIDE, AVENGERS.
IN THE MEANTIME, I HAVE PREPARED A SURPRISE FOR YOU, MY GUESTS.
CAREFULLY CURATED FROM ACROSS THE VARIOUS TIMELINES, EACH CHOSEN JUST FOR YOU. BECAUSE I AM A GRACIOUS HOST.

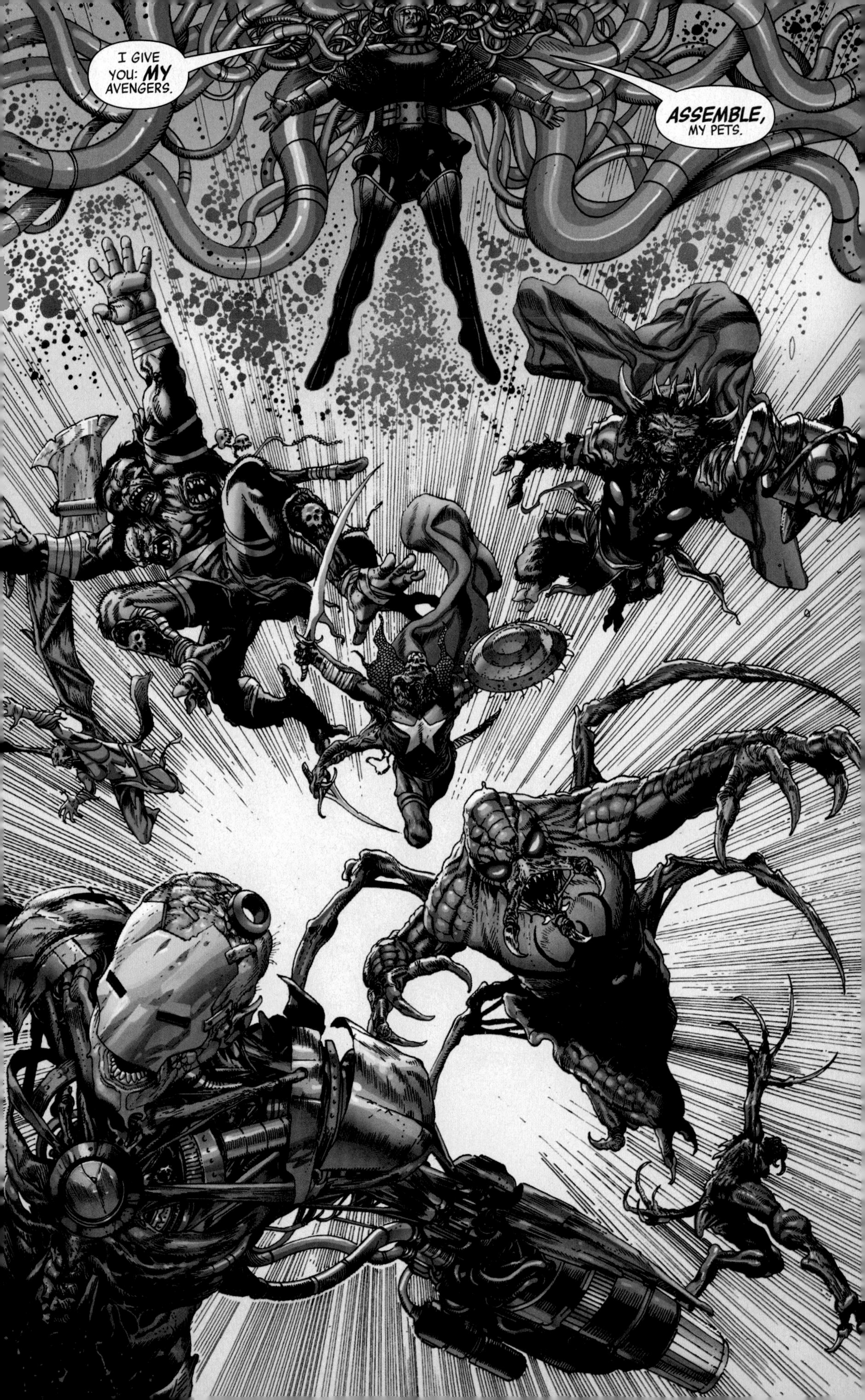
I GIVE YOU: MY AVENGERS.
ASSEMBLE, MY PETS.

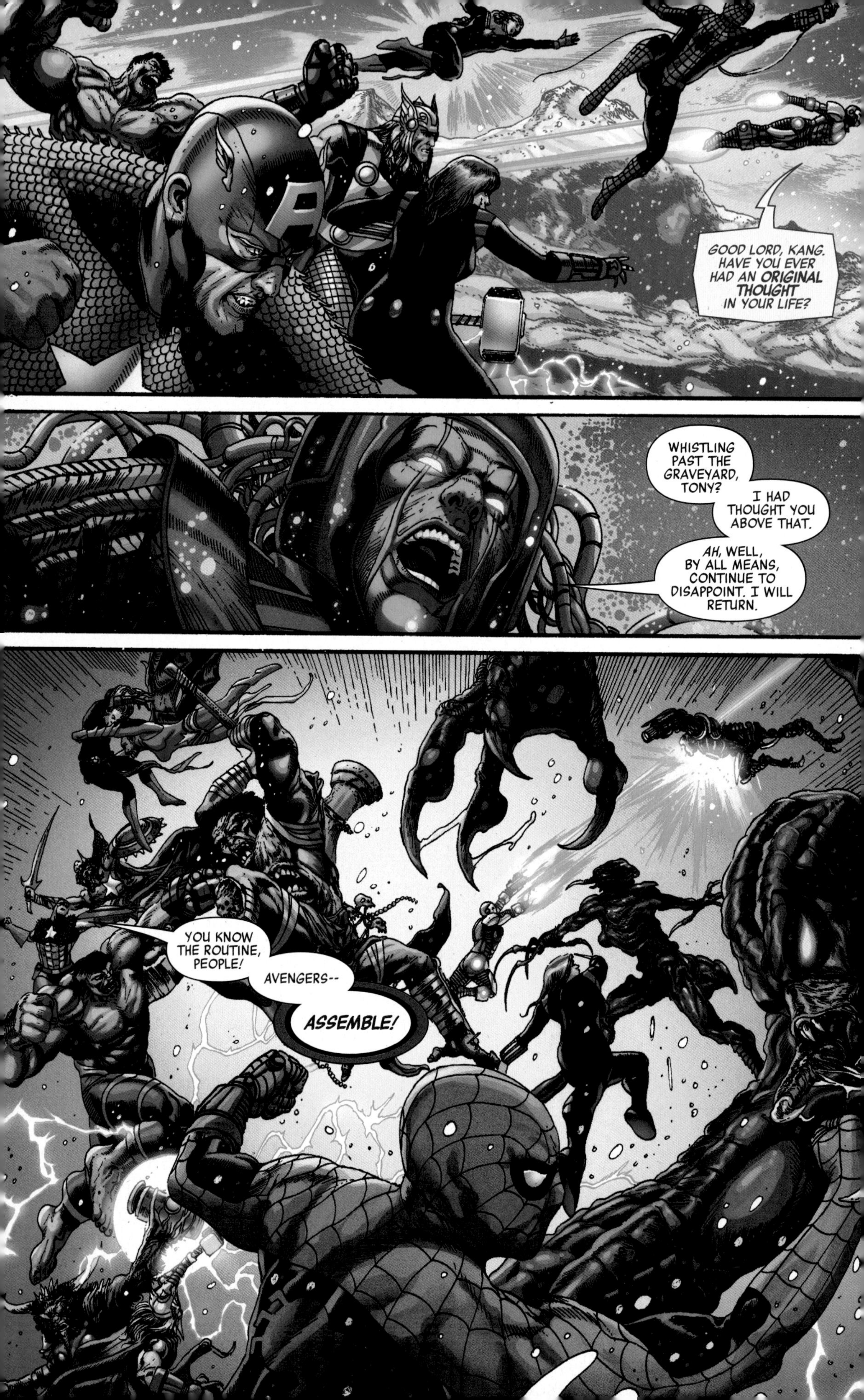
GOOD LORD, KANG. HAVE YOU EVER HAD AN ORIGINAL THOUGHT IN YOUR LIFE?
WHISTLING PAST THE GRAVEYARD, TONY?
I HAD THOUGHT YOU ABOVE THAT.
AH, WELL, BY ALL MEANS, CONTINUE TO DISAPPOINT. I WILL RETURN.
YOU KNOW THE ROUTINE, PEOPLE!
AVENGERS--
ASSEMBLE!

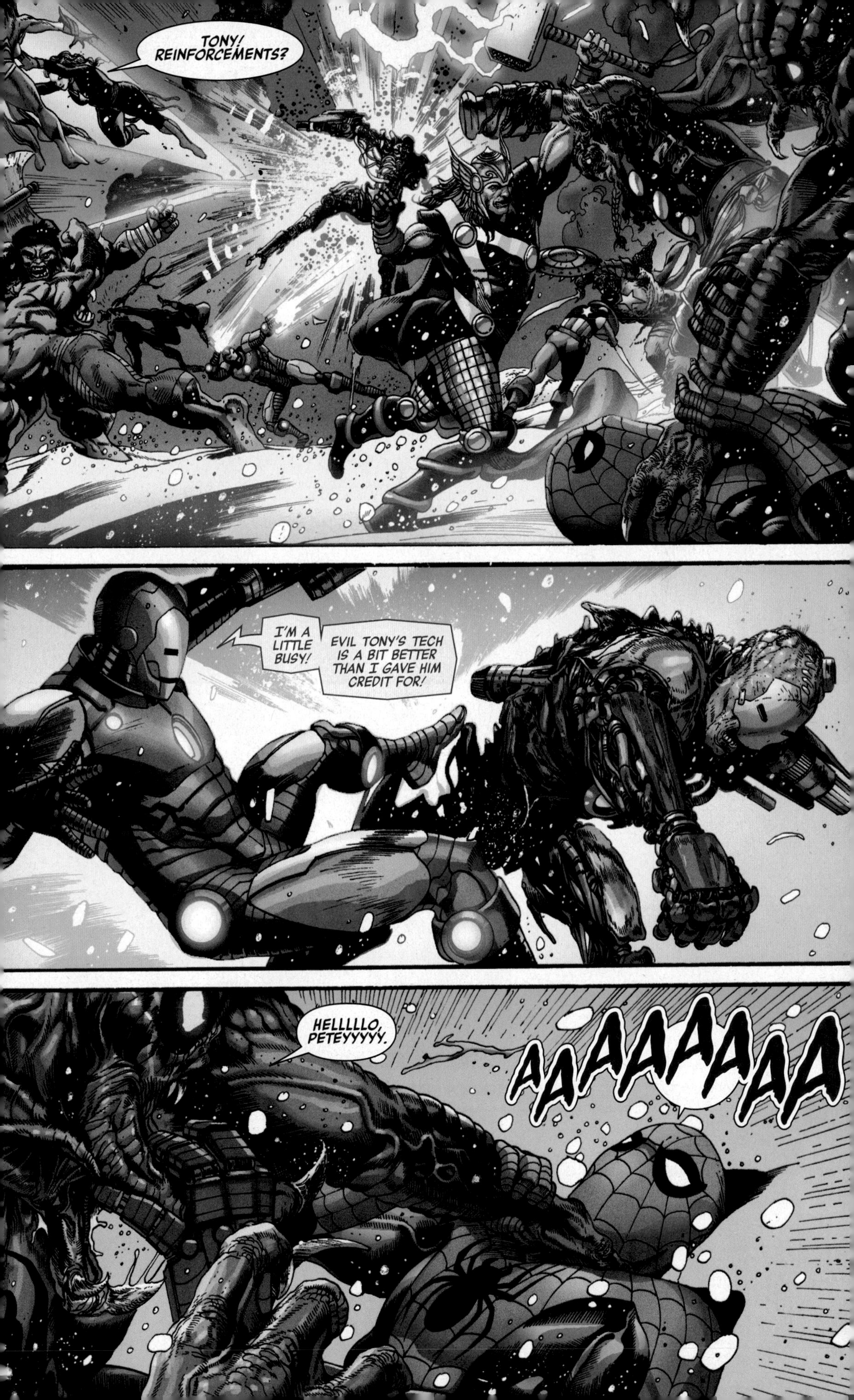
TONY! REINFORCEMENTS?
I'M A LITTLE BUSY!
EVIL TONY'S TECH IS A BIT BETTER THAN I GAVE HIM CREDIT FOR!
HELLLLLLO, PETEYYYYY.
AAAAAAAA

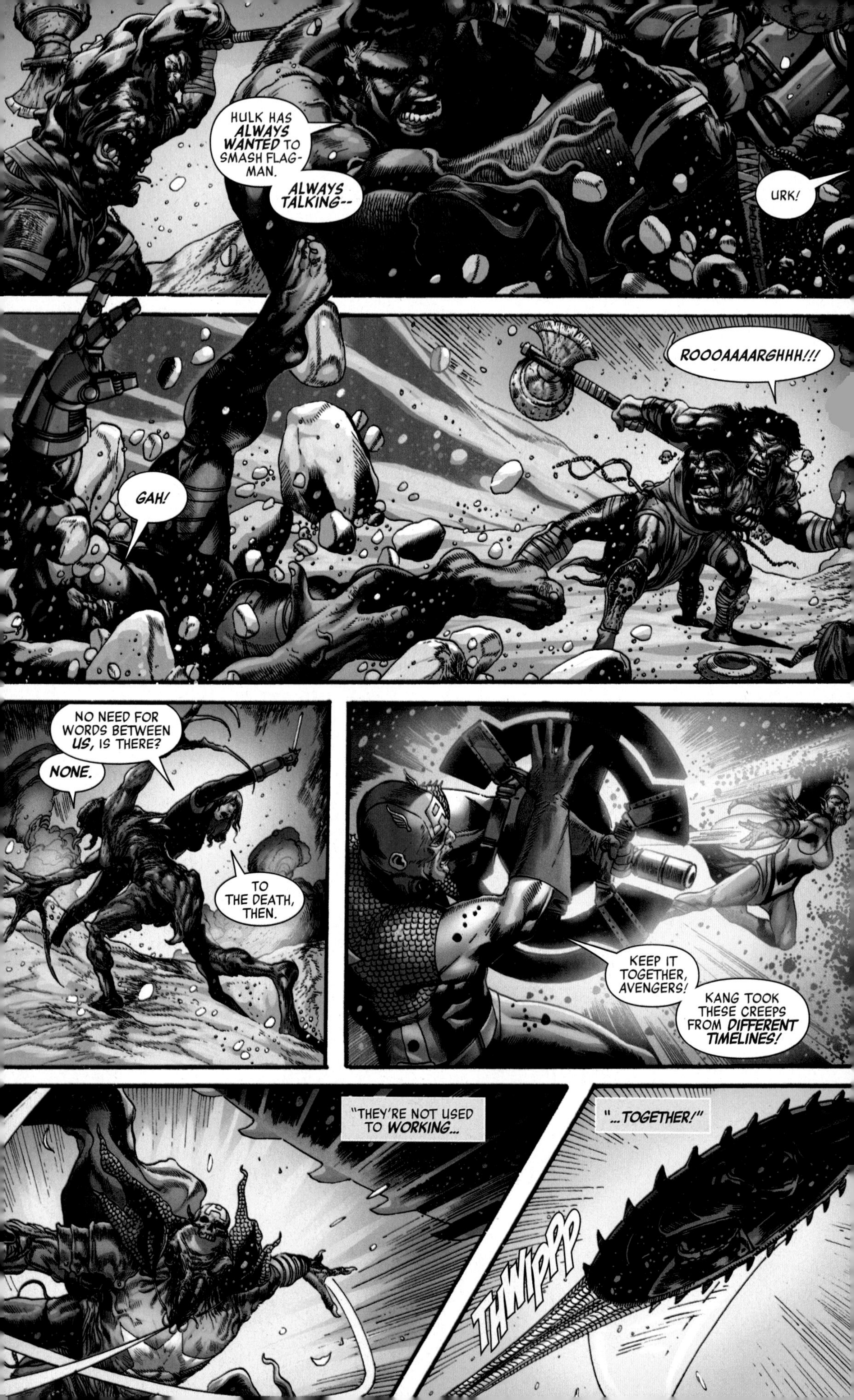
HULK HAS ALWAYS WANTED TO SMASH FLAG-MAN.
ALWAYS TALKING--
URK!
ROOOAAAARGHHH!!!
GAH!
NO NEED FOR WORDS BETWEEN US, IS THERE?
NONE.
TO THE DEATH, THEN.
KEEP IT TOGETHER, AVENGERS!
KANG TOOK THESE CREEPS FROM DIFFERENT TIMELINES!
"THEY'RE NOT USED TO WORKING...
"...TOGETHER!"
THWIPPP

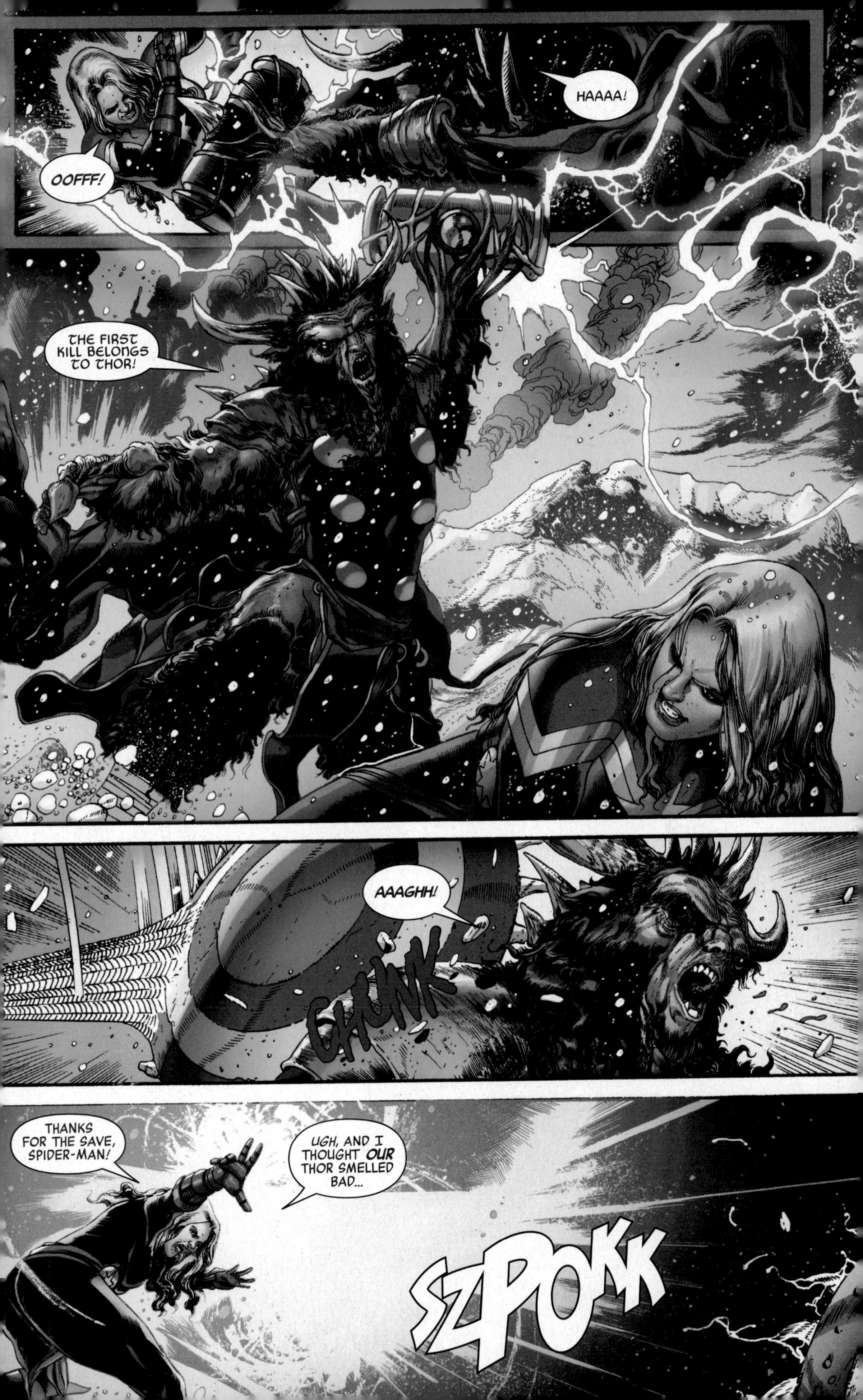
OOFFF!
HAAAA!
THE FIRST KILL BELONGS TO THOR!
AAAGHH!
CHUNK
THANKS FOR THE SAVE, SPIDER-MAN!
UGH, AND I THOUGHT OUR THOR SMELLED BAD...
SZPOKK

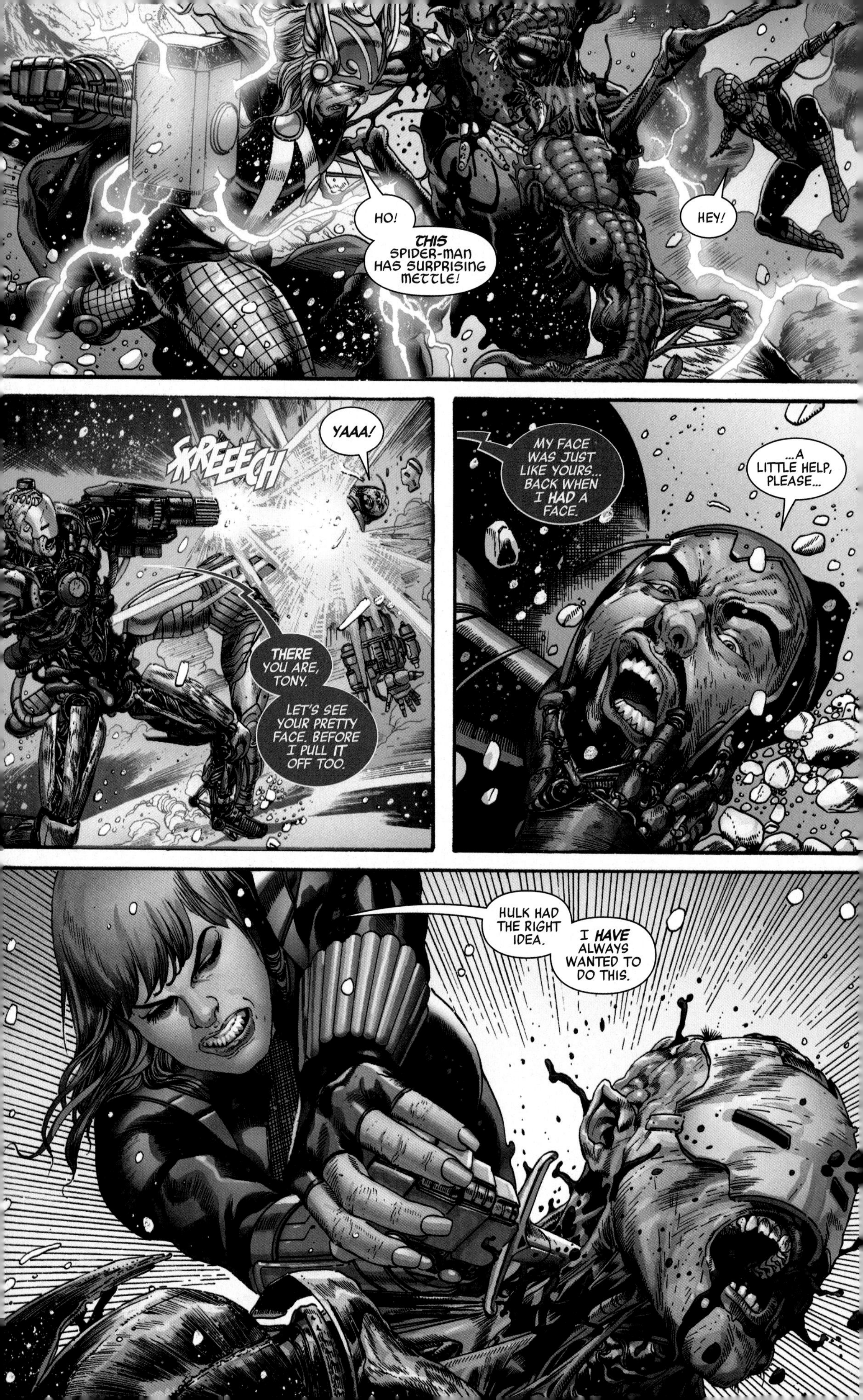
HO! THIS SPIDER-MAN HAS SURPRISING METTLE!
HEY!
SKREEECH
YAAA!
THERE YOU ARE, TONY.
LET'S SEE YOUR PRETTY FACE. BEFORE I PULL IT OFF TOO.
MY FACE WAS JUST LIKE YOURS... BACK WHEN I HAD A FACE.
...A LITTLE HELP, PLEASE...
HULK HAD THE RIGHT IDEA.
I HAVE ALWAYS WANTED TO DO THIS.

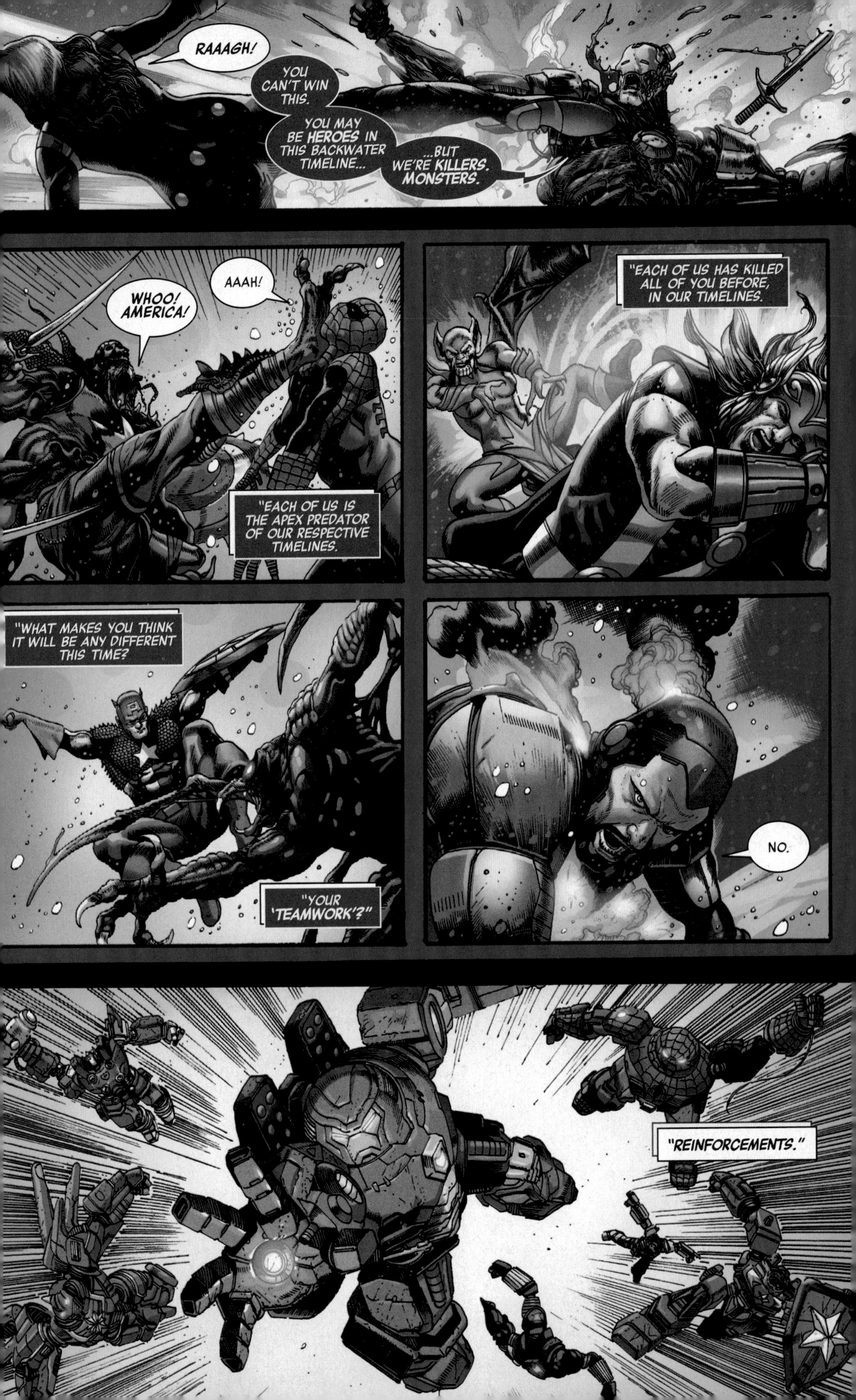
RAAAGH!
YOU CAN'T WIN THIS.
YOU MAY BE HEROES IN THIS BACKWATER TIMELINE...
...BUT WE'RE KILLERS. MONSTERS.
WHOO! AMERICA!
AAAH!
"EACH OF US IS THE APEX PREDATOR OF OUR RESPECTIVE TIMELINES.
"EACH OF US HAS KILLED ALL OF YOU BEFORE, IN OUR TIMELINES.
"WHAT MAKES YOU THINK IT WILL BE ANY DIFFERENT THIS TIME?
"YOUR 'TEAMWORK'?"
NO.
"REINFORCEMENTS."

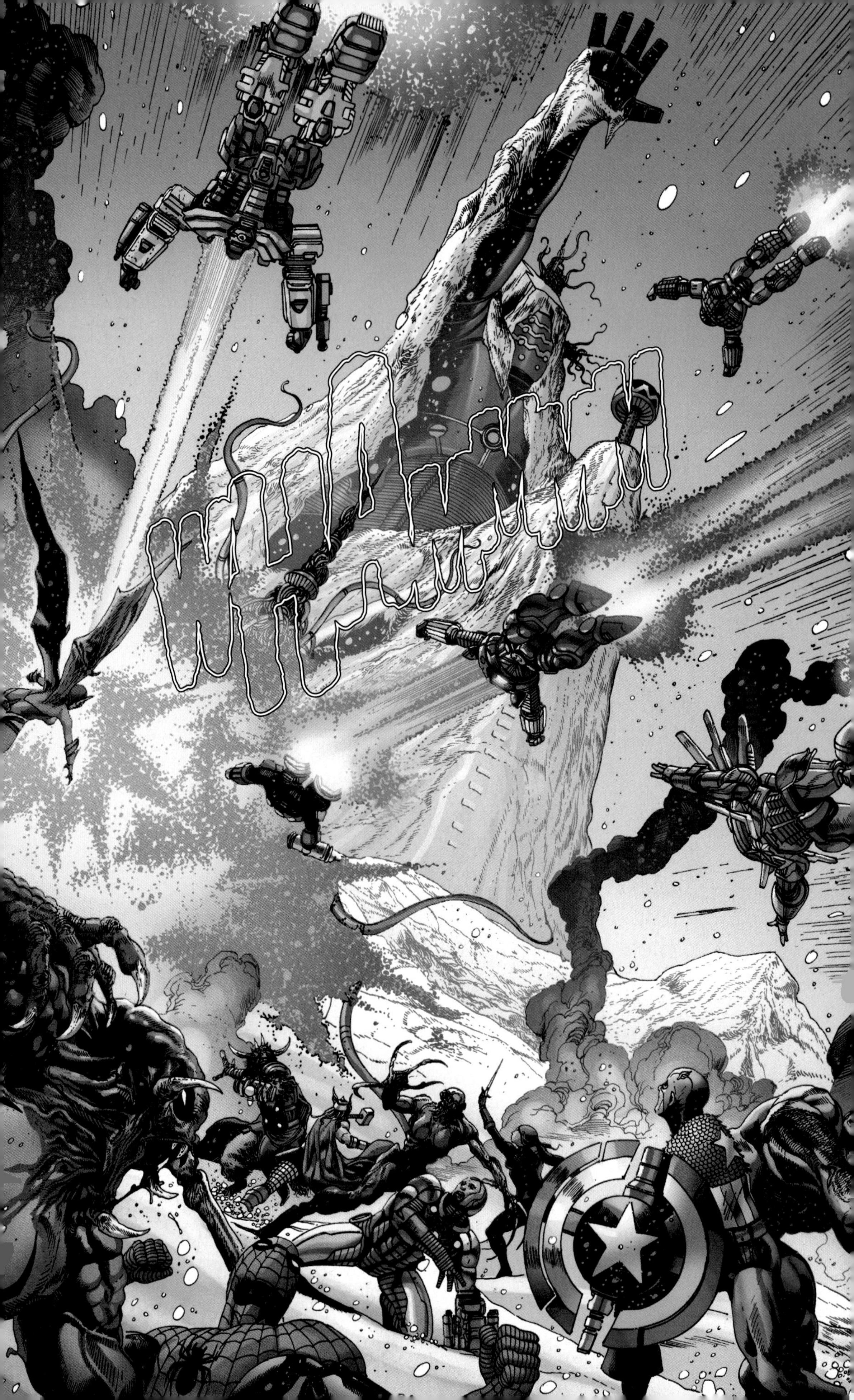

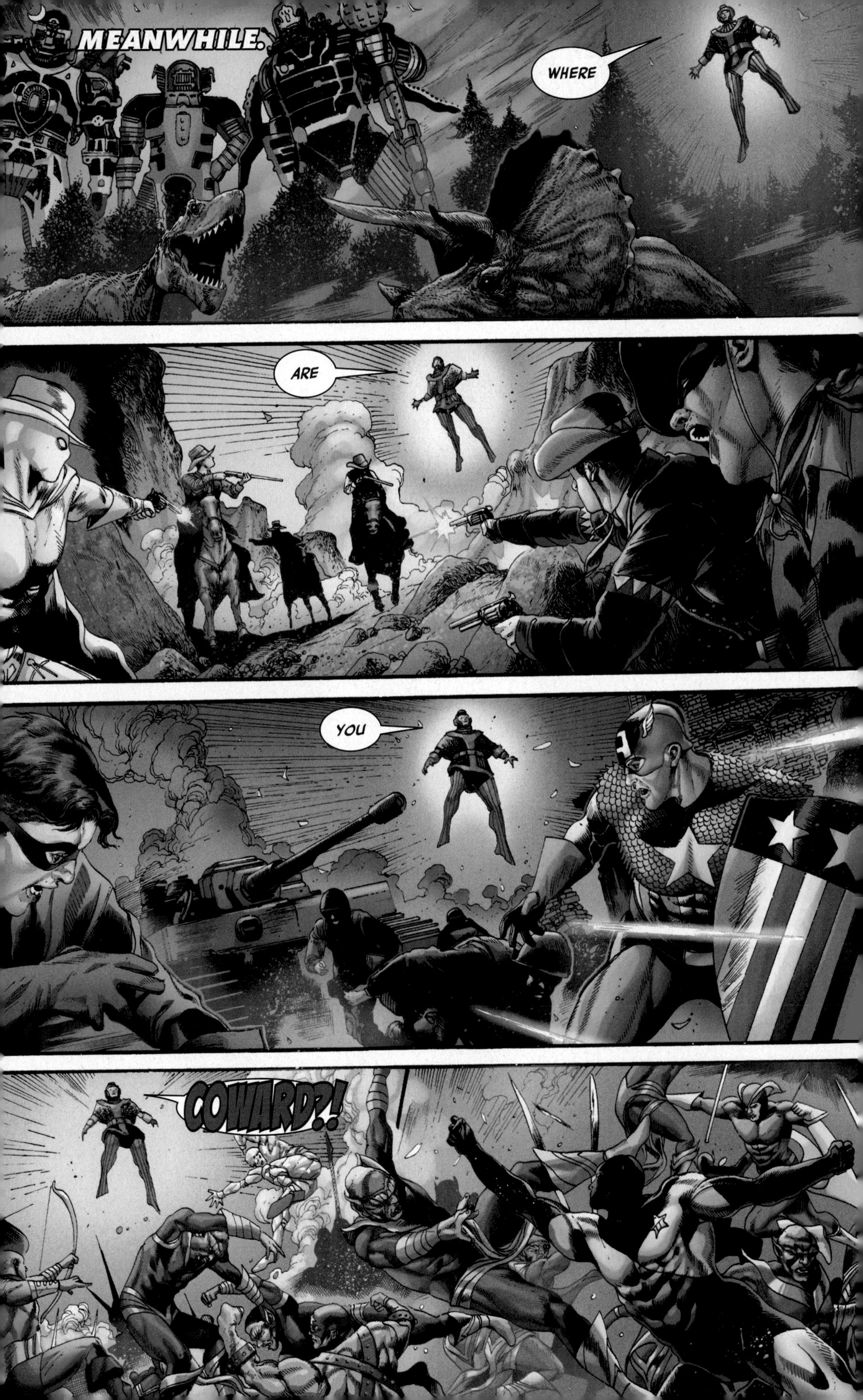
MEANWHILE.
WHERE
ARE
YOU
COWARD?!

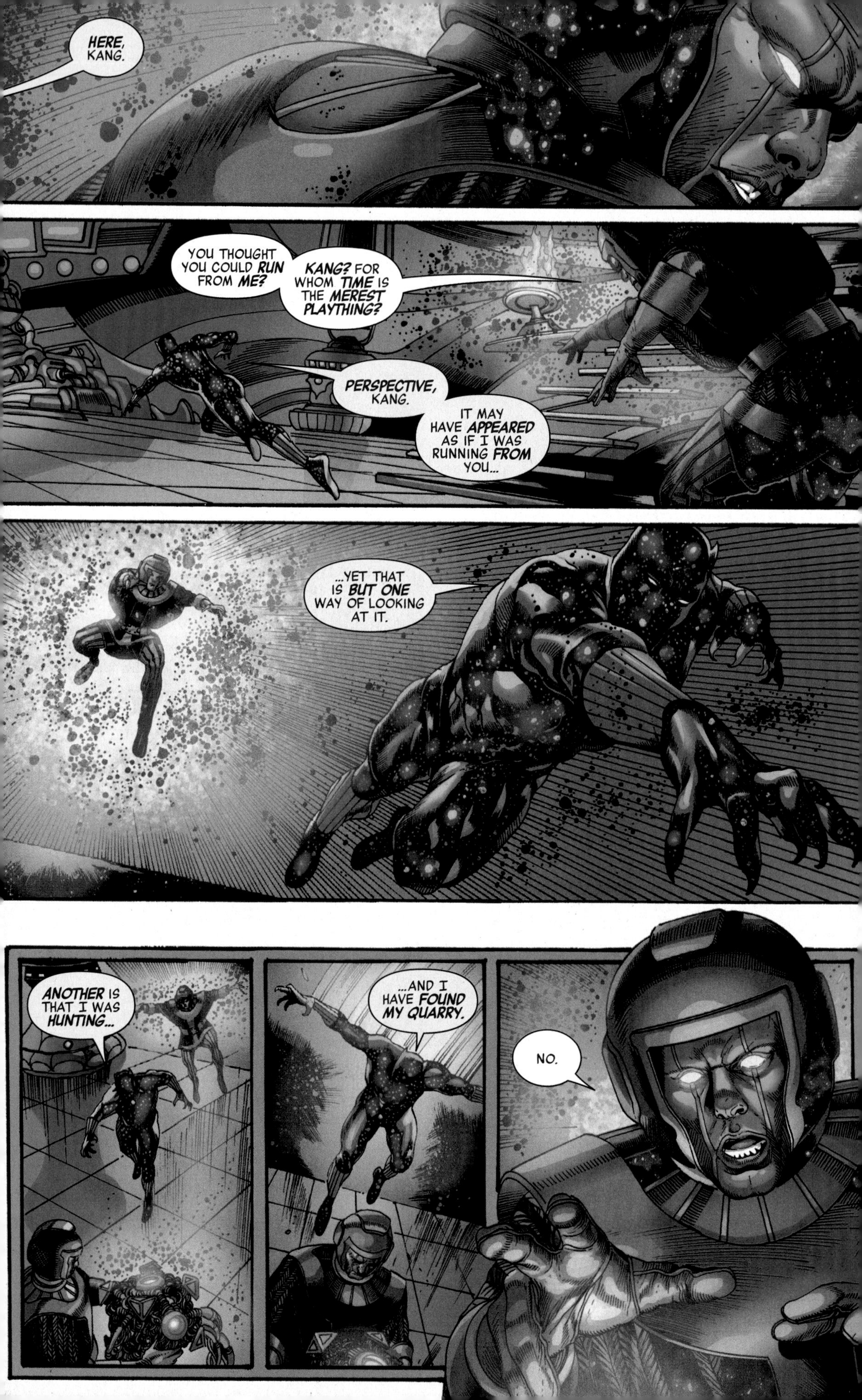
HERE, KANG.
YOU THOUGHT YOU COULD RUN FROM ME?
KANG? FOR WHOM TIME IS THE MEREST PLAYTHING?
PERSPECTIVE, KANG.
IT MAY HAVE APPEARED AS IF I WAS RUNNING FROM YOU...
...YET THAT IS BUT ONE WAY OF LOOKING AT IT.
ANOTHER IS THAT I WAS HUNTING...
...AND I HAVE FOUND MY QUARRY.
NO.

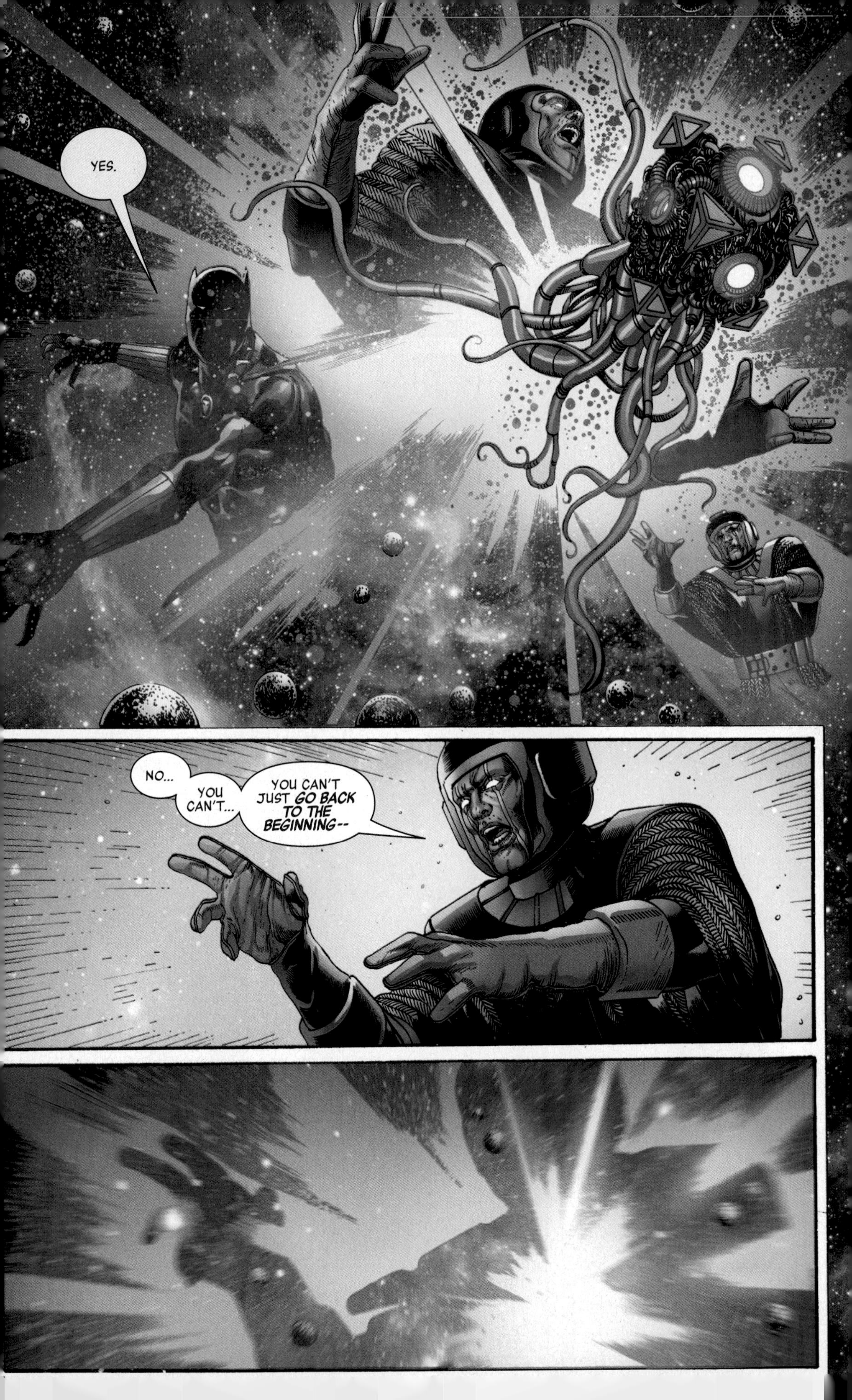
YES.
NO...
YOU CAN'T...
YOU CAN'T JUST GO BACK TO THE BEGINNING--

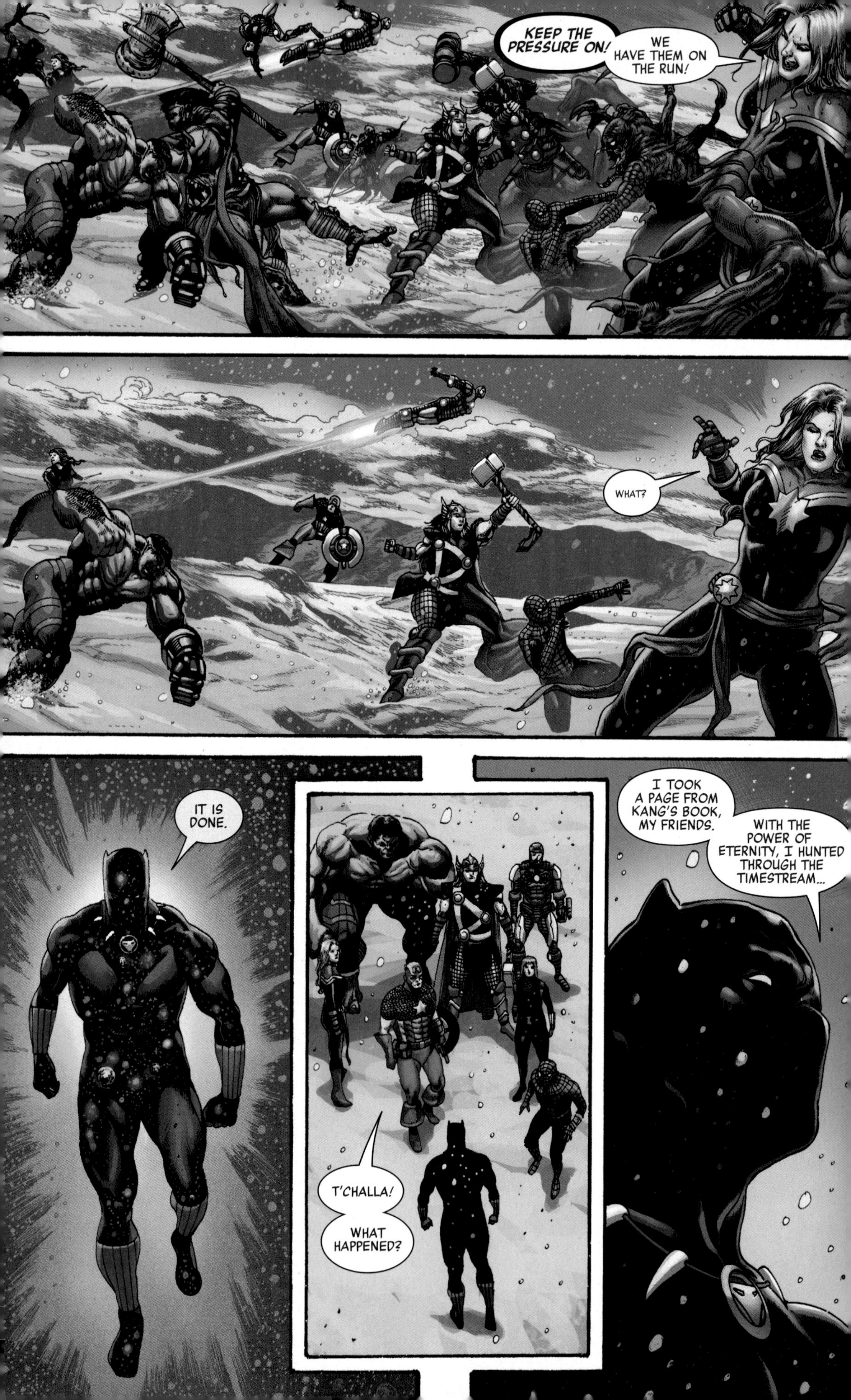
KEEP THE PRESSURE ON!
WE HAVE THEM ON THE RUN!
WHAT?
IT IS DONE.
T'CHALLA!
WHAT HAPPENED?
I TOOK A PAGE FROM KANG'S BOOK, MY FRIENDS.
WITH THE POWER OF ETERNITY, I HUNTED THROUGH THE TIMESTREAM...

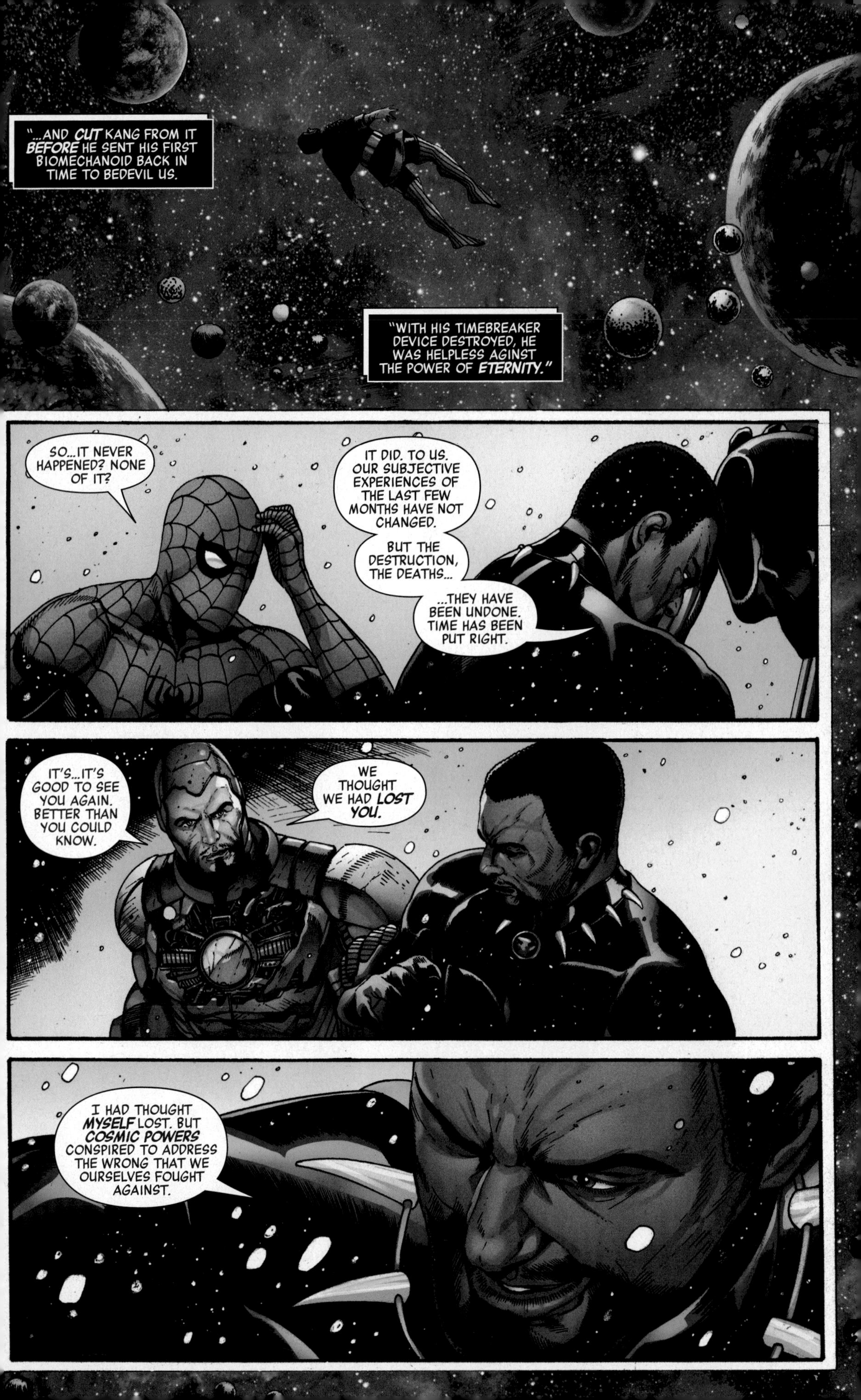
"...AND CUT KANG FROM IT BEFORE HE SENT HIS FIRST BIOMECHANOID BACK IN TIME TO BEDEVIL US.
"WITH HIS TIMEBREAKER DEVICE DESTROYED, HE WAS HELPLESS AGINST THE POWER OF ETERNITY."
SO...IT NEVER HAPPENED? NONE OF IT?
IT DID. TO US. OUR SUBJECTIVE EXPERIENCES OF THE LAST FEW MONTHS HAVE NOT CHANGED.
BUT THE DESTRUCTION, THE DEATHS...
...THEY HAVE BEEN UNDONE. TIME HAS BEEN PUT RIGHT.
IT'S...IT'S GOOD TO SEE YOU AGAIN. BETTER THAN YOU COULD KNOW.
WE THOUGHT WE HAD LOST YOU.
I HAD THOUGHT MYSELF LOST. BUT COSMIC POWERS CONSPIRED TO ADDRESS THE WRONG THAT WE OURSELVES FOUGHT AGAINST.

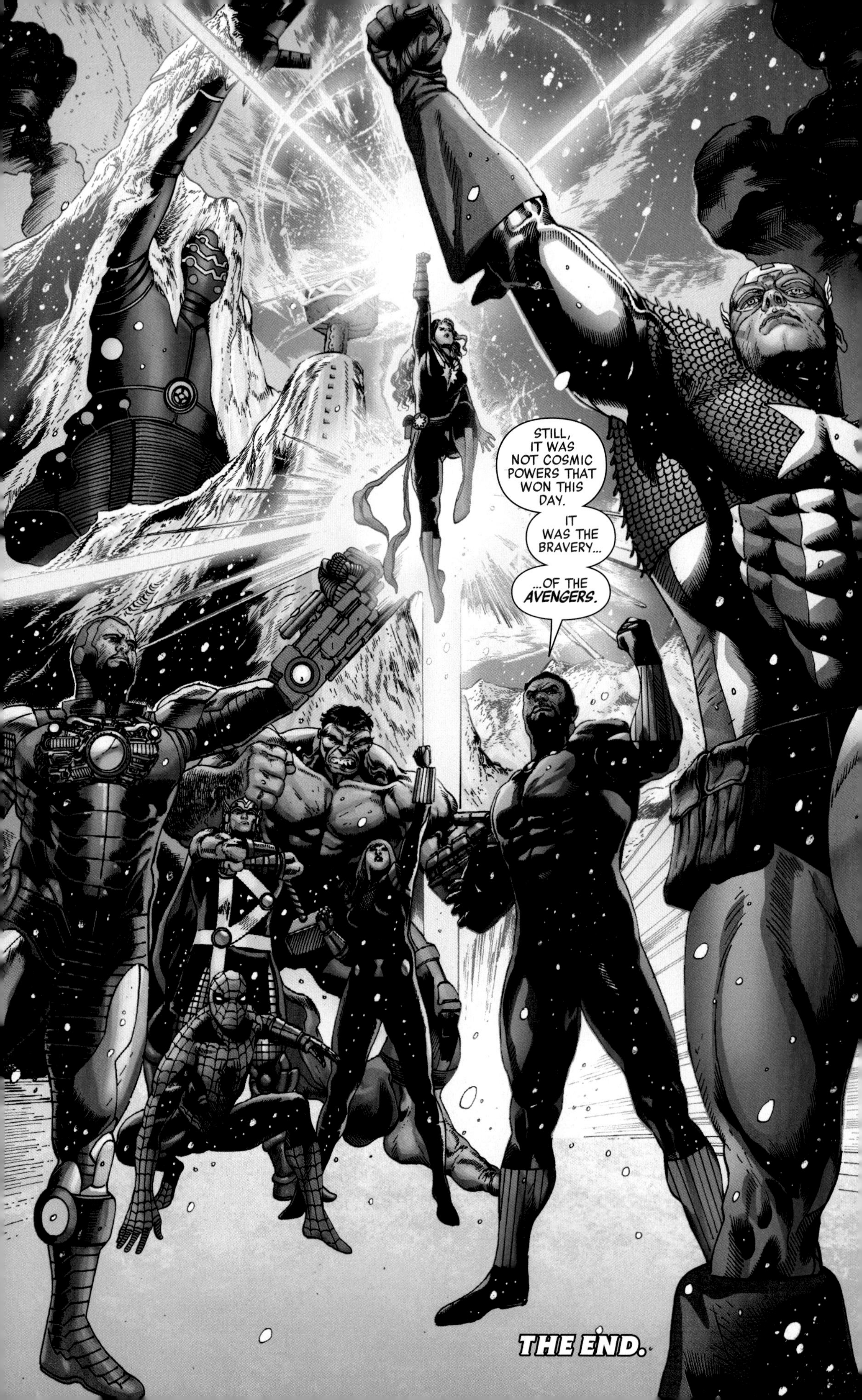
STILL, IT WAS NOT COSMIC POWERS THAT WON THIS DAY.
IT WAS THE BRAVERY...
...OF THE AVENGERS.
THE END.

Jarold Sng
#1 VARIANT

E.J. Su
#1 VARIANT

Leonel Castellani
#1 TOY VARIANT

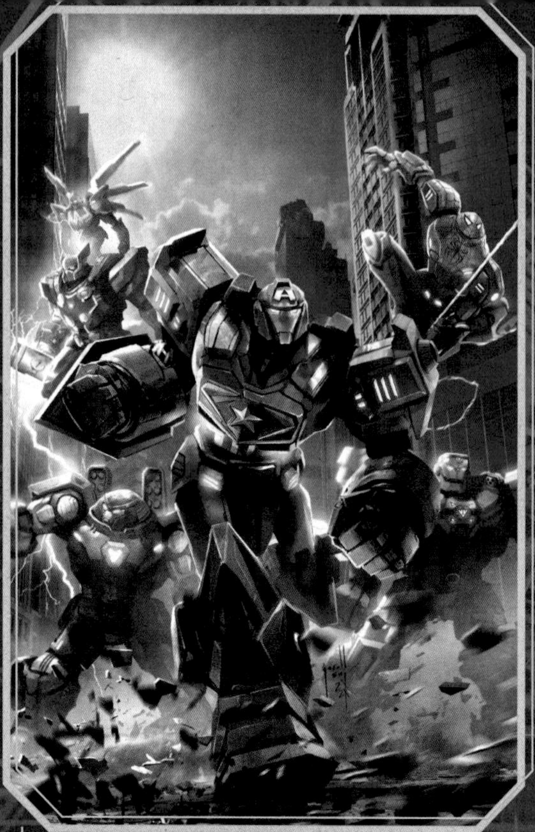

Jarold Sng
#2 VARIANT

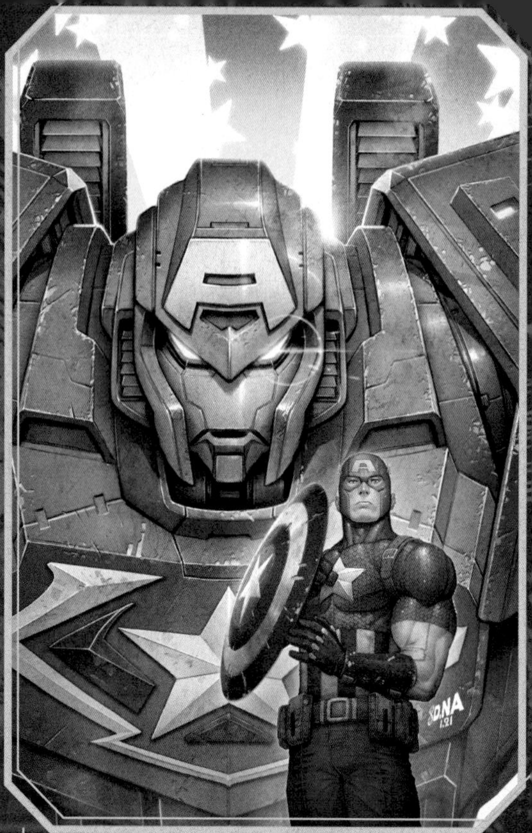

David Nakayama
#3 VARIANT

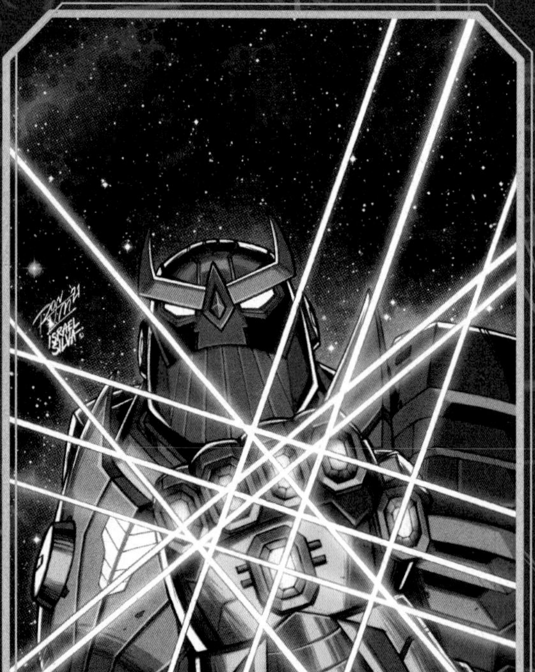

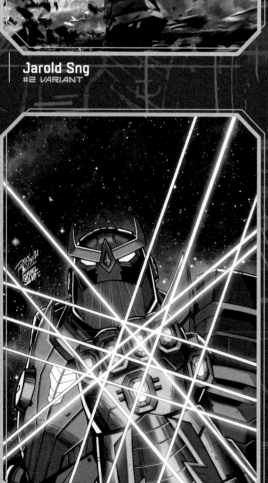

Ron Lim & Israel Silva
#4 VARIANT

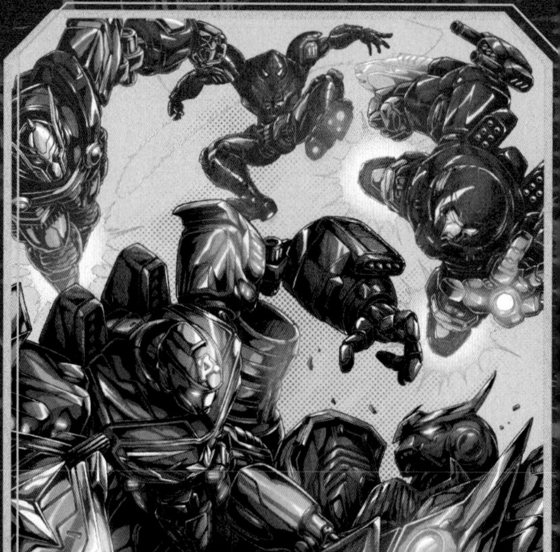

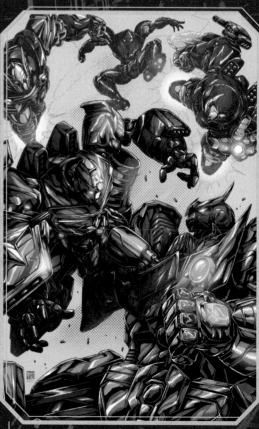

Takashi Okazaki & Rico Renzi
#5 VARIANT